THE
CARE
AND
FEEDING
OF IDEAS

THE CARE AND FEEDING OF IDEAS

Bill Backer

TIMES  BOOKS
RANDOM HOUSE

Permissions acknowledgments appear on page 289.

Library of Congress Cataloging-in-Publication Data

Backer, Bill.
The care and feeding of ideas / Bill Backer. — 1st ed.
p. cm.
ISBN 0-8129-1969-6
1. Creative ability in business. 2. Backer, Bill—Career in advertising. 3. Advertising—Case studies. I. Title.
HD38.B185 1993
658.4′063—dc20 92-38389

Design by Robert Bull Design
Manufactured in the United States of America

9 8 7 6 5 4 3 2

First Edition

CONTENTS

INTRODUCTION

FROM ALL CORNERS of America one hears the complaint that good ideas are in short supply.

Ask yourself when was the last time you encountered an idea—say, in politics, business, or humanitarian work—that moved you in the direction you would like to be going, an idea that provided fresh responses to the wants or needs of the nation, your customers, or the particular group you want to help.

This book deals with those kinds of ideas. It looks at how they are born and how they either get nourished to adulthood or perish for lack of proper care. And why.

The care and feeding of ideas has been a neglected topic in this country, but it shouldn't be. Every brainchild, like every real child, needs a supportive family that knows how to help it grow and prosper. And also understands how to help it through rough times.

In the course of forty years in an idea-driven business, I have had to market many ideas—both my own and those of my colleagues—to people in many different levels of business, some of whom couldn't even identify an idea, much less how to care for it and help it become successful. And I have found that the quickest way to help people learn about ideas is through familiar examples of ideas that worked—and of somc that failed.

The richest source of such ideas, I believe, lies in our popular culture—motion pictures, popular songs, mass products, and especially advertising, the business to which I have devoted my professional life. I have been told that the first rule of writing is "Write about what you know," and that is what I have tried to do in this book.

The story of one particular idea is woven throughout as a narrative, because it stands out as a classic example of the importance of care and feeding at every step of the process. So that idea—which later became one of the classic television commercials of the "Golden Age of Advertising"—is sort of the "hero" of this book. The fact that it made its way onto anyone's television screen is a testament not merely to its own intrinsic value but also to the tenacity and love of its Idea Family. Even two decades on, the commercial still resonates in people's minds, and the words and music are etched in our national consciousness.

You know it as "I'd Like to Teach the World to Sing in Perfect Harmony," but it was born "I'd Like to Buy the World a Coke and Keep It Company." And in between those two titles is the story of what often seemed like a star-crossed path to fame. And as we retrace its steps I will draw on similar tales from other businesses and creative endeavors in all walks of life, to help you grow and nurture ideas in your own line of work.

I begin with a theory about why good ideas have become an endangered species, and later I shall develop some others about how to rescue them.

The first theory is simply this: When it comes to ideas,

WE HAVE THE TALENT BUT WE LACK THE KNOW-HOW.

Our country is full of people who can come up with ideas. But we don't know how to recognize an idea as such, or, if we do, we are in too much of a hurry to take the time to separate the good from the bad. Even worse, we don't know enough about the care and feeding of ideas to nourish them so that they will grow to a meaningful size and become effective.

By not devoting the time to gain knowledge and experience of how ideas happen and grow, we end up making bad judgment calls, and we begin to doubt our abilities. Once bitten, twice shy, as they say, and the easy way out is to keep your distance from ideas altogether. And it's happening everywhere. We just say to ourselves, "Ideas are somebody else's department." We even do that in businesses where ideas are the primary product of the enterprise.

Advertisers today are quick to substitute a new film technique for a new message, and manufacturers are more prone to redesign the package than improve what is inside it.

But today everybody is somewhere in an idea loop. Almost every decision and move you make demands that you have a basic idea, or that you execute one. Or maybe it calls for you to judge an idea (your own or someone else's) or to put one into effect by marketing it.

The difference between your success rate and the next person's may not be how much you know about the marketing data or the legal precedents, but how much you know about developing and handling the ideas that can be sparked by the available knowledge.

But before we get into all that I want to go a little bit further in developing the first part of the theory—that we have the talent, and that most Americans are capable of having good basic ideas.

Right now you might well be questioning that assertion: "Who's he to be saying I have good ideas? I'm not a writer or an artist. I'm a lawyer."

Let me explain that I am talking about basic ideas here—the first step in idea development.

You don't have to be "creative" in the everyday sense of the word to have good basic ideas. You don't have to be in a creative business or profession either.

The people you think of as "creative types," like writers, artists, and advertising people, are mostly in the business of *executing* ideas. They may be no better at coming up with basic ideas than engineers, accountants, or lawyers.

I don't mean to imply that we are all equal when it comes to grabbing hold of good basic ideas. But we are all more equal than we think.

Take, for instance, ideas for new products or ways to make your office procedures more efficient, or new ways to look at the problems that confront your children's school programs—the people who have come up with the good basic ideas in these areas are often people like yourself. Quite frequently they are not our creative writers or our best-known advertising people.

Sure, there are some people who just plain excel in the area of ideas. They seem to start with a God-given ability to recognize every little spark that occurs and grab hold of it. The country folk say those people have a "bent" for ideas. They don't necessarily write, draw, make up songs, or design clothes. They could just as easily be your electrician or the person who sold you your last car as the creative writer who was your best friend growing up.

You may never be quite their equal, but—on the second part of the theory—*you can develop the "know-how"* to be better than you are right now. And you will certainly find it helpful if you become an educated expert at some part of the process, either someone who comes up with and grabs hold of basic ideas, or who creates executions for them, or judges them and furthers them with the follow-up necessary to see them mature and become useful.

But before we get into all that, I think it is time for some disclaimers. Most products hide them on the back of the package—except when the product is a movie or a TV film. Then they say right up front, "May contain offensive material"; "Any similarity to persons living or dead is purely coincidental"; "Approved for mature audiences only"; and so forth.

I didn't want to open this book with the disclaimers. I don't like starting off any positive communication with a "negative" because that can be misleading. It's also bad marketing. But I think disclaimers should be made readily available to the consumer before he or she takes that first big bite of the product. So I'm going to put mine here in the middle of the introduction. That's fair but not too fair.

This is not a "how-to" book. It will not provide you with tried and true recipes for "How to Become a Better Salesman" or "Ten Rules for Creating Better Advertising." There are good books—in hard and soft cover—already written about how to do almost any job in which you find yourself. But they are recipe books, and recipe books have certain limitations.

The best way to explain my view on the limitations of recipe books is with a story from my early days in advertising.

When I graduated from college I kicked around in various businesses (real estate, film production, and music) for several years, and finally ended up in the training program of a large advertising agency—McCann-Erickson. The training program consisted of working in the mail room for about six months and then getting equal time in the department of your choice. We all fervently hoped that the department of choice would elect to keep us on. If not, it was back to the mail room for another stretch and then a go at some other department.

The creative department was first choice for most of us. And to get our shot at the fame and fortune of writing commercials, many of us had to wait much longer than six months for an opening (in my case it was nearly a year). The personnel department justified time in the mail room as "training." We were "getting the big picture," seeing the agency as a whole—how it worked and who did what to whom.

When I finally got my turn at working in the creative department I was hired on permanently. But the salary was still not much more than what I had been earning pushing a mail cart. The result was that five years out of college I was still not earning the kind of salary that gave me much of what is today called "disposable income." The same held true for many of my classmates, some of whom had gone on to graduate school. So groups of us bachelors shared various apartments around New York in order to save on rent and accumulate disposable income for important things like weekends.

In the case of my group, we saved money in another area besides rent—food. We ate out infrequently, and ran a sort of bachelor kitchen three or four nights a week.

Since none of us had ever cooked at home, and neither had the college types we were dating, we began to assemble a vast array of recipe books.

I have always been good at following written directions and became one of the better cooks in the group, such as it was. (But as Paul Foley, my ultimate boss at McCann-Erickson, used to say, "All horses look fast running past trees.") I was hardly on a culinary fast track, but I felt good enough about my relative skills to keep on doing a bit of cooking even after I could afford an apartment of my own and a part-time cook.

My part-time cook was a fabulous character whose father had been the best distiller of illegal whiskey in all of western Tennessee. Even the sheriff said so, according to Edna. But then the sheriff was buying his at a discount.

Anyway, Edna, who ended up a permanent member of the family, brought two qualities into the kitchen that I especially admired—perhaps because I will never have either of them. She possessed a genuine talent for cooking that grew out of a true love of the end product, and down-home, hardscrabble, blue-collar country wisdom. One day Edna applied that wisdom to my array of recipe books which by then occupied over half a shelf in our small kitchen. She was stirring something on the stove and looking up at all the space the books were occupying.

"You know, Mr. Backer," she said, "if you gotta read a book, you ain't never gonna be a cook."

And I feel the same way about recipe books that try to teach you to write or paint by the numbers. With apologies to Julia and James, they can only teach you how to make *their* souffle. If you want to create your own, you must first try to understand why eggs and flour rise—or don't rise—when you do certain things to them, and then begin to develop your own theories, which result in dishes that you create.

So this is a book that attempts to develop theories about the world of ideas: why it operates the way it does, why it works when it does work, and what we should do when it doesn't. Some of the chapters trace the history of certain successful ideas—how they were captured and executed correctly, and what it took to market them. Others reveal instances where people tried to sell ideas instead of marketing them, with disappointing results. Still others show what happened when the ideas were good but the executions let them down or the executors couldn't cope with the ignorance and apathy that face many ideas.

In all of these examples I try to develop theories that explain *why* things happened the way they did. I am far from certain that my theories are 100 percent correct. Frankly, I'd settle for 75 percent.

When you read this book, I invite you to bring a large jug of skepticism to the party and pour it into the punch bowl. That way you will be more inclined to think about how *you* might have made the punch.

Now that I've been so forthright about how this book does not guarantee to make you head of sales or ultimately CEO of your company, and how it will not assure that your next advertising campaign will be accepted and cheered by all concerned or that the next new product you come up with will be a category leader, I think it only fair that you indemnify me from legal action when I make a few promises here and now about what this book can do.

On the way to becoming head of your engineering group or even CEO of your company, or on the way to creating advertising for new products, you are going to need ideas, either yours or somebody else's, and you are going to have to be part of either the team that executes them or the team that judges them, or you are going to have to help pull the process together so that the ideas get marketed. And then you are going to have to exploit the power of those ideas once they begin to be successful.

This book will help you do all of the above.

After reading it, your opinions of your own ideas or someone else's will not only be more soundly based than before, but you will also be better able to articulate them in a manner that others can understand and respect. And your insights on basic ideas and what to do with them will be equally sensitive and thoughtful whether you are looking at five lines of poetry, hearing some lyrics sung to a folk melody, or deciphering the design for a revolutionary new valve. You will understand that behind them all must be an idea that fills somebody's need for something. If that need is shared by a whole lot of people, so much the better. I will concentrate on ideas that are big in the sense of appealing to the masses, but the principles that apply to developing big ideas also apply to those that are no bigger than your company's personnel list or are confined to as small a group as your division.

As I said earlier, my background has been in advertising, so many of the examples I use will come from that field. But the advertising business exposes you to ideas and executions in a lot of other areas, such as new products, music, fads, trends, and ideas in business and politics. So this book won't confine itself to advertising. It examines ideas and executions from all over: how they happened and how and why I think they succeeded or failed. And it will help you think about how you would have judged them or how you might have helped execute them.

I will use the story of one idea—an advertising idea for Coca-Cola—as a sort of tour from which I can depart on many side trips and explore other views in different areas. We will see how and why the idea was born, how it was nurtured and developed, and why it turned out to be so very big. But before we set out on that trip, there is one final disclaimer, the first of Backer's Laws of Ideas:

IDEAS CAN BE DANGEROUS TO THE HEALTH OF YOUR CAREER.

I'm not referring to bad ideas. I am talking about good ones. In fact, in certain environments, the very good, high-profile ideas can be the most dangerous of all.

CHAPTER ONE

The Spark

ON JANUARY 18, 1971, an ill-fated jumbo jet took off from Washington, D.C.'s Dulles Airport bound for London and Frankfurt. It was Pan American Flight 12, and if all went well its passengers would make good connections to the Continent and Near East.

The size of the plane and the nature of its destinations made for a large and varied passenger list—Britons, Germans, Americans, Indians, Arabs, and Israelis.

Since it was off-season, most of the passengers were businessmen and businesswomen. There was a scattering of young people taking advantage of seasonal low fares, and, in addition, there was a young American copywriter/songwriter on his way to London to record some song-form commercials for Coca-Cola.

Most of the passengers on Flight 12 were on tight timetables. There were connections to be made in Frankfurt, or meetings in London that had been arranged to accommodate full business schedules. Time was particularly of the essence for the young advertising writer, who had scheduled an expensive recording session with a popular singing group of the day named the New Seekers. The session was to start at 9:00 A.M. five days after he was due to land at London's Heathrow Airport.

Ordinarily five days to arrange, rehearse, and record material was ample. The problem in this case, however, was that the material to be recorded was not yet written. The songs were to be written in London in collaboration with a successful British songwriting team, plus the head of the music department at Coca-Cola's advertising agency.

Pan Am Flight 12 had left Dulles Airport pretty much on time, but did not land in London on time. In fact, it never landed in London at all.

As the jet approached Ireland it received a message from air traffic control at Heathrow to the effect that no planes were being allowed to land or take off—and that these restrictions would probably remain in effect for some time. London was socked in. And this was no ordinary sock. This was a full-length, over-the-calf, yellow wool job. It was the kind of fog Sir Arthur Conan Doyle would have reveled in; ideal for crimes that would not be witnessed, and therefore could be solved only by being seen in the mind's eye of a master sleuth like Sherlock Holmes. In short, London, all the way out to Heathrow and beyond, was covered by an old-fashioned pea soup.

Somewhere over Ireland Pan Am Flight 12 circled for an hour, then did a one-eighty and headed back west—its destination Shannon Airport, ten miles outside of the Irish city of Limerick. It landed at Shannon smoothly enough in late afternoon.

Had the plane been full of tourists, the disembarking passengers might have seen a silver lining in the gloom of their delay—after all, they had landed in the Emerald Isle—but as it was, the mood of the troop that marched off the jet into the relatively small, plain terminal could best be described as similar to that of the Yale alumni who grudgingly agreed to renew the football coaching contract of the late Herman Hickman, despite several losing seasons. Herman—whose philosophy of life was more Tennessee Mountain than Greenwich Country Club—was heard to quip, "I kept the alumni sullen but not mutinous."

The Pan Am 747 was the first plane of its size ever to land at Shannon. To the nuns who would bring their schoolchildren to see the grounded leviathan next day it represented the excitement of something new. But to the officials at Shannon Airport it represented a major problem.

Even today, when any airport large enough to accommodate the bigger jets has a major motel nearby and a large city a forty-minute bus ride away, two hundred people suddenly stranded and in need of lodging present a situation that needs careful attention. The local motel won't have that many vacancies, and passengers will have to be divided among the larger hotels in town.

But Pan Am didn't want its passengers housed as far away as Limerick. The airline wanted everyone to stay ready to board on short notice in case the fog over London lifted. That meant trying to squeeze everyone into the small, very simple motel that served Shannon Airport in those days.

At that time of year, the motel had a number of vacancies, but not nearly enough for every passenger to have a room of his or her own. The solution was to ask Pan Am's passengers to act like a big family. In short, they were asked to share rooms.

As best they could, the travelers grouped themselves by nationality and sex. But the scene in the lobby of the motel as the arrangements were being made was one of individuals desperate to maintain their privacy and isolation from their fellow man. Some refused to share and chose to sleep sitting up in the lobby. But mostly they began to look around, spot a friendly face, hold out a welcoming hand and join up.

The advertising songwriter ended up sharing a small room with an antiques dealer from the Washington, D.C., area. How the rest of the passengers were paired, he could only guess, but he was aware that as the various pairs left the lobby together, toting whatever overnight bags they had brought with them on the flight, a certain resilience of spirit began to emerge. Anger gave way to resignation, and in a few cases the let's-make-the-best-of-this attitude seemed to soften into maybe-this-could-turn-out-to-be-amusing, or at least less than half bad.

But to the advertising writer there was no chance that the situation would become anything better than desperate. He had a hunk of the client's money committed to that recording session. He had a contract with a major singing group, and that contract stipulated that the group would be paid to record on that date, and there were no escape clauses. The usual "force majeure" clause in the contract covered natural catastrophes to the group or the studio, but not to the writers.

So, here he was in an unknown motel in the middle of nowhere looking for an idea that would enhance what is perhaps the world's best-known product, which at that very moment was being consumed everywhere in the world.

Ideas are like fireflies. Nobody knows what makes them light up, and you can't switch them on and off like the lights in your house. Rarely, if ever, do you find basic ideas in the daylight of your conscious mind. They seem to hang out in the darkness of the unconscious. Then and there, all of a sudden—unexpectedly—they light up. And for a moment, as on a summer's night, nothing else matters except the excitement of the fireflies.

Catching the fireflies and holding on to them is another matter, but seeing them is easy if your eyes are open and in touch with your unconscious. And the next day, amidst all that gloom and desperation, the advertising writer opened his eyes and saw a scene that sparked in his unconscious the basic idea of what would become, arguably, one of the most famous ideas in advertising history.

The advertising writer stranded in Ireland needed a big basic idea—one that would at least involve the entire United States market for Coca-Cola. And in his desperate mood he kept searching his unconscious for a spark.

He had not bothered to stand in one of the long lines that stretched to the two public telephones in the lobby. And when he tried calling London from his room, all circuits were busy. Never mind, he thought. His team in London would certainly hear about the closing of Heathrow Airport and would start to write material without him. But they needed two or possibly three songs, all based on subjects or situations where Coke—"The Real Thing"—fit in naturally and would play a small but important role.

Conversation with the antiques dealer was limited to pleasantries and an Alphonse-and-Gaston routine about who would visit the bathroom first, but mostly the writer's mind was on Coca-Cola and the New Seekers. The group had a warm, friendly folk-song style. They were just coming off of several hits. They hailed from Australia, but were building their careers in London. Was there an idea that could bring all this together for America's favorite soft drink, and if so, could it be seen amidst the gloom that was permeating from a few hundred sulky people stuck in the boondocks outside of Limerick, Ireland?

As he stared up at the ceiling that night, he hoped the idea was there and that it might begin to glow. But if it did, it was so faint he was not aware of its presence. He tossed and turned all night, and next morning, although the sun came out, for him it seemed as dark as ever.

That next day the passengers were not permitted to leave the airport. They could not hire a car for a few hour's drive and a sightseeing tour of Irish villages and Irish fields with forty shades of green. They could not get on one of the buses that ferried more fortunate passengers to and from Limerick. They could only shop in the duty-free shops, eat, snack, talk, and feel sorry for themselves. They had been placed on permanent standby, ready to board the giant jet at a moment's notice when and if the reports from London became favorable.

By mid-morning all the shopping that could be done had been done, and the passengers began collecting in small groups around the tables in the coffee shop. A large, shapely German woman in her early thirties who had been one of the more indignant passengers was now sitting with a small Jewish businessman. In a loud, Teutonic manner she had demanded special treatment in the motel lobby the night before. The businessman and several other passengers had been openly contemptuous of her behavior, which in any case had not been rewarded.

And now, today, they were together, keeping each other company. Their common language seemed to be English with heavy accents, and the common icebreaker was a bottle of Coca-Cola. Perhaps the ice had been broken earlier—while shopping or maybe even the night before in the dingy motel bar after she learned she would not have a room to herself.

Whatever the events that had led to the scene in the coffee shop, there was no question that they were enjoying each other's company over bottles of Coke.

And that scenario was being multiplied throughout the coffee shop. People from all over the world, forced by circumstance, were having a Coke—or a cup of coffee or tea—together. They were not staring gimlet-eyed at each other as they might do over the polished surface of a negotiating table. They were not sitting side by side looking glumly ahead as if in Row 16, seats A and B, on Pan Am Flight 12. They were making eye contact over a Coke, and they were keeping each other company.

The antiques dealer was talking about some of the areas in England where he hoped to find the furniture in which he specialized, but the writer was only half listening. He was watching a composite of the whole world re-forming around him in new groups, based not so much on national boundaries or common business interests as on a desire to keep company with someone else. And in many cases that someone was someone new. And somewhere in the darkness of the young writer's unconscious a firefly lit up, and in that moment he saw a bottle of Coke in a whole new light.

Now it was no longer a soft drink to please a palate with a unique taste accompanied by the pleasant lifting of spirits that caffeine supplies. Instead, it was ten or twelve ounces of commonality between diverse peoples. It was more than an icebreaker between young couples on a first date. It was more than a conversation starter as a remark about the weather might be.

A bottle of Coca-Cola, as he saw it, guaranteed six or eight minutes of a shared opinion about something: "We both like the same drink." Trivial? Perhaps, but still it was a start.

He began to see a bottle of Coca-Cola as more than a drink that refreshed a hundred million people a day in almost every corner of the globe. So, he began to see the familiar words, "Let's have a Coke," as more than an invitation to pause for refreshment. They were actually a subtle way of saying, "Let's keep each other company for a little while." And he knew they were being said all over the world as he sat there in Ireland.

That was the basic idea: to see Coke not as it was originally designed to be—a liquid refresher—but as a tiny bit of commonality between all peoples, a universally liked formula that would help them keep each other company for a few minutes.

To many people the idea that the advertising writer grabbed on to that day might have seemed just average. But he had been in the world of advertising ideas long enough to recognize those that can be big. And he had an inkling the moment he saw it that this idea's appeal might go beyond the United States, that it could be worldwide.

Because he had been trained to execute ideas as well as discover them, the young writer did not stop at the basic idea. He began to write lines on a paper napkin. It was a time of war in the Far East and increased tension between the United States and the Soviet Union. So he started out with thoughts that saw the people of the world as passengers on a large jet and lines like "We must fly together or die together." The lines were obviously too philosophical and too heavy for Coca-Cola or the New Seekers. And others were too long, or just plain didn't say what he was trying to say. But one line hit him as right, and he stuffed it into his pocket for a second and third look during the hours ahead.

Pan Am Flight 12 took off—finally—around dusk, bound for England, but not for London. The fog over Heathrow had not abated but had gotten worse, and news of it had reached as far away as America, where many newspapers featured pictures of presidential aspirant Ed Muskie, stranded and sleeping on a bench in the airport.

The jumbo jet landed in Liverpool at seven o'clock and bused its London-bound passengers to the capital. The north of England was covered with snow. The roads were treacherous and traffic heavy as the bus approached London.

The advertising writer checked into his hotel, the Savoy, a little after midnight and was happy to learn that his collaborators on the project were waiting in an adjoining suite. Roger Cook, the British songwriter, and Billy Davis, music producer/writer on all Coca-Cola projects, had been working all day. They had finished one song and started on another. The tight schedule had forced them to make an appointment with the New Seekers' arranger the following day at noon, even though they did not have all the material.

The writer who had been stranded—and who was ultimately responsible to the Coca-Cola Company for the success of the project—could only thank them and apologize for being late.

He had, however, an idea he liked. An idea he really liked. An idea he thought worth working on throughout the night until the arranger arrived the next day. It was already past the basic stage. It was executed in the form of words—just a few words—a line, in fact. Nothing more than that.

He didn't know it then, but it was an idea that would in the months ahead become the core of one of the most liked and respected commercials ever to be written. For now, it was just a line on a napkin.

It was late and there was no time for much setup of the idea. He said simply, "I could see and hear a song that treated the whole world as if it were a person—a person the singer would like to help and get to know. I'm not sure exactly how the lyric should start, but I know the last line." And then he read the line he had written on the paper napkin.

"I'd like to buy the world a Coke and keep it company."

CHAPTER TWO

Backer's Definition of an Idea

THE LITTLE SPARK of insight that illuminated a bottle of Coca-Cola in a different light, not as a soft drink but as a tiny piece of common territory in which diverse peoples can keep each other company, is an example of a *basic idea*. But it is not a definition of one. Before I go any further, I had better provide you with some definitions of basic and executional ideas, and doing that is not as easy as you might think.

There seems to be no universally accepted definition of what the word "idea" means. My dictionary, *Webster's Ninth New Collegiate*, lists seven definitions, most of them quite different from one another. In fact, it defines the word alternatively as "an indefinite or unformed conception" and "a formulated thought or opinion." This fuzziness continues through the various definitions offered, from the concrete ("a visible representation of a conception," "a plan for action"; "an image recalled by memory") to the abstract ("an entity actually or potentially present to consciousness"; "a transcendent entity that is a real pattern of which existing things are imperfect representations").

Webster's then goes on for nearly 150 words trying to differentiate "idea," "concept," "conception," "thought," "notion," and "impression."

Let's stop and reflect a moment on the significance of all that. You and your associates use the word "idea" every day to communicate in business meetings, political gatherings, creative conferences, sales presentations, new product sessions, social get-togethers, and so on. But which of the many different definitions of "idea" are you using?

We are not just splitting hairs here; the differences are big. The miscommunications that result when different people have different meanings in mind can lead to major misunderstandings, serious frustrations, and the derailment or misdirection of countless projects.

No wonder we see America as a country starved for ideas. What else would you expect? We can't even agree on the meaning of what we're hungry for.

I'm going to challenge Webster's and give you definitions of "a basic idea" and "an executional idea" that have served me well in a business that is supposed to be idea-driven. I won't go back and retrace the etymology of the word "idea." I'm not a language scholar, and even if I were, I would not try to solve this problem with scholarship.

There are millions of people who try each day to keep things moving in a positive direction. That means they have to harness the power of ideas. These people need simple, workday, easy-to-use definitions. In modern parlance, you might say they need to have "basic idea" and "executional idea," or "substance" and "style," made user-friendly.

So I respectfully submit the following pair of definitions:

*A **Basic Idea** is an abstract answer to a perceived desire or need.*

*An **Executional Idea** is a rendering in words, symbols, sounds, colors, shapes, forms, or any combination thereof, of an abstract answer to a perceived desire or need.*

Please hold the questions, catcalls, or applause for a few more paragraphs while I give some examples of how these definitions can help you with your own ideas.

Let's explore first how a new invention might be created for an automobile, given our definitions of basic and executional ideas. I am going to try to invent something brand-new, but it will take years before we know for sure whether it is a good idea or not. To begin, I will start with a 1930s invention that was a success, and I will reinvent it using the definitions I have advanced and then proceed to the new one.

The automobile industry had sold over fifty million cars by 1930. The Federal Aid Road Act had been passed and roads—mostly paved with asphalt—were multiplying. But not fast enough. As *Automobile News* said in its Centennial Celebration issue, "By 1940 . . . the pace of road construction seemed inadequate to cope with the increasing traffic congestion."

And, of course, along with increased traffic came increased deaths due to automobile accidents. According to the National Safety Council, the number of motor vehicles nearly tripled between 1920 and 1930, and motor vehicle deaths increased by more than two and one-half times. Moreover, the number of deaths per ten thousand vehicles, which had begun to decrease between 1920 and 1925, began to increase again after 1926 and on into the 1930s.

PERCEIVED DESIRE OR NEED: There was, then, in 1930 a genuine need for better communication between drivers on the road so as to reduce the danger of collisions. Many people are thinking about the need to make driving less hazardous, but good basic ideas are, as always, in short supply.

Could you have done one? Could I?
Could we have thought in the abstract?
After the fact it's easy.

ABSTRACT ANSWER: Think of the taillights of an automobile as communicators—they give motorists a way to "talk" to drivers who are following.

EXECUTIONS: Put an extra light bulb in a taillight to be ignited when the brake pedal is pushed. Also provide the driver with a handy switch to signal his intention to turn left or right by igniting extra bulbs that flash in the taillights on the left or right side of the car. Today we know both of these executions as "brake lights" and "directional signals," and they are standard equipment on all American cars. Brake lights were introduced in 1933 and directional signals in 1938.

ABSTRACT ANSWERS AS MIND EXPANDERS: I will now try coming up with a new invention using the abstract answer as the wellspring from which new executions must come. This is the ultimate test of abstract answers—the sine qua non. If they are fresh and original, and if the desire or need they perceive is a genuine one, they will lead to new and exciting executions. The number of people who share the "perceived desire or need" will provide the answer to "How big is the idea?"

I went back to my abstract answer, which was, "think of the taillights of an automobile as communicators—they give motorists a way to 'talk' to drivers who are following." Did it provide a fresh insight into solving a perceived need or want? Did it expand my mind and inspire a new and exciting execution? You will have to be the judge. Here is what I came up with when I returned to the basic idea behind the taillights: Brake lights at present merely tell us how long the brake is being hit, not how hard. When the driver up front really slams down hard on the brakes, wouldn't it be wise to have taillights that communicated "hard stop coming up" and flash a special warning in that instance? Or when a driver needs to travel at a much slower pace than is normal on a particular highway, wouldn't a taillight flasher, similar to, but different from, the ones we switch on to warn passing motorists that we are parked or stalled by the roadside, be worth considering?

If you have ever been hit from behind as I have, and been told, "I didn't know you were stopping so fast," you will understand my invention.

Possibilities for executions are endless, for the mind always expands when the abstract idea is fresh and insightful. In this case, highway statistics on accidents would indicate how big the need is. But when you think about it, "taillight talk" is a language that definitely needs to be further exploited.

At this point I need to set the record straight about the lineality of the idea process. I don't want you to think I'm saying that the inventors of brake lights and turn signals consciously went from the abstract to the practical in a regimented sequence. Most good idea people go through the abstract stage without even knowing it. But the originality of their finished ideas will always be dependent on the freshness and originality of the abstract solution to the perceived desire or need.

Also, this book is not just interested in giving you the tools to come up with basic ideas. I know that much of your involvement with ideas will come from judging them and helping the good ones along. But you, the judge, need to uncover and examine the abstract idea underneath the executions that are put before you if you are to analyze them well. In the case above, it may have been a crude engineer's drawing of a design for a turn signal. Would you have encouraged him to go forward with the project if you had been in a position to say "yea" or "nay" at Buick, the company that first introduced the turn signal? Would you have been able to say, "Hey, that is a big idea because it satisfies a need that millions of motorists have"?

Let's turn now to a more explicitly "creative" arena, the arts. I am going to plunge you into an exciting era of America's history—the ten years leading up to the crash of 1929. It was a wonderful era to be living in, if you were rich.

Today's *Lifestyles of the Rich and Famous* seems flat compared to what went on during the years in which you now find yourself.

On the other hand, although there is never a good time to be poor, the 1920s were particularly dismal for many Americans. I realize it got even worse in the thirties but, nonetheless, behind the ragtime beat of the twenties were a lot of small saloons where hopelessness was poured into every glass.

The gateway to America in those years was, as we all know, through Ellis Island into New York. Hundreds of thousands were pouring off the boats and had to make their way as best they could in a big, strange city in a land three thousand miles or more from where they were born. Their backgrounds and languages were diverse. Economics often dictated that families had to be split up after they arrived here. And many of those in their twenties and thirties came with no family at all. Their relatives had stayed behind in the old country.

Everyone who passed through Ellis Island was examined by a doctor, and those who were sick with tuberculosis or trachoma (an eye disease) were quarantined and denied entrance. But there was a more prevalent sickness which the doctors couldn't find with their stethoscopes. It wasn't fatal, but it was debilitating and incurable, at least with ordinary medicines. The sickness was, of course, loneliness. And the immigrants were not the only ones suffering. The country people, many of them dispossessed sharecroppers and drought victims, were migrating to the cities in droves.

A big city is a lonely place when it's only ten miles from home. But when it's a hundred miles or three thousand miles or more, and you have no family and friends there, the real condition that results must be described as "acute loneliness."

Suppose you had been the curator of a prestigious New York museum at the time and were constantly having to judge the painters of the day. You want to exhibit the good ones, and if your budget permits, you would like to acquire representative pictures by the very best of them for your permanent collection.

As a curator, you have a good eye for execution—color, brush technique, composition, etc. But do you have a good sense of basic ideas, abstract answers to perceived desires or needs? The artist himself may never have consciously gone through the abstract state to get to his painting—he may never have consciously said to himself, "I perceive a desire or a need there"—but if an abstract answer to a desire or need is present in his painting, can you recognize it?

If so, you would have been ahead of most of your fellow curators in New York. They took many years to recognize Edward

Hopper. He was middle-aged before museums began to purchase his paintings. Yet today he is recognized as superior to most of his contemporaries, whose paintings were triumphs of style but lacking in substance.

In the twenties and thirties Hopper chose to paint the agony of loneliness. Those critics who insist he was extolling the joys of loneliness have never been alone in a foreign land and pinched for money. His paintings were not political. He flatly denied that he was ever trying to make a statement with them. Despite himself, the paintings addressed a basic idea by definition.

This same idea showed up in other artistic endeavors of the time. Imagine yourself as a proprietor of one of the biggest music stores in America, with a prime location on Broadway. It sold sheet music almost by the ton, and as many records as any two other stores put together. But when a sales representative of Irving Berlin Publishing—or maybe Mr. Berlin himself—came in to plug some songs for you to order in sheet music or record form, would you have gone overboard for "All by Myself"? And later on for "What'll I Do?" and "All Alone"? Most of what Berlin was writing in those days sold well, but in 1924 and 1926—the years that they came out—"What'll I Do?" and "All Alone" sold over a million copies in sheet music alone. Those numbers were big even for Berlin. A million-selling record is still considered big today, and our population has doubled since 1920.

Using my definition of a basic idea and an executional idea, let's judge Hopper's *Sunday* (1926) and *Automat* (1927), along with Berlin's "All by Myself" (1920), "What'll I Do?" (1924) and "All Alone" (1926).

PERCEIVED DESIRE OR NEED: People who are alone and lonely in the world want to feel that someone out there shares their agony and understands it.

ABSTRACT ANSWER: Make loneliness a theme in painting or song.

EXECUTIONS: Create paintings of ordinary people surrounded by a world that is realistic except that there are no other people in it, or create songs to be sung in the first person about everyday people in everyday surroundings who are alone and feeling the agony of loneliness.

There are, of course, many other successful executions expressing loneliness in painting and song. Because this book is concentrating on ideas and executions that have mass appeal, I am selecting songs and paintings from a time when the need for them was especially great. For ideas, as with everything else in life, timing is critical. It can determine how big they are.

Like Hopper, Berlin was not consciously thinking "mass appeal" when he wrote the first of his loneliness trio—"All by Myself." He wrote it for just one person, his mother, Lena, whose husband had died some years before and whose family was able to visit her only infrequently. But the song "took off," and Irving Berlin understood that he had touched a basic nerve in the public, so he wrote two more loneliness songs.

If you have never seen Hopper's paintings or listened to Berlin's songs, it is more difficult for me to ask whether or not they fulfill the basic definitions I have set up. It's easier with a directional signal for a car. We have all used those. I can only urge that you borrow a copy of a retrospective book on Hopper's art and judge for yourself while listening to "All Alone" and "All by Myself" from an album of Berlin's classics.

Also, I must admit that in final execution, Hopper failed by my definition of a big idea because his paintings were never made available in cheap reprint form to the general public of the time. Perhaps, like Berlin's sheet music, they would have sold a lot of copies. And they certainly sold well later on, in the years of the "Me Generation," the mid-seventies and eighties. The loneliness of that decade came more from being psychologically uprooted from family and friends than from physical separation. But it was loneliness, nonetheless, and Hopper was, in a sense, "rediscovered" by the public.

In the final analysis, mass ideas must be executed in mass form to reach their full potential, even if their creators do not see them as mass ideas themselves. The intensity of the need or desire as exemplified by the loneliness of the era certainly affected Hopper's executions and helped make them the kind of art that lives instead of dies. The same goes for "All by Myself." It was sung at Berlin's one hundredth birthday tribute on national TV, and it sounded as fresh as the day it was written.

When style has real substance beneath it, it has the force and intensity to last without burning out.

No matter where you are—in business, in the arts, in marketing, or in advertising—you must have some definition of a basic idea and an executional idea to go by. Otherwise you won't be able to separate the two, and you will be a good judge neither of what you have created nor of what you must say "yea" or "nay" to in the course of your day.

My definitions of basic and executional ideas have served me well, and I resubmit them here for you to use just as they are or as starting points for you to develop some definitions of your own.

> *A* ***Basic Idea*** *is an abstract answer to a perceived desire or need.*
>
> *An* ***Executional Idea*** *is a rendering in words, symbols, sounds, colors, shapes, forms, or any combination thereof, of an abstract answer to a perceived desire or need.*

CHAPTER THREE

The Idea Family

THINK BACK TO the sixties if you're old enough to remember them. (If not, I will sum them up for you in a few sentences.) They were years when idealism dominated cynicism among America's youth and the answer to most of the world's needs and wants was "All you need is love," courtesy of Paul, John, Ringo, and George. Today, it's difficult to imagine a time when peace was worth more than money or a sports car to a large segment of the population, but the sixties was such a time.

So people back then, especially young people, felt a need and a desire for anything that might promote better understanding between various peoples of the world, even if it was only a universally liked bottle of soda pop that helped those people "keep each other company." And, as I have said, answering that perceived desire or need in the abstract was the basic idea on which the stranded advertising writer's proposed commercial rested.

The line "I'd like to buy the world a Coke and keep it company" represented a partial rendering in words of this abstract answer to the perceived desire or need. So the line was the start of the executional idea, a start that would dictate the tone, mood, and form of the more complete execution that followed. It did not, however, represent a finished execution per se. But during those early hours at the Savoy Hotel, the nucleus of a very talented Idea Family began to assemble, which would move the execution along in a way the world would later take to heart.

Before I go any further, let me explain about Idea Families. A basic idea is like a newborn babe. It needs a family that extends beyond the immediate parents if it is going to grow and live up to its full potential. Fathers and mothers can't take an infant all that way by themselves. Along the way they are going to need help—teachers, doctors, dentists, coaches, etc. The same applies to a basic idea.

A basic idea will never grow without the help of people who can provide executions that make it practical along with other people who put their faith—and often their money—in it and say, "We'll back it, or we'll use it." What all these people together represent is what I call the Idea Family.

The Idea Family consists of many different kinds of people representing many different skills and interests. They are attached to each other not by shared genes, but by a mutual attraction to an idea in some stage of its development. And unlike the family that shares a gene pool right from the start, an Idea Family grows as the idea grows. The size of each Idea Family and the roles played by the individual members depend on the nature of the idea itself, the category into which it falls, the number of people it hopes to influence, and how far the original parent can take it before needing outside help.

Technically speaking, a small idea with a rich parent needs no extended family. For example, if someone has basic ideas that he feels he has the talent to execute in blank verse, he can pay to have a limited edition of his poems published and distributed among his friends.

But when one is dealing with big ideas that seek to address the needs or desires of large groups of people, those kinds of ideas just don't reach their potential without some sort of an extended family.

How far the parent of the basic idea takes it before others join the family depends on both the individual parent and the category into which the idea falls. For instance, in the fine arts the basic idea and the executional ideas usually come from a single parent, as in the case of a painter, a sculptor, a poet, a serious novelist, a playwright, or a classical composer.

In the more popular arts and in pure entertainment the original executors may well be teams—but, they, too, carry the basic idea well on into execution. Semiclassical composers like George Gershwin, who was not capable of orchestrating basic musical ideas like "Rhapsody in Blue," fall into a second category—the category of teams such as songwriting teams, playwriting teams, screenwriting teams, advertising art director/copywriter teams. All of these original parents are also capable of taking their basic ideas into the first stages of execution.

But somewhere down the line these parents have to expand their Idea Family. The playwriting and screenwriting teams need directors and producers. The songwriters need singers and producers. The painters need patrons or galleries, the novelists need editors and publishers, the politicians need speech writers, the inventors need designers and marketers, and in the end all of them need someone to put up the dough.

As I say, all of those who gather around somebody's newborn brainchild are part of an Idea Family, but those who gather around first and help clothe the babe with executional ideas I call Uncles and Aunts.

Later on come those who are interested primarily in getting the kid into college, that is, moving the idea along toward its intended destiny. I call these people the Godfathers. They are the account people, agents, and lobbyists who act as conduits between the original family of Parents, Uncles, and Aunts and the final Judges of the idea. And those Judges are the last team of people the idea must pass before it gets to its public—the studio heads, agency clients, the backers of Broadway shows, etc. They are the ones who have to put their money and reputations on the line and adopt the graduating brainchild. You might say they are the ones who offer him or her a job. I call them the Surrogate Parents.

It turned out that "Buy the World a Coke" would need an Idea Family of five Uncles, plus several Godfathers and Surrogate Parents, before it could become an advertising success on television. And it assembled a very special and, in my opinion, ideal Idea Family along the way. Not only was each a talented and mature professional in a particular field, but together they represented a polytypic group, and the importance of this type of variegated family for big ideas cannot be overestimated.

I have always felt that clones of any race, class, creed, sex, or economic background make less effective mass marketing teams than teams that have a broad balance. And I don't mean just for mass marketing of packaged goods. I'm including motion pictures, TV shows, pop songs, department stores, and especially politicians and their ideas for our betterment or detriment. Over the years, many experiences have strengthened my faith in the need for balanced teams. One early experience remains vivid to this day.

It happened in the mid-1960s, when I was part of a team that presented a large agency's credentials to the General Foods Company.

At that time, General Foods was considered one of America's premier marketers. It had built such famous brands as Jell-O and Maxwell House coffee. But with all the momentum of fame and fortune behind it, General Foods had not recently fathered any new brands that were making it big.

And as I say, I remember certain details of our presentations to this day. The room was set up like a drab little theater. There were twelve or perhaps fifteen people in the audience, and as they filed in they each dutifully shook our hands and introduced themselves. They were proper and courteous, and I should have been very "up" for my part of the presentation. Instead, I was a mess—all over the lot, distracted, and without enthusiasm for myself, my creative group, or the agency for which I was working.

I was the third presenter—after the agency's chief executive and its president, who gave the "How Big and How Important We Are" part of the presentation. My part was to present the "How We Think and How We Execute Our Ideas" portion. It would involve my showing a reel of commercials—all illustrating consumer benefits in a variety of ways. In between the commercials I would stop and discuss why we had done what we did. But while I was sitting in the darkness, only half listening to my colleagues (I already knew what they would be saying), it began to dawn on me that Jell-O, my favorite summer dessert, was in trouble. It was being marketed by a group of clones.

I had just met the dozen or so big guns who were in charge of judging marketing and advertising ideas, plus developing new products, for the largest food company in America, and they were all the same person. They were graduates of Yale or Princeton, and later Harvard Business School. Tanned, trim, and Protestant, they were all dressed by Brooks Brothers, Fenn-Feinstein, or J. Press. To judge by the conversations among them before the meeting got under way, they were all tennis players in the summer, squash players in the winter, emotional about who was summering on Fisher's Island these days, and unemotional about Jell-O.

I don't mean to knock Yalies or Princetonians—I'm a Yale graduate myself—and, furthermore, I don't want to deride the Harvard Business School approach to marketing a product. But I felt strongly then, and more strongly today, that it takes all kinds of people to fully explore the magic of an idea like lime Jell-O. And the reactions to the various commercials and the different ideas behind them confirmed my fears. Because there was not a variety of reactions. There was one reaction. The executives nodded in unison, shook their heads in the same places—mostly where the commercials departed from being serious—and asked the same questions.

But Jell-O is an "everyperson" product for every season. Every mood, every age, every income group. And when the changing times would begin to dictate that these Ivy League clones understand the School of Hard Knocks, I was certain, they would turn Jell-O over to Ozzie and Harriet, who were on their way out, not in. And that's what happened.

After the presentation, the General Foods people politely showed us the door. They were obviously underwhelmed by what they had seen and heard. We were not a uniform lot, and my part—which only hinted at what I am now saying openly in the pages of this book—undoubtedly clashed with their corporate culture.

As the years passed, and as General Foods products continued to slip in market share, the more I became convinced that my gut instinct had been right.

BIG IDEAS NEED IDEA FAMILIES THAT ARE BROAD BASED.

And that is what "I'd Like to Buy the World a Coke and Keep It Company" had all along the way up to and through its TV debut.

As you have no doubt realized, the young writer stuck at Shannon Airport, the Father of the idea, was me. The background that I brought to the Idea Family was a silver spoon—not one from Tiffany or Cartier, but rather one from a silversmith's workbench. My mother's line was started in this country by a Huguenot silversmith who landed in Charleston in the early 1700s.

I don't believe he was an artist of an artisan since no signed "Legaré" pieces have been found, and his children became successful farmers and politicians. (My mother refused to connect the word "politician" to our family and always referred to Congressman Legaré and Ambassador Joel Roberts Poinsett as "statesmen.")

My idols growing up, however, were the songwriters who wrote for the masses, not the classes. For me it was Irving Berlin, not Cole Porter. I thought, and still do, that to write songs America sings was a high calling, and during my years in the Navy and later on at Yale, I continually wrote songs and musical skits and shows—middle-class, cozy, happy, very easy to sing and hard to forget. The fact that America began to stop singing songs in the late fifties and to merely listen to them instead left me with a pocketful of impossible dreams and a head full of tunes. So by the time I was stranded in Ireland I had begun writing musical commercials in a unique form I called "song-form commercials." They were very successful, and today, most of the "Oldies but Goodies" collections of musical commercials include more by W. Backer than by any other writer.

In addition to me, the Idea Family for "Buy the World" would include a very special pair of Uncles to help with the executional idea.

Each one would bring to that next stage of idea development a different viewpoint about what the various peoples of the world might wish for each other if they were "keeping company" over a Coke. Billy Davis, for instance, brought his experiences of having grown up black in Detroit with a grandmother as a surrogate mother. He had toured as one of the Four Tops and knew what it was like to be locked out of all-white hotels in towns where there were no available accommodations for a touring black singing group. (There were actually Five Tops in those days. Their tour schedules were so full, and travel between stops took so much time, that sleep was often out of the question unless there was at all times an alternate Top standing by to substitute. Before the days of TV, people didn't know what the Four Tops looked like and, as Billy said, in the South in those days, all black men looked alike anyway.) Before that, Billy had been one of the many talents who were close to Berry Gordy when Motown Records was starting up, and his writer's royalties, which came from the Motown songs he helped write, had been very helpful during some of the lean years between Motown, the Four Tops, and being artists and repertoire (A&R) director of Chess Records, the title he held when I cajoled him into trying the agency business.

Roger Cook's experiences were of growing up middle class, not in America, but in Bristol, England, at the time John, Paul, George, and Ringo were teenagers in Liverpool. And like them, Roger had had ambitions to be a performer. He started performing as a singer with a band called the Blue Mink and as "David" of David and Jonathan. But bookings were slim at times, and during one of those periods he had ran into another singer named Roger Greenway. Cook asked Greenway, more out of politeness than genuine interest, "How's it going, mate?" When Greenway answered, "I got troubles," Cook responded, "You've got your troubles, I got mine." And within days the two of them had written what would later turn out to be a classic pop song with a title inspired by that chance meeting. After "You've Got Your Troubles" hit big, Roger wrote for his living, although he would always fill a singing booking if asked.

Together the three of us represented the sort of diverse and proven talents that I believe make ideal Uncles and Aunts for an Idea Family. But when I presented my one line to them at midnight in the Savoy Hotel, we were not yet an Idea Family. I had to get the other two to join me, so that we could complete my executional idea.

CHAPTER FOUR

Executing Words and Music

"EXECUTE" IS A schizophrenic verb. It may well be the most schizophrenic verb in our language.

As I have been using the word, it means "to complete or put into effect" or "to make according to a pattern—as a work of art." But, of course, it also means "to put to death—legally."

The three of us in Suite 611 of the Savoy Hotel had less than forty-eight hours "to complete or put into effect" the Coke idea for a recording session in a manner that was so effective it would not be "put to death—legally" in the future.

If you have been Father or Uncle to ideas at all, you know that many good ones have been put to death legally in the boardrooms and back rooms of corporate America. Our system often lets the best die young, instead of the worst, because catching the firefly and sparking the brainchild are only part of what ideas are about. Along the way they will need all the help they can get, and a "proper execution" is an essential part of that help. That's execution, of course, in the positive sense of the word.

I cannot say that either the basic idea or the start of its execution was greeted with instant enthusiasm by the two people I was hoping to recruit into my Idea Family. And, in fact, I had not expected the ideas for Coke to be accepted at once. They aimed too high and were too far-out to be easy.

Professional executors know firsthand that "the higher you climb the harder you fall." It is always easy to get approval when the assignment is "climb a small mountain." But we've all seen documentaries that show how silent and thoughtful the pros become when the assignment is "climb the Himalayas." So my two pros were at first silent and thoughtful.

Finally, I began to sell—but it was soft sell. With real professionals you never use hard sell when it's your basic idea. "Guys," I said, "I know this idea reaches a bit. After all we're only selling a bottle of pop here. On the other hand, think of all the times you have personally used Coke as a social catalyst, as a disarmer, or maybe as a peace offering. If you stop to think about it, offering someone a glass of Coca-Cola is really the world's most accepted way of saying, 'Let's sit down and chat, let's get to know each other better, I want to be your friend. . . .' "

They both began to realize that the basic idea helped make a bottle of Coca-Cola relevant to their everyday needs and wants in an entirely new and fresh way. They had both used the soft drink many times as a simple social icebreaker, especially with members of the opposite sex. But this idea went beyond that. This one said that Coke's universal popularity can be used to establish a bit of commonality between peoples who are separated by gaps in culture, geography, economics, and age, as well as sex. And since Roger and Billy had to deal with those gaps every day, and had helped narrow them many times over a Coke, they said to themselves, "I believe it, it's true." And in this way they became Uncles to the basic idea.

Because people in power often fail to understand what good basic ideas are all about, in the course of our business lives all of us often have to work on executing basic ideas that we do *not* believe to be truly relevant to people's wants or needs. But, in my opinion, the better we are at executing good basic ideas, the worse we are at executing bad ones. We try because, unfortunately, that's often "part of the job," but the enthusiasm of the prideful professional cannot be artificially summoned to do dreck. "Garbage in, garbage out" holds for basic ideas as well as computers.

The line itself, "I'd like to buy the world a Coke and keep it company," demanded even more reflection than the basic idea. Was it a musical idea? In pop songs "he" always bought "her" a Coke. But "the whole world"? Wasn't that a bit ridiculous?

"I understand your concerns," I said. "Up to now the world has never been personalized in song. It's been 'Love makes the world go round,' 'What the world needs now is love sweet love,' and so on. But if we can arrive at universal things that everybody in the world wants, can't we treat the world as one universal person? Let's at least try. What have we got to lose except some of the Savoy's fancy engraved stationery?"

Because Billy and Roger were pros, and because they realized that the basic idea was both big and original, and that my beginning of the execution was organic to the basic idea, they were willing to go ahead. And because they were pros they saw all the pluses of the basic idea and the start of the execution. But they also saw the pitfalls that would lie ahead. However, we were no longer a parent and friends. We were a family of executors with a desire to complete the idea, not kill it.

The brainchild we had adopted was unabashedly naïve, and no one tried to change that. Professional people accept the shape of a line that sums up an idea. It was what it was. It was Dorothy and Toto longing for their rainbow. It was a bit of unrealistic idealism that would someday have to face a series of very realistic worlds. We all understood that. We would worry about that next month in the boardrooms and on the airwaves ahead.

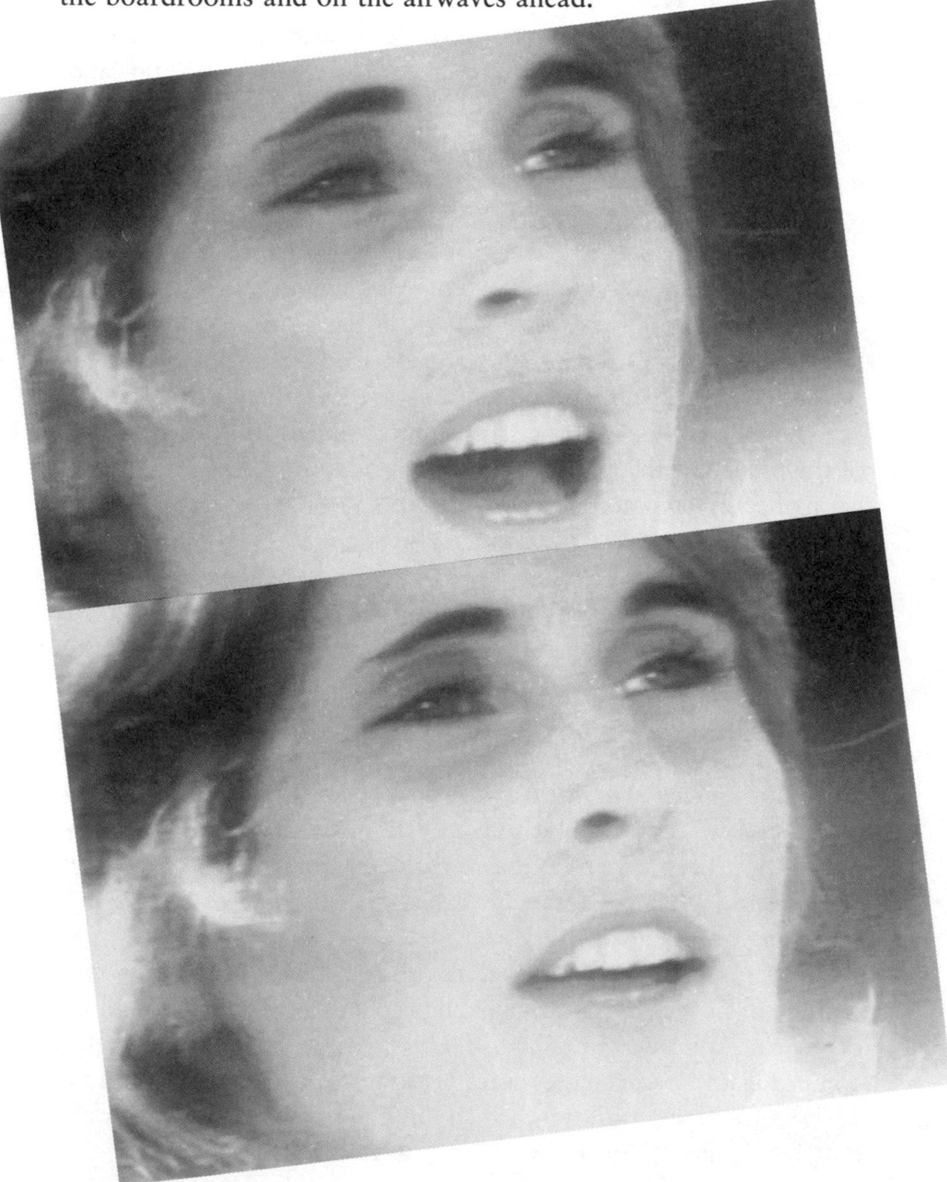

For now—it was put stars in your eyes and pretend you had the power to "buy the world a Coke and keep it company."

I said, "I see a structure like that of a song where the singer wants to wish a number of good things for a loved one. I know that structure is so idealistic, it isn't used very often. But it has worked in the past once or twice. Like in 'More I Cannot Wish You' from *Guys and Dolls*."

So we began to think of all the things we could wish for someone we wanted to get to know and to help. Our someone was of no particular race, color, creed, sex, or country of origin—like our diverse

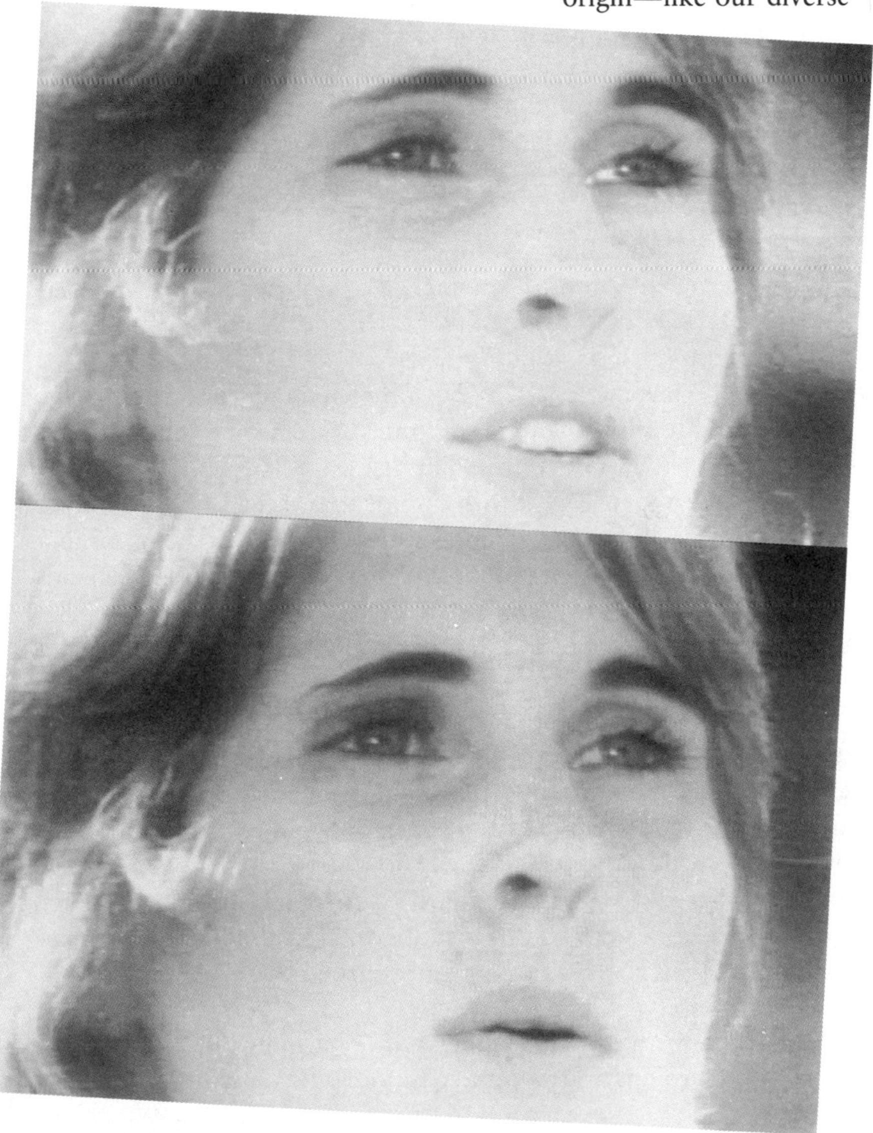

threesome. Our someone was everyone and was named "The World." And during the next hour and a half the differences in our background paid off. Those differences allowed us to come together, like the symbols on a slot machine do every so often, and hit a jackpot.

For the first ten minutes we sat silent, slumped in the over-stuffed chairs and sofas, trying to decide what each of us would wish for The World. And then we began to open up. The first thoughts, however, were weak, and after twenty minutes or so of rejecting one another's shallow, top-of-the head ideas we became silent again. Then Billy Davis gave us one from deep inside.

"You've got nothing if you don't have a roof over your head," he said very quietly. "The first thing The World needs is a home." Neither Roger nor I would have thought of that. To us a roof over our heads had never been in question. It was a given. I put the idea into the rhythm pattern of my line. "I'd like to buy the world a home," I said.

We all liked it. But then Billy continued, "How many people can afford to *buy* someone a home? We don't want to be just for the rich. How about, 'I'd like to *build* the world a home'?" So those became the first words of our lyric.

I can't remember exactly who completed the first line with the words, "And furnish it with love," but I do remember quite a long conversation about how we couldn't just leave The World with any old home. We had to leave it with a home that was a little bit special. We finally agreed that every home in the world should be furnished with love—and at that time we knew there would be no disagreement beyond the walls of the Savoy with that style of decorating. The calendar may have said 1971, but culturally we were still, after all, living in the sixties.

Roger Cook supplied the next line. It was a line characteristic of a highly professional British lyricist. Hearing it at first, Billy and I both thought it a bit too poetic. I said it sounded like poor man's Wordsworth, but after we tried a dozen or so more prosaic descriptions of the setting we wanted for The World's home, we realized we had better stay with Roger's poetry. After all, the home was to be furnished with love, so it was fitting to surround it with "Apple trees and honey bees and snow-white turtle doves." Now we had Love and Peace.

I added the next line. It ended with "harmony" because I love the word. Harmony was becoming an out-of-date word even then, and today it has virtually disappeared, replaced by "we must work together." But working together isn't the same thing as working in harmony. The first implies "getting along while disliking one another and arriving at a compromise." Working in harmony recognizes working toward an agreed-upon goal—or sound in music—while recognizing and respecting the fact that each person—or note—has a right to be a different pitch. Also, I must admit, I needed a rhyme for "company," which was coming up.

So the next line was, "I'd like to teach the world to sing in perfect harmony," and the verse ended where it had all started, with "I'd like to buy the world a Coke and keep it company."

After that would come the chorus of "It's the real thing, what the world wants today is the real thing." That was the basis of the campaign music and lyrics I had written for Coke three years earlier, and which had tied all our ideas together since that time.

Now what we needed next was a lead-in melody for our lead-in words, and Roger and Billy had one handy. They had written it while I had been stuck in Shannon—a simple, almost bell-tone melody. They wrote it to go with some words they had written about apple pie and motherhood and Coke all being part of America. I had felt Coke was already there, so to speak, and that we would be talking to ourselves with lyrics like that. So we dumped the words. But the tune came in handy. Very handy.

(On my return to New York, I would tell the chairman of our company about the mom-and-apple-pie lyrics for Coke. He felt it might be appropriate for Chevrolet, and took it to them. They liked the idea, I guess, because they ran it as their big advertising campaign for three or four years.)

As for us it was now almost one o'clock and we were ready to meet the arranger and the New Seekers the next afternoon. We had not sat down with the purpose of writing—or executing—a hit. When you try to do that it never happens. We had merely done our professional best to draw from a basic idea an execution that was warm and romantic so that it would translate into a New Seekers song.

Though none of us realized it, the basic idea to which we had just added an executional idea in less than an hour would shape our futures almost more than anything we would ever write. It would help bring Roger Cook to America. Later on, as an American citizen—I was proud to provide one of the references called for on his citizenship application—he came up with big hits like "I Believe."

The idea would also establish Billy Davis's reputation as a top music producer far beyond his former stomping grounds, Chicago and Detroit. He would become a name in New York, London, and Nashville as well. And it would help me become cofounder of a major advertising agency.

It turned out to be that kind of an idea. But it would need the help of more executions, additional Idea Family members, strict attention to detail, and careful avoidance of the negative pull of Backer's Laws of Corporate Gravity before it got to where we wanted it to go.

CHAPTER FIVE

Backer's Law of Gravity

I WONDER, AS I look back, if "Buy the World" could have survived the battery of idea killers it would run up against in a typical marketing organization today. I am not at all sure it would have.

I have a theory about why there were fewer obstacles in the paths of ideas twenty years ago. Back then most of our companies were still young and growing. And growing companies have fewer levels of bureaucracy and a higher percentage of entrepreneurial types in their ranks than do older companies.

Today's manufacturing and service companies are more interested in staying in control of the continuous flow of business that represents a sort of "river of life" for mature companies. The flow is like a stream or river that gets its water from a continually melting glacier or a series of ever-replenishing springs. The flow is comforting, relatively predictable, and satisfying. You make the product, place it in its channels of distribution, do the normal things that keep the channels of distribution open (like advertising and motivating the sales force), you send out bills, pay your people, stay on top of the paperwork necessitated by state and federal regulations, stay on top of the cash flow, try to make a profit and pay dividends.

I don't mean to minimize the brains, skill, and energy it takes to do all this; I itemized the flow merely to illustrate that it doesn't call for capturing, judging, or executing big ideas on a daily basis. In fact, ideas tend to disrupt the smoothness of the flow itself.

Throughout all of this, the level of flow in the channels is pretty much a constant. Of course it varies, but never by much. And downstream it finds its usual dam and generates energy—or profits.

The system is designed to maintain the status quo, and it does. And the people who maintain the riverbanks mostly do a good job of preventing erosion. But there is no mechanism to absorb ideas when they come along.

Ideas are like thunderstorms. They don't come in a predictable manner. They are not continuous. They start with a flash of lightning and then the skies open up. Before you know it, some weather reporter is warning of flash floods in the area. Why flash floods? Simply because there are no channels to accommodate the sudden new flow. There is no active division continuously on alert with the skill and energy to channel the new flow into productive areas—like reservoirs to be used in the future for irrigating crops or generating power. Instead the flow is often wasted by banging against the present dam that is already at capacity.

In today's mature companies that's exactly what happens to many ideas. They are forced into channels whose main, everyday course is to keep the existing flow moving in the right direction. And when all of a sudden a big wave of new water comes cascading down their channel, the people in charge say to themselves—consciously or unconsciously—"Hey, man, this new torrent of ideas could erode my riverbank. I could be blamed and look bad." And they begin to feel the pull of Backer's Laws of Gravity.

It's not their fault, it's the organization's fault. Backer's Laws of Gravity are not inevitable, but they seem that way in many organizations. Let me explain the laws themselves, and how I came to discover them.

Some ten years into the business of trying to market ideas and getting more than my share of the lumps along the way—at least that's the way I saw it—I began to ask myself why it was all so hard, or to put it more positively, why wasn't it easier and more fun? Was it me? Perhaps it was. Certainly others were having a much easier time than I was, albeit with somewhat lower rates of success. Was it karma? Was I star-crossed?

I couldn't buy that kind of thinking then or now. I know too well that I have always been luckier than most. Nine times out of ten, when things go wrong the person I have to blame isn't Lady Luck. She likes me and always has. I'm the one who is at fault.

I finally came to the conclusion that there was something about "The System" itself that I didn't understand and that I had better figure out.

After many discussions with those around me who were sadder, perhaps, but certainly wiser to the ways of Big Business, I began to formulate "Backer's Law of Human Gravity" and its corollary, "Backer's Law of Corporate Gravity."

I want to confess here and now that neither has been officially recognized by the scientific community, and probably won't be. Because unlike Newton's Law of Gravity, Backer's Laws have some happy exceptions. But to understand Backer's Laws you have to first understand that Vince Lombardi was wrong. Winning isn't everything. It isn't even the only thing. Losing is everything.

Winning is everything only in the short run. In America, over a bit of time, losing almost always beats out winning in our memories.

Ask anyone in America what comes to mind when you say "Napoleon." The majority will answer "Waterloo." Waterloo! Why Waterloo?

Napoleon lost only three major battles in his entire military career. He won over a dozen. At Austerlitz, for instance, he defeated the Russian and Austrian armies combined. Later on he took Moscow. Ultimately his Russian invasion ended in disaster, as did Adolf Hitler's. But Napoleon, at least, was not stopped at the gates of Moscow as the Germans were.

Napoleon started his professional life as an obscure corporal and ended up emperor of Europe. The history books call him "one of the greatest conquerors of all time." But the man on the street remembers him for his final battle, which he lost, at Waterloo.

Richard Nixon's ideas about how to deal with an emerging China are generally conceded to have been brilliant. One could theorize that had Watergate never occurred, neither would Tiananmen Square. Yet Watergate happened. And if you ask the man on the street what he thinks of first when you say Richard Nixon, the answer will be Nixon's Waterloo—Watergate.

The Rose Bowl has been contested regularly since 1916. And there have been approximately 350 touchdowns scored in the games. But the names of the players who scored those touchdowns have mostly been forgotten, at least by the average person. The football buffs remember them, but not the rest of us.

However, in 1929 a California player named Riegels recovered a Georgia Tech fumble, was bumped around, turned around, and was so confused that he ran sixty yards the wrong way to within a yard of the wrong goal line, where he was finally tackled by a teammate. His name was remembered by all America for many years—far longer than the names of the official All-Americans who scored in later games. His first name was never recalled—just the nickname that brought to mind his most memorable feat. And that nickname was, of course, "Wrong Way"—"Wrong Way Riegels."

In ensuing years he even lost his last name and was remembered as "Wrong Way Corrigan"—after a flier who had also become famous for going the wrong way.

I use "most memorable" in the sense that Backer's Law uses it when it theorizes that the corporate and political game we play is all wrong. Why? Because the game's rules have been influenced by Backer's Laws of Gravity.

If you are skeptical about what seems to produce high profiles in our country, as well as in your company, try the exercise yourself. Take Jimmy Carter, whose ideas about an energy policy for America are making more sense every day—especially since they don't demand Desert Storms—and ask yourself what is he best remembered for, great ideas? Or losing?

Don't we remember Pearl Harbor in song, story, and history more than the triumphant landings on the coast of Normandy?

You may not agree that Backer's Law of Human Gravity is a real law, but when you think about it, you must admit it deals with a side of human nature that is worth examining.

I don't mean to imply that we don't worship success. We do. But I must remind you that you and your ideas will rise with success and be remembered for it only until you have your first big failure. Then the law sets in. It doesn't always take over, but you will feel the pull of its gravity. And when I say "your idea," I don't necessarily mean an idea of which you are the Father or Mother. You could be anyone who is asked to join an Idea Family along the way to an idea's maturity—you could be like this typical executive, for instance, in the company where the idea is being marketed.

One day he is happily tending his flow, keeping his banks clean of trash that might look unsightly or cause erosion, and the next day an idea comes tumbling down the stream, making all sorts of waves and overflowing his banks. And he is asked to judge it, and if he approves, to join the family. He is not really a qualified judge. He has had only limited experience and no real training in judging basic or executional ideas. On top of all that, he has exhibited no native talent for judging ideas by joining up with one or two of them forcefully before they have been successfully brought to maturity. He is probably not by nature or temperament an entrepreneur. He was on the way out of his previous job when he luckily landed this one. He has a wife, a mortgage, two kids with a third on the way. He is everywhere in the company, in all companies, and at all levels.

For him the pull of Backer's Law of Human Gravity is always present. And when a new idea comes along, the bigger and fresher it is, the more that law tugs at him.

They say Isaac Newton got the idea for his Law of Gravity while sitting under an apple tree and watching the apples fall.

I discovered the basis for Backer's Law of Human Gravity during a writing session I had with Ray Charles in the early seventies. We were working on a Coca-Cola commercial, and the idea was to make people feel good about the ordinary times in their lives, as opposed to the special times. The lyrics were about a man who has begun to realize that the pleasures found in one's own backyard are often the best:

> I've been around most everywhere
> And I've seen most everything
> And I want to tell you
> How glad I am
> Just to be home again.

The problem we were running into was that Ray's ideas for the musical execution of the idea differed from mine. Ray kept hearing it really bluesy, and consequently, sadder than I heard it.

In a situation like that it is often wise not to press the point, but to change the subject to a tangential topic.

Ray was at the piano in his California office studio playing and singing as only he can—about a tired man coming home, and I was finding him so exciting as both a person and a performer that it was hard to interrupt him, much less find fault with his blues-based tune. So I hit upon a good, and I say, tangential question.

"Ray," I asked, "why is it that the Top Forty always has more sad songs than happy ones?" Ray stopped doodling at the piano for maybe four beats and then gave an answer that was so perceptive, it made my big question seem suddenly very small.

" 'Cause there's more sad people than happy people," he said.

Thoreau had said it in a more literary fashion: "The mass of men lead lives of quiet desperation." But Ray's way of putting it became the basis for Backer's Law of Human Gravity. Since sad people can identify with failure more easily than they can with success, and since there are more sad people than happy people, Backer's Law of Human Gravity says:

FAILURE CARRIES MORE WEIGHT THAN SUCCESS.

There is, of course, one obvious exception to that rule. It does not apply to an environment where happy people are in the majority. And by happy people I mean those motivated by praise and recognition of their successes, however small. And by making light of their mistakes as long as those mistakes do not stem from lack of interest. Think about that when you select or create an environment.

As for Ray and myself, we compromised. Ray kept the blues chords and let the melody soar a bit on the words "How glad I am to be home again." And he promised to sing them in a way that would make a listener believe he was glad to be home again. And in the studio two days later he lived up to his word—and then some.

Backer's second law, the Law of Corporate Gravity, is an outgrowth of the first. Given our superior memory for failures, we have produced a peculiar scoring system for both the political game and the business game.

After extensive calculations that compute the laws of probability with the lessons of business history, including my own experiences, I have concluded that the corporate/political game is most akin to baseball, but different in that each player is scored separately, and the scoring is such that every game ends up a minus-sum game—not a zero-sum game but a minus-sum game. Let me explain.

In today's corporate game you get one point for a single, two for a double, and so on. However, you are docked ten points for striking out. That means a strikeout can wipe out five doubles or two home runs and two singles, etc. Since no one can hit that consistently, all players end up losing. There are no winning players. But there are winners. The winners are the nonplayers who sit in the stands instead of stepping up to the plate.

As the players drop off the corporate roster one by one, they leave the field, and in the end the only ones left are the nonplayers. At the end of the season, when bonuses, trophies, and titles are awarded, the nonplayers are the only ones present to step up to the mike and make speeches.

The result of these dynamics is that when you and your team are presenting ideas and executions you must remember this—a majority of the audience will more than likely consist of people who never stepped up to the plate with a basic idea or an execution of one. And they have learned not to be co-opted by them, either. So with insight developed by watching the corporate game for many seasons, they have come up with their own survival manual, and the first sentence reads: "Better to reject than be rejected."

If the above discourages you, just remember—some good ideas have been successfully marketed to those people. And some real players have risen to the top by virtue of being a Father or an Uncle to a successful idea or two. But as you and your team plot your strategy for marketing a basic or executional idea, it will be helpful to remember that those you will face instinctively understand Backer's Law of Corporate Gravity:

HE WHO SHAKES THE CORPORATE TREE DOESN'T GET THE FRUIT.

CHAPTER SIX

Is God Really in the Details?

THERE ARE MANY ways to avoid the pull of Backer's Law of Corporate Gravity. One way is to completely and carefully execute all your basic needs in every detail—including shape, tone, finish, attitude, etc. But to do that takes money, and to get the money you have to have a reputation and be trusted. The three of us who had expanded my lyrics in the Savoy that night were in that position—we had the budget necessary to give full attention to the details and to keep them organic.

I think it was Frank Lloyd Wright (some say it was Mies van der Rohe) who is credited with saying about architecture: "God is in the details." Wright selected or designed everything that went into his buildings from moldings to doorknobs because he felt that the basic idea of a structure would never be realized unless all the elements in it were an outgrowth of the original thought.

Wright's statement about God being in the details is often abused by people in an idea loop. When the basic idea comes from a Frank Lloyd Wright, and a Frank Lloyd Wright designs the details, then God is in them. But a building based on an inferior idea—or on no idea at all—won't be blessed just because attention is given to every detail involved.

A necessary skill in judging executions is to be able to go back mentally to the basic idea, determine once again that it is a good one, and then see if the executions are a natural outgrowth of it. God is in the details only if they hark back to a good original concept and thereby help to advance it. Otherwise you are heading for trouble.

You can't take a Frank Lloyd Wright element from one building and expect God to approve it in another. Even if the details were created by a genius, applying them to an inappropriate idea—or to a bad idea or no idea at all—won't make *you* look like a genius. A great deal of money, time, and talent is wasted every day on details that were very effective in communicating one idea but are not organic to the one being judged. On the other hand, many good ideas never reach maturity because not enough money, time, and talent are spent on the details of their execution.

In the months ahead you will surely be involved in deciding whether or not an execution is "good," "worth the money," "too expensive," "a breakthrough," "appropriate for our group or company," and so on. You use words and phrases like that every day of your life. And what you are really doing is judging executions and the details that have gone—or are about to go—into them.

You may sit in a budget meeting next week to approve a budget for an event as large as a worldwide sales meeting or an architect's rendering of a proposed redo of the entire third floor of your office building—or as small as the proposed budget for a photographer to shoot the cover of a new record album.

Or if you are in marketing, you may be judging the new cabinets for the TV sets your company will manufacture, the packaging for a new hair care product, or an advertising campaign that calls for hiring a million-dollar rock star.

In private life, you could well be discussing how to throw a party or how to organize a meeting to raise money for a political candidate or a favorite charity.

In all these cases you have to judge the costs of details, and which ones are necessary to the idea and which are superfluous. You'll be asking yourself—or at least I hope you will—whether the proposed executions take their cue from the basic idea or from the egos of those who joined the family after the idea was already in place.

But for now, since we are at a spot in the story of "Buy the World" where our Idea Family first began to address the nitty-gritty details, I have taken a detour into the world of executions and perhaps gotten slightly ahead of myself. If so, I apologize.

It's easy to look back on a personal success and say that everything you did was done for a good and rational reason. And because it's easy, I will probably fall into that trap in the pages ahead. I am going to describe in some detail the next steps in executing "Buy the World" and probably leave you with the impression that every move was thought through and made without the influence of blind emotion. But it wasn't.

If I had read a book on the care and feeding of ideas, more of the moves probably would have come from the brain instead of the gut. On the other hand, knowing what I know now, and having written a book about it, I might well have screwed up the next steps to such an extent that the idea would never have surfaced on national radio, much less worldwide television.

I cannot tell you how to develop a "gut feel" about executions. I can only give you a theory that says, up to a point,

THE MORE EDUCATED THE GUT, THE TRUER THE FEELINGS.

I don't know where that point is exactly, but I have learned that an overeducated gut has no feelings at all.

My gut gave me a clear warning that a song about a bottle of pop that opened with the line "I'd like to build the world a home and furnish it with love" was walking on thin ice. Let it get one ounce too heavy and it would fall through and disappear into the cold black hole of public derision. I would like to say, "But I well knew that the risk was worth it because I was certain that if it didn't fall through the ice, we would have a hit on our hands." But that wasn't the case. What I can only repeat was I knew I had a big idea ("big," at least, for the small world of advertising) that would be a standout if our Idea Family could bring it off.

In this case the details that would be most important would be those that would give the basic idea its "tone of voice," just as the details in a Frank Lloyd Wright interior are responsible for continuing the feeling of the exterior into the inside of the structure to give it its ultimate validity. Without the right tone of voice, "Buy the World" would become unbelievable—even a joke; a piece of communication that had no validity at all.

To arrive at an opinion about a tone of voice for any communication—be it a song, a story, a building, or a full-length feature film—someone has to decide, "Whose voice is it?" Was "Buy the World" the voice of Coca-Cola, or a much bigger voice—a voice of the times in which we were living, and of which Coke was a very natural part?

I decided it was a voice of the times in which Coke would join believably because it was natural that the Coca-Cola Company would wish for an ideal world where consumers could enjoy its product and where the product could play—in a minor way—an active part. I've never been afraid of portraying decent, honest emotions as long as they are not being used to manipulate people toward a point that isn't true. Sure, Coca-Cola is a profit-making corporation, but that fact did not preclude it from expressing such wishes, even if enunciated in human and very idealistic terms. The portrayal of the product as a bit of commonality between diverse people was—and is to this day—as honest and as real as it was in Shannon Airport. Therefore, I resolved to have the song sung with as much emotion as if it were a true hit folk song of the day—or even a hymn.

But before we even got to the recording studio, my small Idea Family wrestled with the problem of how the heck do we keep the details organic to our basic idea and not to some other idea—like a previous song of the New Seekers, or a preconceived notion of what a Coca-Cola commercial should sound like.

Keeping the details organic to the basic idea is always difficult in advertising, but "Buy the World" would have had it easier than many commercials, as far as the sound track was concerned, except for the fact that it ran into family problems.

Whenever the executions of an idea involve talent, ipso facto, that talent becomes part of the Idea Family. Whether its the Italian designer who executes Ford's idea for a new small car, the actors who portray someone's idea of what really happened in Dallas the day JFK was shot, or the singers who must project an idea that a certain bottle of pop is more than sugar and water—they each become custodians of the basic idea.

Conventional wisdom says they can "make or break" the ideas. But that is not 100 percent accurate. Certainly any performance on their part that does not move the basic idea toward maturity can temporarily stunt or stop growth. But the idea can still be revived. On the other hand, a great sauce can hide a multitude of sins in the meat, and certainly a brilliant execution can partially save a mediocre idea. In the end, however, good basic ideas tend to bring out the best in talent—if it's the right talent for the job and if the right go-betweens are there in the Idea Family to build a bridge between the basic idea and the execution.

In show business and its first cousin, advertising, these go-betweens are directors and producers. In business they may be engineers or top managers. In politics they seem to be consultants and advisers. (Today the number of people involved in executing a basic advertising idea seems to have grown geometrically. I also suspect that ideas in the worlds of entertainment, manufacturing, and politics are facing an increased number of people who get in on the act as well. In politics, for instance, there were so many cooks involved in creating a broth for a Democratic candidate for president in the 1970s and '80s that the result was judged to be slop rather than soup by a majority of voters in four out of five presidential elections.

Certainly "Buy the World a Coke" would need some careful bridge-building between the members of a popular singing group who had not hitherto done a commercial and weren't really sure they wanted to do one and the executional idea of the commercial itself. And equally certain was the fact that the Father and Uncles who gathered in London's Trident studios had done their best to write words and music that grew organically from the basic idea. But the tone of voice in which their words and music were about to be rendered would represent a whole new set of details. And the power to assure that anyone, much less God, would ever bless them was not entirely in their control, even in the event that they were correct in saying "the voice" would be bigger than Coca-Cola's. It would try to be the voice of the times—the end of the sixties.

CHAPTER SEVEN

Keeping the Execution Organic

IN ORDER FOR a human voice to be transferred onto a roll of magnetic tape, it must travel—at a minimum—through a microphone, a length of insulated copper wire, an amplifier, and a recording head. In a modern recording studio, complete with filters, limiters, and special frequency boosters for a dozen or so different inputs, what happens to the sound waves generated by the vocalist standing at a microphone can be comprehended only by a sound engineer.

But what happens to the performers we can all understand.

The performers are sealed in a room designed by an architect who saw his client as a sound wave, not a person. The aesthetics are dictated by how the room looks to the vibrations of a steel guitar instead of the eyeball of a human being, and the result is an atmosphere that tends to dehumanize the performance.

The unreality of the decor is not the only element the performers have to overcome. Another problem is the absence of a live audience. There is an audience, but it is sealed away in a soundproof box called a control room. The people inside can see the performers through a glass picture window that looks out on the recording room, but all they hear is the sound that travels into the control room via copper wires, amplifiers, etc., into the control room's speakers. There is no human interaction while the performances—called "takes"—are going on.

It wasn't always that way. There was a time when a recording session was full of glamor and the entire atmosphere was wall-to-wall electric. Today, most of the electricity is siphoned off by the wires that run into the many amplifiers involved.

What changed the scene was the rise of electronic wizardry and the fall of the big bands.

A full orchestration played by live musicians together with live vocalists is a sound that occurs very rarely today outside of the opera house. It still happens in some big-name concerts, a few club acts, charity balls, and places like New York's Rainbow Room. Otherwise that sound is the passenger pigeon of the music world. People think they are hearing it in a few of today's pop recordings, but mostly the sound has been recorded in steps and enhanced electronically every step of the way. The string section was added later, for instance, and four live violins were doubled and tripled electronically to sound like twelve. Or maybe the entire string sound came from a synthesizer.

However the ultimate effect is produced, the singers almost always sing with the prerecorded sound of the key instruments coming to them via earphones instead of from the live players. That way the effects of human error are minimized. A sour note in a guitar lick, for instance, won't mess up a take that involved the singers or two dozen or more musicians. It will necessitate the rhythm section playing another take, but doing that will merely use the time and salaries of five or six people instead of twenty or more. And when all the rough spots have been ironed out, the rhythm section can go home and the next layer of instruments—the brass section, for instance—can be added if the arrangement calls for it.

Since the New Seekers' musical arrangements had their roots in folk music, their sound did not require a "big band," and building an instrumental background for our song was not particularly difficult. Nonetheless, we did not attempt a live recording with singers and instruments all playing in the room together. Following standard practice, we prerecorded the musical tracks and then proceeded to add the vocals.

I might add here that as studio recording has become more advanced it has demanded a degree of precision in musicians that touring groups seldom possess. Performers of pop or rock music who perform "live" on stage need different skills from studio performers. The stage performer is called upon to dance around and move within the music while relating to the audience. Even if he is a keyboard player he has to project, but doesn't have to play or sing nearly as well on stage as he does when recording that same song in a studio while hoping for a hit single.

The result is Milli Vanilli. Behind most touring groups there ... musicians who help make the studio performance ... Milli Vanilli carried the practice of usi... s about as far as it can go—right u... bers on stage. Milli Vanilli is mere... at started to form with the adv... een building ever since.

...techniques were not so electron...

vanced as they are today, but the factors that tend to take the heart out of an emotional performance were already in place—no live instruments and no live audience. So even in 1971 when the material to be recorded was the voice of someone wishing something nice could happen to the whole world (in other words, if the material was to be warm), the recording session would stir up a conflict between technology and humanity. And our job was to keep the execution organic and to see to it that, ultimately, humanity would triumph.

I had started the execution with the words "I'd like to buy the world a Coke and keep it company." I had bundled my brainchild in warm clothes. You might say the team that helped the execution grow had added cashmere and goose down with lines like "I'd like to build the world a home and furnish it with love" and "Apple trees and honey bees and snow-white turtle doves." Now we had to keep the hand of technology from tearing our clothes apart. If God was to be in our details, we had to take care of these concerns.

We had analyzed our baby pretty thoroughly before sitting down with David Mackay, who arranged most of the New Seekers' songs. The lyrics were first and foremost a wish, but not one of your ordinary, self-centered, please-make-me-rich-and-famous kind of wishes. Ours was a wish for the other guys. May he and she have a good roof over their heads, be wrapped in four secure walls, surrounded by a garden peopled with friends who want to keep them company over a bottle of Coca-Cola.

So we told David to make the arrangement warm and universal. Resist the temptation to editorialize on the idea with an arrangement that is tender or cute. And above all plan to start the song with Eve Graham, your lead vocalist, unaccompanied by the men in the group. We had realized that what we had was more a woman's wish than a man's. It was *House and Garden*, not *Field and Stream*. So the opening line of the wish was going to be sung by Eve alone, and the group would join her in singing the second line.

Five months later, when a lovely young blond girl, a total amateur, would lip-sync on film to Eve Graham's voice, the wisdom of our instructions would be appreciated. Eve's was a voice that ...ld wish the world a home, and five hundred million listeners al... ... the world would know she meant it. If every brainchild co... ...such an understanding family, there would be far fewe... ...ts.

As Billy Davis, Roger Cook, and I sat in the control room of Trident Studios in London, however, our problem was that for the first time the details of execution would slip out of our hands. We couldn't sing the song. We could only make suggestions and hope the singers would see fit to join our Idea Family.

But the first takes that were piped into the booth were horrible, and not for the usual reasons. In most cases, poor rehearsals occur because the talent is unfamiliar with the material and is stumbling around with the notes and the rhythms of the lyrics.

The New Seekers, however, had rehearsed the material before the session and their first takes were practically note and letter perfect. The problem was, they didn't understand the material, and it wasn't their fault. It was mine.

I had skipped the rehearsal the day before for no good reason, except that I was running out of gas. The time spent in Ireland, the all-night session at the Savoy Hotel, plus a writing session the following afternoon on a second piece of material for the New Seekers (a more typical party song for Coca-Cola) had left me exhausted and making excuses for myself. But if you're the Father of an idea, don't allow yourself an excuse other than "force majeure." When your brainchild graduates to the next level, you must be at the ceremony. Uncles and Godparents are great, but the fire will always burn brightest in the memory of the person who first saw the firefly.

As I listened to the takes, I knew what was wrong. The New Seekers had forgotten why they were there. They were there to be "the New Seekers"—a warm, believable pop/folk group. However, they were trying to be a typical jingle group—belting out the material as if each word had the same weight of meaning and putting accuracy ahead of feeling. In short, they were trying to be "the voice of Coke" instead of "the voice of the times." (Years later, when the Coca-Cola Company revived "Buy the World," the revivers changed the tone of voice to the voice of Coke halfway through the commercial. They ended with an aggressive tone summed up with the words, "Can't beat the real thing." The commercial lost its impact because it lost its tone of voice. They screamed louder but the commercial got smaller and I writhed when I saw what they had done to my song.)

It's expensive to stop a session and ask the talent to reinterpret the material. It is also dangerous. When performers are asked to step outside of their area, they become understandably insecure and consequently more prickly than usual. And when a pop group is doing their first commercial they are outside of their area from the start.

The alternative is to edge them quietly, take by take, in a new direction without letting them know how far away they are from understanding the producer/director's interpretation of the material. I call that the "That's great guys, now let's add a little whatever" approach. My impatience usually shows through when I try the "That's great, etc." opening. I'm better at something like "Let's take five and get together in the studio for a minute. I'm coming on out." In this case, I knew it could be a lot longer than five minutes. But I saw no other way.

So we all went into the studio, pulled chairs around in a circle, and I proceeded to explain how our ideas for Coca-Cola were executed not as jingles but as short songs.

The idea for our song-form commercials had grown out of a need to be more contemporary than the competition without saying, "We are it" or "We are for those who think young." I had felt that the people at whom those statements were aimed were exactly the ones who were likely to be turned off by them.

At the same time, I had become aware that Coke, as an integral part of the American scene, often appeared in the lyrics of pop songs of the day. One that I still remember was the hit "Palisades Park," sung by a pop star, long since eclipsed, named Freddy Cannon. The lyric, as best I can remember it, contained lines like:

> We ate and ate
> We danced around
> To a rockin' band
> At a hot dog stand

All that song needed to be a perfect piece of material for Coca-Cola was to change the first line to include the word "Coke" and add the word "because" plus a reason:

"Because things go better with Coca-Cola, things go better with Coke."

Coke could then be as contemporary as the scene and the lyrics and music that describe it.

And I, working with some of the best songwriters of the day, had proceeded to write song after song about scenes in which a bottle of Coke fit naturally—and which would go a little better with a Coke. They were scenes of good times, hot times, and thirsty times.

As I sat there explaining all this to the New Seekers, it occurred to me that Roger Cook and his partner Roger Greenway had worked with me to create the very first example of this type of song some years earlier. I had written solo and also with many other writers in the meantime, but here Roger and I were back together reciting and singing the lyrics that had helped get the basic idea started by executing it so well. It's nice to be home, I thought, as Roger and I sang for the New Seekers the first Coke song we had written:

Come on waitress,
Bring me what I'm needin'
I got a truck outside,
It's got a heavy load
Never mind the menu
I'm not eatin'
I'll have a Coke
And then I'll hit the road
Cause things go better with Coca-Cola . . .

It was never destined to top the charts like "Buy the World" would, but then again, the idea wasn't as ambitious.

Many times since then I have been asked which was the better of the two campaigns I launched for Coca-Cola—"Things Go Better with Coke" or "It's the Real Thing."

They were very different in conception. "Things Go Better with Coke" is a simple promise of a reward that Coca-Cola can deliver, within reason. It can't get you a raise or make the rain go away when it is spoiling your Saturday golf game. But a lot of tiny moments throughout the day, including having a meeting with the boss and discussing a raise, can be lifted with a glass of Coca-Cola. "It's the Real Thing," on the other hand, is a fact, not a promise. You had to build a promise on it every time you used it.

Today the Coca-Cola Company has eviscerated the campaign by pushing "It's the Real Thing" into the realm of conjecture. "You can't beat the real thing"—that's like saying, "You can't beat honesty" or "You can't beat true love."

Any phrase that opens with the words "You can't beat" becomes personal opinion at best. It invites challenge. When Bing Crosby sang Cole Porter's "True Love" to Grace Kelly it won an

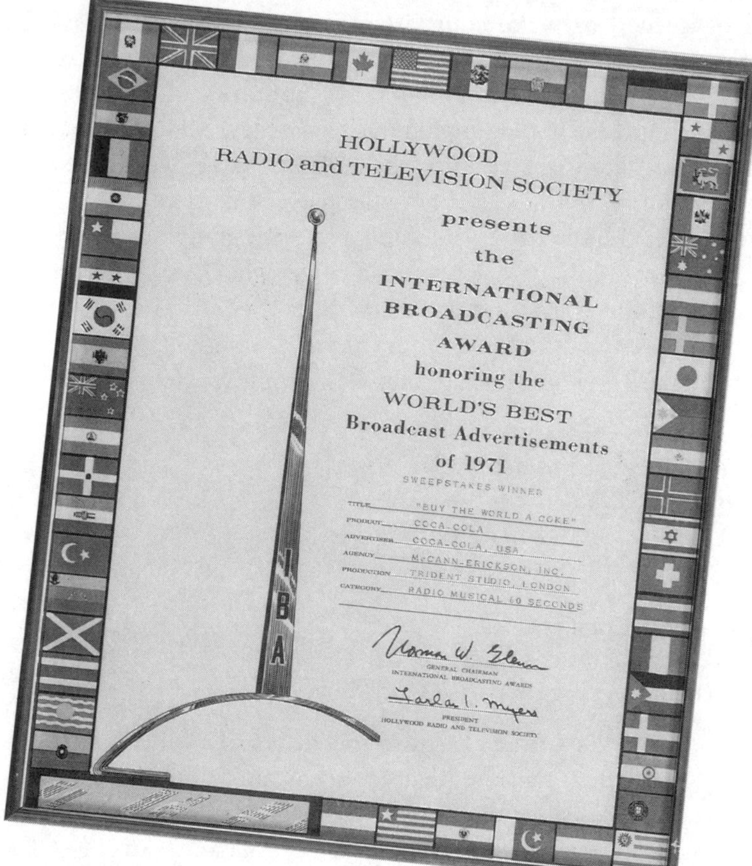

Oscar. I'll guarantee a song called "You Can't Beat True Love" never will, unless someone writes it as a tongue-in-cheek country song.

The idea of building a campaign on the fact that Coca-Cola is the "Real Thing" in soft drinks grew out of listening to the pleas of the sixties. "Take us away from plastic to basics." Also, several new generations had become soft-drink consumers since Pepsi had been introduced and they were now asking which cola was "the original." And so the basis of the campaign was right for its times. But a promise to make the moment a little bit better is right for all times.

More high-profile TV commercials were built on top of "It's the Real Thing" than on "Things Go Better," and the self-styled experts who hand out awards handed out more to "It's the Real Thing," if I remember right. But in my book, "Things Go Better with Coke" was better advertising.

Different as the two campaigns were, they shared some important common denominators—they were both true, they were both expressed in the language of consumers, not advertisers, and they were both designed to keep building the brand. Maybe that's why one lasted ten years and the other on and off for twelve.

I took thirty or forty minutes to go over the history of Coca-Cola with the New Seekers. I had to convince them to be part of the Idea Family and to understand that what they were singing was not a jingle. The subject of a jingle is a product:

> Pepsi-Cola Hits the Spot (or Is the Choice of a New Generation)
> The Heartbeat of America Is Today's Chevrolet
> Coke Is It

The subject of our songs were thirsty truck drivers, kids who wanted to go downtown, boys who wanted to meet a certain girl—and now someone whose heart went out to the world. In all of them, Coke would help, but it was never the whole song and never the entire answer.

Had the New Seekers been American, our job would have been easier. But to the New Seekers (and it turned out later, to "marketing experts" all over the world), the American attitude toward Coca-Cola was met with justifiable skepticism.

They asked many questions, like "Who is the 'I' in the song, the one who sings 'I'd like to build the world a home'? Isn't it the Coca-Cola Company?"

"No."

"Is it anyone who would want to build the world a home?"

"Yes. Wouldn't you like to build the world a home?"

"Yes."

"Wouldn't anyone of good will?"

"Yes."

"Okay then, so wouldn't you want to sit down and keep company with the world?"

"Yes, but over tea, not Coke."

"Unless, guys, you are American. The universal drink of America is Coca-Cola. And for the next couple of hours you are American, and you are up to making that transfer of nationality because you are talented and have universal appeal.

"And because your checks will come from the Trust Company of Georgia, U.S.A."

Then they understood, and the details of tone, style, emotion, and attitude were organic in every detail to the execution idea.

But in the end, the execution *did* get changed. The change was a minor one involving the lyrics, but it brings me to a major point about the kind of scrutiny the lyrics in some of today's popular recordings are getting, and I think it is worth discussing here.

Eve, the lead singer of the New Seekers, felt strongly that the word "build" didn't "sing" as well as "buy." The way she was emphasizing the "I" of "I'd like to" seemed to give the line a nice internal rhyme with "buy" that was lost with "build." She agreed that Billy Davis had been correct when he said that "build" broadened the meaning of the line so it involved more people than just those who could afford to "buy" someone a home. Any group of people, regardless of race, color, creed, or depth of pocket, can get together, pick up hammer and nails and help build someone a home—a point that the organization Habitat for Humanity has been making most eloquently since 1976.

There was no question that "build" was more precise on paper, but in the melody, in the rhythm pattern, and in Eve's vocal cords, "buy" was the better of the two. Which brings me to the larger point: You can't judge lyrics solely by how they look on paper. Because they aren't written to be read. Good lyrics are written to be sung, and the writer understands that they are a part of a whole that includes melody, melodic pattern, and the rhythm of the song. Good lyrics are not poems set to music. They are like the black plate in a set of copper plates for four-color prints—they need the other plates to provide the color that brings out the mood, the tone, and above all, the emotional meaning. That's why lyrics are bad carriers of precise messages and why, when woven into the right melodic pattern and turned over to the right singer for execution, they are often the best conveyors of emotional ones.

We shouldn't amputate lines from lyrics and lyrics from their melody and rhythms for judging purposes. A recording should be judged as a recording. Censor the song itself, if you believe in censorship, but don't print the lyrics in some newspaper and judge them the way you would prose. Their vocabulary has been limited by the constraints of rhyme, melody, rhythm, and the limits of vocal pipes. Leave them as a part—a very important part—of an art form America knows more about, and does better at, than any country in the world—the popular song.

So we had to agree with Eve. "Buy" gave the opening line more impact. We had no idea it would someday be the opening line of a worldwide song hit that would lead to printed sheet music and choral arrangements. Had we known that, perhaps we would have stayed with "build," which is how the sheet music reads.

The inescapable conclusion to all this, however, is that having a good basic idea is seldom enough. You have to be articulate to get it executed organically all the way to the finish and you have to involve Uncles and Aunts all along the way who really care. In a funny way, that's a sad thought. I keep wondering how many wonderful songs never got sung, how many great paintings never got hung, how many film scripts never saw a camera unslung—in short, how many sparks never lit their intended fires, because their Fathers and Mothers lacked the ability, the energy, or in some cases the fierce desire necessary to get all the good organic executions they needed to see their sparks burst into full flame.

CHAPTER EIGHT

How Bureaucracy Kills Ideas

THE MUSIC, THE arrangements, the attitude of the vocals—they were all, finally, where we felt they should be: each one growing organically from the basic idea and the original executional idea. "Buy the World a Coke" was as ready as it was ever going to be to face its first judging session. And there we knew it would have it easier than most ideas, because it was not going to face a bureaucracy.

I have no statistics on where or why most ideas die. But I have a guess based on experience. Many ideas perish because they were weak to begin with, others because they were improperly clothed in executions that were not strong executional ideas or, if they were, they were not organic to the basic idea. In some cases the Idea Families were not in harmony with each other or with the basic idea. But I would guess that more good ideas, well executed and professionally marketed, have been killed by bureaucratic practices than by any other force.

No one legislated the practices. Probably no one even saw the bureaucracy creeping into the company. It certainly didn't happen overnight. But it happened.

A business organization is like an automobile engine—if you run it at slow speeds for too long it begins to gum up with sludge. You need to blow it out every so often with an up-to-the speed-limit spin on an open road.

When "business as usual" prevails in a company year after year, year after year the company begins to gum up, too—not with sludge, but with bureaucracy. Only bureaucracy isn't as easy to get rid of as sludge. It holds on like epoxy glue and resists all changes of speed. In fact, change of any kind represents a threat to a bureaucrat, and since any fresh idea—basic or executional—represents change of some kind somewhere, the bureaucrat comes to work each morning with a prejudice against ideas.

And let's face it. Eighty percent of what mature companies do every day is not look for new ideas, but conduct "business as usual."

I'm not knocking them for that. Our tax system rewards short-term profits more richly than it does long-term growth. So stockholders, boards of directors, and ultimately company executives proceed on the philosophy of "a bird in the hand is worth two in the bush," and the emphasis is on managing the day-to-day flow of work as flawlessly as possible.

What I do complain about is their failure to recognize how bureaucracy flourishes over the long term in an environment of "business as usual" and how the longer it builds up the more resistant it becomes to changes of any kind and how receptive it becomes to fear of failure and the negative pull of Backer's Laws.

So the invisible mottoes on most office walls begin to read:

Don't Drop the Ball.
Mistakes Cost Money.
Don't Goof Up.
Reward the Player with the Fewest Errors.

You might sum up all of these as "Failure Carries More Weight Than Success."

Organizing to do "business as usual" breeds bureaucracy because it seems to demand that you divide the company into a series of territories—or responsibilities—and build clearly defined fences or lines around each one. On an organization chart these territories look like boxes or squares with lines of authority running up to fewer and fewer boxes.

Ultimately all work flows through these territories as if it were a continuous stream. And the people in the territories monitor that flow, add a drop here, remove a drop there, and concentrate on not spilling.

Ideas have no place in such a system. They make waves in the channel. They are risky. Their effects cannot be completely ignored but must be minimized at all costs, because remember,

FAILURE CARRIES MORE WEIGHT THAN SUCCESS.

So to keep ideas from messing up your career you have to become adept at filtering them.

As I have said, the people at the edge of the flow don't want a big rise in level. They try to view every new idea as merely an added trickle in the channel, because both logically and emotionally they want it to be a trickle and not a big exciting wave. They themselves don't make waves and they don't want ideas that make waves.

There are two standard ways the failure avoiders reduce a big wave of an idea to a harmless trickle. Filter and age it (translation: sit on it) or divert it out of the channel (translation: kill it).

To filter and age an idea you treat it just like a batch of Jack Daniel's whiskey. First filter the trickle—through layers and layers of an inert substance—then let it lie around for a while and age. After that it must be labeled. In the case of Jack Daniel's, the inert substance is hardwood charcoal, which has the ability to filter out impurities and thus, as they say, "smooth and mellow the whiskey drop by drop." But when it comes to ideas in large organizations, the inert substance takes the form of layers and layers of bureaucracy.

Unlike charcoal, these monitors of the daily work flow have little or no ability to distinguish which substances in the idea or its execution are impure. What is impure to them is whatever will be considered impure by the guys downstream. And that gang has no definition of impure either, so they try to outguess their next level. They filter what substance is left and send the idea along so smooth and mellow it cannot be harshly criticized. But it has become so small and bland in the process it will be indistinguishable from all the other ideas that are filtering through a thousand other similar bureaucracies. But it is now safe, and in the end it will die of its own dullness.

People in the business of parenting or uncle-ing ideas in any and all areas will happily cite many examples of this bureaucratic filtering process in private—but are reluctant to be quoted in print. In print they can become identified as "whistle-blowers" and get what whistle-blowers get the world over—the gate to the street. The example I will give you is safe, however, because it goes way back to a time before this particular company had been reorganized from the top down to remove many levels of bureaucracy (though probably more to cut costs than to facilitate the flow of ideas). The company was the old General Motors—the General Motors of the sixties.

I have been Father, Uncle, or Godfather to ideas for companies in almost every area of American business—automotive, oil, food, soft drinks, beer, whiskey, snacks, banking, electronics, tobacco, fast food, and what is known in my business as "hard goods"—refrigerators and other appliances. But of all the companies I ever worked with, General Motors in the sixties was the least concerned with ideas that met the needs of their buyers. The "desires" they felt they could manipulate—and they could and did for many years. But big ideas are almost always influenced by a certain compassion for people, and I found none at General Motors.

The agency I was working for, McCann-Erickson, had the Buick account. Buick, of course, is a General Motors car, and represented a major piece of business at the agency. So when Buick sneezed, McCann-Erickson caught cold. I was never privy to what caused Buick to sneeze in 1972 as I was not active on the account, but the pollen that sets off these kinds of attacks is generally caused by the blossoming of someone else's sales at your client's expense. When McCann-Erickson caught cold the epidemic was agency-wide, and though I was not involved with the account on a day-to-day basis, I suddenly found myself in Detroit looking at sketches for the new Buick and listening to rationales for why it would be the way it would be. These seemed to boil down to the fact that Buick was viewed by the car-buying public as "a car for doctors and bankers," types who didn't want to be tagged as Cadillac people.

But the times they were a-changing. The idealism of the sixties was fading and the "me" generation was beginning to stir, although they were yet to be defined. The new generation of car buyers, including doctors and bankers, didn't want a car that was reliable, respectable, and dull. So the Buick Division, now run by its former head of sales, had restyled some models to make them appear younger, more sleek and modern, and less respectable. One might say flashier and less tasteful, as well. But the changes were mostly cosmetic, or as I was later to say—unwisely—mostly chromatic. They had added a lot of chrome to exchange boxy lines for speed lines and to separate different color tones. But they had also added some touches in the interior that made it more convenient and easy to occupy, especially on long trips. And it was still extra-spacious because the exterior had not been streamlined, just made to look like it had.

I don't know why the campaign that I submitted was chosen. Was it the best of a bad lot? (All horses look fast running past trees.) Or did someone in the first level of flow monitors see something in it and decide to take a chance? Whatever the reason, I found myself in charge of "The New Campaign for the New Buick"—seven words that added up to one small lie. Because the car wasn't new, and by the time the campaign hit the air, it wasn't either.

My thought had been that the new Buick buyer, unlike the old doctors and bankers, would be driving more often for less utilitarian reasons than his predecessors; more often for the sheer fun of it. And since the interior was more enjoyable to ride in than that of previous models, and superior to that of more streamlined cars, my basic idea was to say, "View this car as more enjoyable than other cars for *all* concerned—passengers as well as drivers." And the executional line in which I wrapped the basic idea was, "Getting there in life is half the fun." The line has been used since, but it was fresh at the time. We all know that the climb up any ladder involves some sacrifice and misery. But in an ideal world, compassion will play a part at every rung of the ladder, so getting there should involve some joy along the climb. Besides, it was a time in America when hopes were on the rise and people were seeing bright futures.

Interiors given priority over exteriors? Couples instead of families? Skiers, not country clubbers? Guitars instead of lush strings? This was not typical advertising for the General Motors of the sixties, and anyone interested in outguessing his superiors down the line could not be blamed for wanting to filter and mellow it a bit.

Anyway, I gave the line a lot of horsepower with a catchy tune and a happy beat. The storyboards were full of young people enjoying the interior and each other, and before I had time to collect any further thoughts I found myself in a big room in the General Motors building in Detroit, surrounded by flow monitors. It seems the campaign had been Godfathered without my knowing—or up to that point caring—past the initial stages of approval.

To keep the executions organic to the basic idea, the destinations—which were the other half of the "fun"—had to be just that—fun, in the contemporary sense of the word. The people "getting there" and the music that accompanied them had to have the "new era" approach to fun as well.

They had to be going to places like ski lodges and out-of-the-way eating spots in the country—the further away from mansions and country clubs, the better. And all the while they had to be enjoying the comforts and advanced gadgets of a big, roomy, plush interior to the rhythms of music and lyrics with a contemporary feel as well.

I think I am better than average at explaining both basic ideas and the necessity for having their executions grow organically from them down to the last detail. But in the weeks that followed my first meeting with the flow monitors, I ran up against a line that to this day I cannot combat: "Bill, this is Detroit."

"But guys," I would say, "a house party in a ski cottage isn't sinful—these couples can wear wedding bands."

"Bill, this is Detroit."

"But the exterior of the car isn't new at all, just the interior."

"Bill, this is Detroit."

"Can't I just mute the guitars instead of losing them altogether?"

"Bill, this is Detroit."

And so it went.

The line about Detroit came, to my surprise, from the agency's Godfathers, not the flow monitors. The Godfathers had long since decided that maintaining their relationship with the flow monitors was more important for their careers than the fate of any one idea—or ten of them. For their part, the flow monitors just said things like "We don't go for that kind of music."

In the end, what went on the air was a standard GM car commercial—forty seconds of running footage and twenty seconds of static beauty shots interrupted by a few interior close-ups. The beauty shots were, naturally, shot at destinations like country clubs, mansions, and all-family resorts. The one that got to me the most was a city park. "You want a park!" I moaned. "Why a park? You can walk to a park. You don't even have to drive." But the park had a pond that would reflect the chrome speed lines while the Buick was standing still, and in the early seventies parks were still considered safe places to park your Buick.

Luckily for me the campaign was hardly on the air before it was taken off, not because it was totally bland and dull—which it was—but because the first big gas crunch had come along. (It's an ill wind, as they say, that blows no one any good.) This campaign promoted "frivolous driving," the agency said. So they threw out most of the driving shots, took all the static shots and cut them together with the line "Wouldn't you really rather have a Buick?" and were back on the air in a few weeks. The fact that the New Buick, like hundreds of other automobiles manufactured here and abroad was still loaded with "frivolous horsepower" was never discussed. After all, how wasteful can horsepower be when it's parked by a pond in a park?

Not all bureaucracies are as entrenched as General Motors was in the sixties, so there is always a hope in the heart of an Idea Family that its idea will emerge, like good whiskey, with some of its character intact. If it does, however, it must still go through an aging process in most organizations. They want to "sit on it" for a while.

"Think about it for a few minutes" or "look into it a bit

further" are often wise next steps. But "sit on it a while" is an idea killer.

Ideas, I have always argued, tend to be children of their time. Unlike whiskey they can often lose some of their impact if they sit around and age. And unlike whiskey, if you can label them they are probably not worth labeling. Identify them, by all means, categorize them, if you can. Simplify them? Yes. But organizations should contain the kind of people who understand that if you can label an idea easily it is not original. That doesn't mean people in your organization should drop it. They just better understand that me-too ideas don't achieve the impact of fresh ones. But whatever you do, don't ask the people—your people—to paste a label on every executional idea.

Original ideas, and here we are talking mostly executional ones, resist being labeled.

People in organizations that encourage treating ideas in this fashion say that the system is designed to knock off the rough edges of an idea and its executions before it reaches top management—which is, of course, what happened to "Getting There in Life Is Half the Fun." The problem is that rough edges are often necessary to put sharp ideas in focus. So a system of people in boxes who knock them off early on is not calculated to produce high-profile ideas and executions, just more cars in parks.

Had "Buy the World a Coke" faced that kind of a system with layer upon layer of people bent on avoiding failure it would never have survived.

I think it will certainly be productive at this point to zoom in and take a close-up shot of a typical filterer and see firsthand why he is like he is. He's a junior or mid-level manager in the kind of company I have just described. For the sake of simplifying the use of the pronoun I will make him a man, but he could be either a man or a woman.

First thing we notice is that only a small part of his time—probably less than 20 percent—is used in being an active part of an idea loop. That 20 percent may well be the most important part of his job. But since senior management doesn't recognize it as such, our filter manager doesn't realize its importance either and you can't blame him. What is important to him is what is important to those up the ladder, or in my analogy, down the stream.

He is everywhere throughout all mature organizations. He could be a member of the Water Authority for the City of New York, a junior manager in the promotion department of MasterCard, a mid-level executive in a worldwide computer company like IBM, or an assistant brand manager in Coca-Cola USA.

Wherever he sits, he faces the following three problems when it comes to being a productive member of an idea loop: (1) his everyday job, (2) the focus of his organization, and (3) his previous background.

In his job, he is like a weekend golfer who is expected to compete successfully in major tournaments 20 percent of his time—or one day a week. Maybe he has the ability. But both mentally and physically he can never be on top of his game because he just doesn't spend enough time at it.

If his organization based their promotions and salary increases on his golf scores, he'd find time for extra play in the summer, when the days grow long, at driving ranges at night, and on vacations. He would never be the equal of a pro who does nothing but golf, but if he had some native ability, he would at least be a competent amateur instead of what he is now, a drag on the game.

But his organization does not base their evaluation of him on his ability to play golf, that is, to judge ideas. They judge him by how well he seems to do the 80 percent of his job that involves keeping the everyday flow going smoothly.

On top of that he faces a system that is in constant flux because the key personnel keep changing at the top, which means changes all the way to the bottom.

By my count over half the junior and mid-level managers in today's marketing companies change jobs—though not necessarily employers—every two years. Since most big ideas take over a year to reach maturity, the second half of many a manager's term involves ideas that he can never see to graduation. And chances are the next guy won't feel the same way about the brainchild. After all, it's not his!

As for those ideas our manager joins up with in his first year of duty, they will be far and few between. He doesn't know the ropes of his job the first year, and more than ever he will be subject to Backer's Laws of Gravity and inclined to say "no."

How come his job tenure is shorter today than in the sixties and seventies?

My theory is that the feeding frenzy for LBOs and mergers that occurred in the eighties produced more major changes in personnel at the top than usual. It also produced shifts in corporate goals.

When the guys at the top are more worried about paying off the banks than they are, for instance, about having their organization come up with ideas for extending the influence of their brands, the thrust of that kind of thinking spreads very rapidly through all levels, and the negative pull of gravity described in Backer's Laws grows stronger and stronger.

So neither the priorities of his job nor the focus of his organization is helping our manager avoid the influence of Backer's Laws. And neither is his background.

His background has prepared him for 80 percent of his job, but not for the 10 to 20 percent of his time that he spends in an idea loop. His courses in business administration or engineering dealt with tracking cash flow or the flow of electrons, but not the flow of ideas. As a consultant in an idea loop he is a help, but as a participating family member he brings no useful training or experience to the table other than the ability to say whether it will work or what it will do to the numbers.

This is not to say that engineers and MBAs don't make good idea people. Many of them do, of course. They can be some of the best. But their college degrees don't necessarily guarantee they will be competent members of an Idea Family. Unfortunately, their degrees do guarantee that they will rise in today's business organizations and so they will often be expected to be exactly that—competent to judge, add to, and subtract from ideas both basic and executional.

I am, obviously, more conversant with what goes on in idea loops that involve advertising than those that involve city government or international trade. So for a tight close-up of a specific idea filterer I am going to put "Buy the World a Coke" up against a hypothetical assistant brand manager in a contemporary company, also hypothetical, that might be marketing Coca-Cola today.

He begins his day with a meeting with his advertising agency to review some advertising "pool out" scripts for the campaign that he has been running for eighteen months. What the campaign is all about is explaining to the consumers the fact that his brand is "The Real Thing" in colas, and that fact gives it special powers to please people. He has reserved a mini–conference room on the floor above his office, and he and the representatives of his agency are gathered around the large dining room–sized table. The team from the advertising agency is a typical idea team—consisting of a Father, an Uncle, and a professional Godfather.

The process of marketing ideas has been institutionalized over the years. There is now a whole set of people—professional Godfathers—who act as go-betweens for the Idea Family and the Judges and Juries who are the next part of the idea loop. As I said earlier they are often more interested in moving the idea along than in the quality of the idea itself. The good ones won't hire on if they think the idea is bad, but they seldom have the emotional attachment to it that the blood relatives have.

Regardless of the nature of their attachment to the Idea Family, these go-betweens are important connections in many idea loops. As I have pointed out, agents occupy this role in Hollywood. In Washington it is the lobbyist who makes and keeps the connection. And in the agency business it is the account person. All of these Godfathers are pragmatists, for their own sake, and rightly so. In the big scheme of things, they know that their continuing relationships with the Judges and Juries are more important to their careers than the life and death of an idea, even though the Idea Family may be paying them. There are exceptions to this lack of emotional commitment to the idea among agents and lobbyists, and there definitely are among account people in advertising agencies. Unfortunately, those Godfathers—and they are few and far between—who are willing to risk a relationship for the sake of an idea they believe in often burn themselves out faster than their cohorts. Their careers can suffer, and sometimes they even find themselves on the street without a job. In the end it is the Judges and Juries who have the power of money, position, or masses of votes. So the film director who has a script idea, or the association of conservationists lobbying for a new view of timbering public lands, or the advertising art director/copywriter team with an idea for a new execution will be less important to the Godfather in most situations than maintaining the long-term relationship with the power source.

In an ideal situation, push never comes to shove; both parties are given an honest connection by the go-between. But the world of ideas is no more ideal than any other world. So, today our assistant brand manager will probably be taking his serious signals not from the idea's Father and Uncles, but from the family's hired-on Godfather.

Our idea filterer arrives fifteen minutes late—to emphasize the fact that this is his territory—and starts the meeting with the usual "OK guys, whaddaya got for me today?" What they have is a rough set of lyrics about someone who wants to, among other things, buy the whole world a bottle of soda pop and promote better understanding among people. This is all set up first by the Godfather.

If he is reluctant, his reticence may well ooze from every pore as he stands up to review what is currently running on radio and TV. This is to remind everyone that what is out there now is doing a damn good job. (Inference: Why take a chance with something as kooky as you are about to see?) He then goes on to say maybe it's time to "explore" some approaches that are a bit more "daring."

With these words he has sent the proper signals without getting caught by the Father and Uncle of the idea. He has said "explore" and "daring." Forewarned is forearmed. Both the account executive and the client are already well aware that ideas can be dangerous to the health of their careers. The assistant brand manager has thus been forewarned by a fellow careerist whose aims are similar to his and whose job depends on building a long-term relationship.

The Father of the rough lyrics and the Uncle (who may be a music writer/producer) read their lyrics with genuine enthusiasm, but perhaps with no tune, because they can't sing and have no money to produce a demo track. They then proceed to ask for an investment of a not inconsiderable sum of money to finish the lyrics and team them up with a tune or an arrangement in the style of one of the day's most popular singing groups. No guarantee our assistant brand manager will like the results, of course.

He took no course at business school that prepared him for this type of proposition except, perhaps, a course in probabilities. And the probabilities here can be assessed easily and quickly:

1. There are at least six points along the way where failure in this project is more probable than success, starting with the distinct possibility that the basic idea won't sell soft drinks.
2. Then there is the probability that the boss—his boss—won't think the idea will sell soft drinks even if it will. After all, the lyrics are a long way from "We taste the way you want us to taste," or "We are it," which is where the boss would really like it to be. He isn't even comfortable with "The Real Thing" which sounds to him more like real leather or real wool.
3. There is the probability that the words will never communicate properly. Why can't they just say, "Sit down and share this soft drink with someone right now—at a special price"?
4. There is the probability that even if the lyrics and music are okay, the Advertising Review Board (made up, in this company,

of nine sixty-year-old guys from various divisions, plus two from the board of directors) will think this approach is "too far-out" for the product.

5. There is the probability that even if this idea eventually becomes the "commercial of the year," and even turns into a song that soars high above the competition, attracts worldwide attention, and boosts sales significantly, that someone higher up will grab the credit, and it will not boost his career.
6. Finally, there is the probability that if it is a dismal failure, he will get all the blame.

To sum up, the probability of failure in this project is larger than the probability of success. Who needs this kind of risk?

Not someone in his particular position.

In short, he is in an environment where Backer's Law of Corporate Gravity is exerting a pull that is impossible to resist. The people at the top are maintenance men like him. If they realize that there is no such thing as standing still in today's highly competitive business environment, they have never signaled that fact to the rank and file. You either move ahead with the help of ideas, or you slide backwards. But that has not been registered and trademarked as an integral part of the company culture. So Backer's Laws prevail unchecked, and a good job of maintaining the existing flow is what merits a promotion and a raise in this mythical but not atypical company.

Everywhere the vibes warn, "Don't step up to the plate!" "You might strike out!" "Stay in the stands!" "The hitters have to strike out sometime and that will put them out of the ball game and probably out on the street."

Our manager does not, of course, share his list of probabilities with the Father and Uncle of the idea. Instead he says, "Develop the idea further. Talk to the singing group. Maybe they will record a version on spec?" (Even a rank amateur should know they won't.)

Meanwhile, peace groups are parading in front of the nation's capital, flower children are calling for more understanding among peoples, the time is rapidly ripening for the fruit of this idea to be plucked. But what is that to him? He is in a bureaucracy, and in a bureaucracy it's safer to kill an idea than to join its family.

CHAPTER NINE

Playing Idea Doctor

THE BUREAUCRATIC SYSTEM'S ill effects are not limited to the negativism it generates toward anything new. A bureaucracy also does damage to the people who work in it, especially those people who have the kind of energy and hands-on mentality that causes them to rebel at their roles—or lack of a role—in the system. Mostly the rebellions are internal, kept inside where they eat away at the people who don't have the courage to make a break for it and escape the system. They hang in there wasting their most productive years, unable to help themselves or their company. And unknowingly they become hazardous to the health of ideas.

Bureaucracies get bigger and fatter as they get older, so each job within the flow of an old bureaucracy becomes smaller and less significant. And corporate fat tends to make restless people even more restless.

Let's take the typical flow monitor in our last chapter and give him a different psychological profile. He is energetic and secretly ambitious. But his job has no meaning. It's too small to be important. So his entrepreneurial streak is growing bigger and stronger every day. He has kept it well within himself up to now because the management of his company is no longer entrepreneurial and is nervous about that kind of thinking in the ranks. The popular belief in the large corner offices of this company is that entrepreneurs along the banks of the flow can only make for trouble.

But along comes some idea like "Buy the World a Coke," and it unleashes the hidden force within him. He is bright enough to see "something in it." There is "something there," he says. I have put these phrases in quotes because when a Judge says, "There is something there," he provides a few life jackets for an Idea Family that can keep them afloat. But the words are also a signal to beware. If the family members are wise and professional they can make this guy a Cousin, and that's good. But they have to know how to contain the relationship so it doesn't go any further.

In this situation, or in any similar one, our mythical Idea Family must analyze what is in the mind of the manager. At this point he might well be saying to himself, "If I take a flyer on this idea, I had better make it mine." He knows very well that "success has a thousand fathers, but failure is an orphan"; if he goes along and stamps this idea with his insignia, he will never duck the blame if it fails. But "there is something there," he says to himself, and it could be a winner: "I am going to think positively. How can I own it so that if it is a success, it won't have a thousand fathers—just me and the original family? I must stamp it with my contribution. Besides, being a contributor to this idea could actually be fun, and I don't have much fun in this job. In fact, I don't really have a job."

What he is now up to may be fun for him, but it can be ruinous to the idea unless he is an extremely professional manager with a very healthy ego. Or unless he is in a company with extremely savvy leaders. It's not all his fault that he wants to be more than a Cousin. Bureaucratic bloat and corporate fat have squeezed all meaning out of his job.

What is our manager supposed to answer when his little daughter asks him, "What did *you* do today, Daddy? Look, I drew this picture."

Should he tell the truth? "I sat in four meetings and said what I thought my boss would like to hear in two of them. And in the other two I wasn't ever called on to speak because I have no practical function. I was there to 'absorb information,' as they say." "I stood for no ideas, no particular standards of human behavior toward others inside or outside of the company." "I played the game of office politics on the sidelines, but not the game of winning, which is what the company is supposed to be about." "I yinged and tomorrow I will yang." "They are all playing the same way." "They won't catch up with me."

Is that what he is supposed to tell his little girl? Maybe a simple "No, honey, I didn't paint a picture today" is a better answer.

He is a closet entrepreneur smothered in corporate fat. His responsibilities don't call for him to accomplish anything, or at best very little. Like too many people in too many companies he has too little to do, especially when it comes to satisfying the good old American urge to see the result of one's activities. He can't see or feel the results of what he does because they end up minuscule, fragmented as they are between so many people. No wonder that when he sees a chance to contribute to an idea, he seizes it.

Most people are frustrated artists, writers, lyricists, interior decorators, architects, inventors, creative chefs, or coaches anyway.

They want to create something, and the fact that they feel they have a latent talent for this is perfectly understandable. Their ideas fall mostly in the executional area, because in their daily lives they have to exercise their sense of style or execution constantly. They purchase clothes, they decide on colors for a new car or a living room paint job. They purchase records and books, and they have opinions about the executional styles and the executors.

But when their private creative taste or sense of style is spurred on by dissatisfaction in their jobs, they often fail to curb this urge and become unwelcome Uncles to ideas instead of welcome Cousins or family Judges. And most often they insert themselves into the executions, not the basic ideas.

When someone fathers a basic idea that fills a desire or need held by multitudes of strangers, he or she should be free to choose the family that will help with the creative executions.

This time, our manager sees a chance to add some color himself to the dull picture of his life in the workplace. He has convinced himself to resist the negative pull of Backer's Laws. That's extremely helpful, indeed, absolutely necessary for the future health of the idea. But unless he is, as I say, a truly professional Judge with a very healthy ego, he is about to commit a sin that is just as destructive to ideas as fear of failure: He is about to use his position to force his way into the Idea Family and "doctor" the idea.

My stepfather, a pediatrician, was a doctor of the old school. He devoted one day a week to a free clinic for the poor. He paid house calls and was on constant duty, so he was out of the house and office quite frequently. Every so often, when patients would call to seek advice for minor ailments that might be afflicting their children, only to find him temporarily unavailable (there were no car phones in those days), my mother would offer her own remedies. My stepfather happened to overhear her at this when he arrived home one night. He wasn't truly angry, but I do remember him chiding her with only half a smile—"Mama," he said, "do you know what the penalty is in this state for practicing medicine without a license?"

Unfortunately, there is no penalty for practicing "idea doctor" in any state, and in very few companies.

Certain account people I've known in the advertising business have become very adept at capitalizing on this human desire to be creative, and they use it to co-opt Judges into unwittingly becoming contributing members of the Idea Family and, thus, into losing their objectivity as Judges. I would guess that the better lobbyists, talent and literary agents, political staff and speech writers all do the same thing. It takes a special skill on the part of the go-between to keep the contribution benign, but it can be a useful sting. Because once you tempt a Judge into becoming a contributor, no matter how small his contribution, you have him. I am sure agents and lobbyists do the same thing. Turn the Judge into an illegal doctor for one minute and it is very difficult for him to extricate himself from the rest of the process.

If you're going to be a Judge or a member of the Jury, you can't be the medical expert who testifies and sways opinions.

Clear, concise criticism is what all-powerful Judges should present, and the culture of the organization should make that clear. That culture, of course, comes from the top. The shape of the long shadow cast by the man or woman on the hill is what, in the end, determines the configuration and intensity of any corporate culture. It is that culture that must assure that critiques of ideas should be rendered only by those sufficiently mature to step into the shoes of the people for whom the basic idea and its executions were intended. If the person at the top is so busy looking for the light at the end of his organization's tunnel that he can't see to it that ideas are being judged by qualified people, then the flow of ideas will slow to a trickle and his organization will suffer from what I call Tower Tunnel Vision. It takes years of training to begin to think and feel like your market, instead of yourself, and it also takes a mature person who can keep his creative bents from bending the style or direction that someone else's executions have taken. Without a culture that demands this quality of training and talent in its people, and outlines a sort of invisible "Bill of Rights" for ideas, they will never grow and flourish. And whether or not any given culture provides the proper atmosphere in which to grow ideas is the sole responsibility of the guy in the tower. At least that's my opinion.

If you think I'm making a mountain out of a molehill, try looking at it through the eyes of an Idea Family.

Human beings are naturally territorial, and some bit of territory comes with every job. Try to understand the dilemma of a creative family bringing you their brainchild. They are defenseless folk who must travel through many strange territories. If you allow the chiefs of those territories to become hostage to their own fragile egos and unchecked desires to play amateur player or playwright, or if they become hostile to good ideas and executions because they don't feel the risk to their careers is worth taking, then you have severely limited the options of a creative family that is trying to get to your territory with something worth your while. And I'm presuming you *want* ideas to flourish and to get to you eventually.

Our family can turn back, of course, in which case you will never be exposed to their idea. They can say, "when in Rome," and do it the way your Romans want them to do it, in which case you get to judge a camel instead of what might have been a tiger. They can try to sneak through under cover of darkness. Or they can fight. The last two will inevitably leave the idea team with enemies who will follow them with daggers drawn, waiting for an opportunity.

In the kingdom of ideas, territories with all-powerful chieftains serve a useful purpose for a weak executive only. They protect the core territory of someone at the top who is so insecure about his own prowess as a Judge or his ability to assemble a good judging team that he doesn't want new ideas to reach him. If you were in that category you wouldn't be reading this book. So I can safely say to you, "Limit some of the powers in the territories and give some to ideas."

"Buy the World a Coke" did not have to face an organization full of people imprisoned by bureaucratic bloat and corporate fat. It faced a lean organization in which everyone had a real job and no one needed to add "Idea Doctor" to his or her title. That's why it was able to survive. That's why many of the big ideas of what is now called advertising's Golden Age survived.

"Buy the World" sailed through to its ultimate judge and jury—the public. But there it ran into trouble.

CHAPTER TEN

Trouble-shooting an Idea

ON FEBRUARY 12, "I'd Like to Buy the World a Coke" was shipped on reels of magnetic tape to Top 40 radio stations all over America. On the same tape were the other commercials we had recorded in London and in the United States during the preceding months. Three days later the tapes were being played on the air.

Had "Buy the World" hit the radio air waves with a bang, the TV commercial that followed would never have been executed in the manner that made it famous. It would have been more conventional. It probably would have featured scenes of diverse people having a Coke together. But the radio commercial did not hit with a bang. It was met with a deafening silence from the public and with worse from the Coca-Cola Bottlers. From them it got a whimper. They felt it didn't "sell hard enough." (Any company whose products are partially produced and wholly distributed by franchises needs their enthusiasm to be effective. And that enthusiasm was particularly important to the Coca-Cola Company, because its bottlers are major contributors to the advertising budget.)

I was stunned. My child had failed—and I had had such great faith and had rallied so much support.

Wise marketers of mass products keep in constant touch with their consumers. The Coca-Cola Company talked with theirs via a continuous program of focus-group interviews and telephone tracking studies. Also, their public constantly wrote letters "To the President of the Coca-Cola Company, Atlanta, Georgia" expressing their likes and dislikes for certain advertisements.

The legendary Robert W. Woodruff, who was chairman, CEO, and largest single stockholder of the Coca-Cola Company during my early years on the product, had a philosophy about Coca-Cola advertising that was the best one on which to build an indulgence brand that I have ever come across. Since that time, I have not met many brand managers who agreed with it. But most brand managers don't worry about the long-term health of a brand. They will be working on some other product or will have moved up or on before the wheezes in their brand have turned into pneumonia.

Woodruff's philosophy, which was framed and displayed prominently in many key executive offices during the early days of his chairmanship went something like this:

"The purpose of Coca-Cola advertising is to be liked."

There were those in both the agency and the company who paid lip service to Woodruff's belief about advertising, and not-so-secretly ignored it when they could. But I followed it, and whenever I was permitted to do so, the results have spoken for themselves.

While not all of those in management at the Coca-Cola Company believed Mr. Woodruff's "to be liked" philosophy down to their toes, they at least felt it to their kneecaps, and "Buy the World" was expected, like all Coca-Cola advertising, to be "liked" by its public.

"Buy the World" was not disliked. It just plain produced no reaction at all, except, as I say, among certain groups of bottlers.

Reexamining an idea is much more difficult than examining it in the first place. It is even more difficult after it has been partially executed. By then, you are no longer unbiased.

First of all, while at the beginning it was just a tiny spark, it's now your child. Second, after an idea has been executed, it becomes very difficult to separate the basic idea from the executional idea. Third, there are the footsteps in the hall.

They say a quarterback is finished when he starts hearing "footsteps behind him." And the same holds true for Fathers in the world of ideas. Only the footsteps are not just behind them. They are all around, in the halls and corridors. They are the footsteps of the nonplayers who are waiting to dock you ten points for failure so that they can move up automatically when you are out of the game.

And there's another possibility, too, the possibility that footsteps or not, you just plain came up with a real bummer—a lousy idea that got carried all the way to finished execution because you marketed it brilliantly each step of the way.

In the process of marketing ideas we all make mistakes in execution as we go along. But these missteps can be retraced. However, if they lead you all the way back to the original idea—where the compass was located in the first place—then there is no way out. The mistake was in the basic idea, and you are finished. It's like a house: if the foundations are cracked, whatever you have executed on top of it will fall apart in the first high wind.

If it's a play, you can call in the script doctor. If it's a new product, you can call in the engineers. But if it's an advertising campaign—against which millions of dollars have already been spent—there is no honest way to cut your losses. You don't just declare bankruptcy and walk away. Many do just that. And when they do, the only place for them to go is to the sidelines where nonplayers sit. They can join the ranks of the armchair quarterbacks who win by your losing. But if you're going to ever again be the Father of an idea and assemble and lead an Idea Family to help it grow, bury your own when they fail and do it all by yourself. But first it's perfectly fair to go back to square one and reexamine the basic idea and subsequent executions. Where did it fall apart?

I repeat, it's a difficult undertaking because your judgment is now colliding with emotions. And where the waters were clear before, the idea at the bottom of the spring is now covered with the froth and foam of executions.

Three out of five times when I've refused to admit defeat and have gone back and tried to rescue the basic idea, I have wasted my time—and occasionally some of my credibility, and some of my agency's or my client's money as well. But I always learned from the exercise. And anyway, I'm too stubborn to quit.

My grandfather on my father's side once insisted that it made sense to build a twenty-story office building in the middle of a cornfield. The newspapers of the day dubbed him "Crazy George." However, he stubbornly clung to the concept and built the Heckscher Building in the cornfield.

The building, magnificent to this day, is now called the Crown Building. What was the cornfield is now the southwest corner of Fifth Avenue and Fifty-seventh Street in Manhattan.

What I always derived from that story was that the Backers had good ideas. My mother, on the other hand, said it proved the Backers were stubborn and were the source of my stubborn streak. She, a Legaré from Charleston, South Carolina, had wangled a scholarship to Cornell in 1916, an era when Charleston ladies-to-be graduated from Ashley Hall School for girls, made their debuts in the Hibernian Hall on Meeting Street, and if they pursued any studies after that, they were conducted in an all-girl's Southern college and were most likely in the fields of Southern history or the arts. Mother, on the other hand, went to Cornell and majored in agriculture with special emphasis on dairy cattle.

She stubbornly insisted her choice of a college and a career indicated that the Legarés were practical, but not stubborn.

I use the above as a convenient excuse to this day. I was born and bred stubborn on both sides of my family. The late Paul Foley, who headed the Interpublic Group of Advertising Agencies, used to say, "Bill has a whim of iron." But, as I say, it's not my fault.

So it was in the genes that I would not walk away from "Buy the World" without a long, clouded-by-emotion, second look at both the main idea behind the commercial and its musical and lyrical executions. I started with the basic idea. Mentally, I walked around it a hundred times while riding in cabs and forgetting where I had instructed them to go, or while shaving and cutting my face, or while walking in the halls oblivious to the greetings of others.

I had no doubt that the perceived desire/need was a genuine one. But could a bottle of what is primarily sugar and water fill the role I had envisioned for Coca-Cola? Was my abstract answer really not an answer? Maybe it was a phony hype motivated by a desire to make a product seem more important than it was.

And yet Shannon Airport was true. I had seen it with my own eyes. More than that, I had lived it. So had Billy and Roger.

The gulf between myself and an introspective antiques dealer would by the very nature of our interests be wide—yet over a couple of Cokes it had narrowed. So had the distance between the elderly Jewish gentleman and the hard-faced German woman. I was not over-promising. Pushing the envelope, perhaps, but not breaking it. The problem had to lie in the execution. But where?

Frankly, I had been suspicious from the beginning that the first bars of the tune sounded more like a children's piano exercise than a song about hopes and dreams. And yet no one else in my highly professional and accomplished Idea Family had agreed with me. I had to respect their opinions.

Were lyrics like "apple trees and honey bees" too fanciful? If they were, they should have elicited some objections from the public instead of apathy.

Obviously all of the above was on my mind when I joined Sid McAllister for our regular, bimonthly state-of-the-account lobster dinner at the Palm Restaurant on Second Avenue in New York. Sid was head honcho on the account with the official title of Senior Account Director. My idea of a good senior account director is someone who is a superb Godfather to all major ideas on his account. Most account directors shun this duty because it's dangerous. Sid was an exception. He was Godfather, cheerleader, "laundry and morale officer," psychiatrist, and drinking buddy to all the Fathers and Uncles of ideas on Coca-Cola business. He had been a journalism major at college and was an excellent writer, a credential that made him welcome as an idea doctor when our ideas came down with pneumonia.

When we were able to, Sid and I always secured a small table halfway up the stairs because, while it was cramped, it was kind of private. Also, the waiters passed very close to you going up and down the stairs, so one could always get their attention by pointing a threatening fork toward a strategic body part. The topic of conversation, after the lobsters were ordered and gossip exchanged, was always Coca-Cola advertising in general, plus the latest sales figures. But at this dinner, the subject was narrowed to just one piece of advertising—"Buy the World a Coke."

Sid, like me, had been a big fan of both the idea and the execution, and had thought long and hard about exactly why the reception had been so flat.

Let's face it, most advertising is met with apathy at best. But music and lyrics like ours were different. It should have aroused something more—either approval or disdain. It was definitely not low-profile communication. It was not "just another commercial."

Sid had talked to some bottlers and various people in the research departments of both the agency and the company, and none of them had any real answers. We weren't in trouble. We could have let the commercial fade into the general din of radio and removed it from the air after three or four months. Most radio commercials don't last much longer than that anyway, and shouldn't. We had had some in that category, but we hated to see this one go that way. And so we talked on.

Finally, Sid came up with a theory. "Bill," he said, "I wonder if they get it." The "they" Sid was talking about was the public. "I have a feeling they just don't get it."

Sid's theory was at least something concrete. You can wrestle with a thought like that when it is about a piece of communication. And we did—back and forth, up and down. And we came to the conclusion that "Buy the World" was asking too much of its audience.

In almost any form of communication there should be something that presets the mind for what is to come. Movies describe themselves as comedies or psychodramas. Even before titles flash on the screen there are sequences that begin to set the mood of what is to follow.

One goes to an art exhibit at an important museum expecting to see paintings that somebody of consequence considers good. Take one of those same paintings and hang it in the lobby of a hotel or in a restaurant and see how many heads it turns. The average mind just isn't set for great art in those locations.

Good workshop theater does well Off-Broadway, but not on. Why? Because on Broadway the audience is preset for something bigger than they experience in less formal theaters.

Why do we introduce guest speakers? Why do disc jockeys talk about a song before playing it? Why does the host of a TV show say, "And now here's so-and-so with the weather report"? Why not just cut to the person and the weather map?

The answer to all these questions is that the target of the communication prefers to be preset—to get ready to laugh or to be impressed with something really big or different, or simply to learn that tomorrow will be sunny all day.

People expect commercials in commercial breaks. They are preset to be bored or perhaps entertained mildly and maybe given some bit of product information that relates to their wants or needs. Or maybe they are preset to go to the bathroom. What they do *not* expect is that they will be asked to think or to have to use their imaginations.

Radio was always the medium that gave one's imagination the best workout. You had to put the face to the voice and fill in the rest of the scene that was suggested by the sound effects. The lyrics to songs were less explicit in the early days of radio than they are now, and consequently I suspect they were more important.

With the coming of TV, which is a complete medium, our imaginations have become weak and flabby from lack of exercise. We who have been in the advertising business for a long time can see the deterioration of imaginations from generation to generation. Today, people—especially young people—are not willing to conceptualize. They want it all spelled out.

In focus groups, when an interviewer begins with "Now I want you to imagine that these drawings are really a finished TV commercial," they can't do it. They discuss the drawing in front of them, nothing more. They can't—or don't want to—imagine what the finished pictures might be like in mood or feeling. They just aren't used to being involved with concepts or theater of the mind.

Soft-drink advertising, on radio especially, had traditionally set its audience up by singing about happy feelings and situations like parties and picnics where soft drinks are consumed in quantity. But suddenly, with no warning, out of nowhere, we were hitting the public with a tune that was almost childlike in its innocence, and a set of lyrics about wanting to buy the whole world a home. How the heck can the whole world fit in one home anyway? Plus, the fact that the home was to be furnished not in Chippendale or Danish Modern, but with love. And furthermore, it was to be surrounded by apple trees and honey bees. And what was Coca-Cola doing there anyway?

We were at the end of Finian's Rainbow without the pictures of Glocca Morra. Our singing voices had no faces attached to them. And no location other than a fantasy home that wasn't even built yet. It too was just a dream.

We had left too much to the imagination. We had not preset the minds. We had not set up the fact that this was a commercial that saw things differently and you needed to use your imagination—if you still had one—in order to relate to the special thoughts it contained.

By the time the last lobster claw had been cracked and picked clean, Sid and I were pretty sure we had put our fingers—a bit greasy at this point—on the problem.

Now, we now had only two courses of action—either advise the client to drop the radio commercial (we had enough others to fill the gap) or create a TV spot around the song and convince Ira

"Ike" Herbert, Coca-Cola's director of marketing, to produce it. (Ike would later rise to president of Coca-Cola USA and executive vice president of the Coca-Cola Company.)

And if we took the second course there were two ways we might proceed.

The easy way would be to view the project as "experimental," and try to tap into some experimental production money that Ike Herbert would make available from time to time. But this course had one major disadvantage: experimental projects are hardly ever labeled "Rush—Perishable." And we knew that "Buy the World" was perishable. It was a child of the times, a wish that would resonate best with the idealism of the late sixties and early seventies. But later on who could predict? We weren't wise enough to foresee the selfishness of the "Me Generation" to come, but we still felt strongly that the time was ripe for a lyric that opened with "I'd like to build the world a home and furnish it with love."

Yet if we didn't label the project "experimental," we would have to label it "for real," and reserve a future slot in the up-and-coming commercial schedule for the TV spot—no matter how it turned out. And there were some big, ominous, black holes in our schedule for the summer, which is the big selling season for any refreshment product. They would need some solid filling.

The main campaign for Coke—"It's the Real Thing"—had been pretty well explored and mined. In the area of its primary meaning, there wasn't much left undone. We had pictorialized about every scene of "real things" to which our market could relate—and some to which it couldn't. The campaign was beginning to repeat itself and needed executions based on new insights. The basic idea wasn't stale, but our executions were beginning to make it look like it was. People who don't understand the difference between basic ideas and their executions often throw out the baby with the bath-water in these situations. Ike Herbert was too smart to do that at this point. Still, we all agreed with him that it was time for a whole new look at the executions. But to go down to Atlanta and say we would be able to fill one of those important summertime slots with a television commercial based on the "Buy the World" radio track was taking a big risk.

Frankly, I don't find risks a thrill. Early on I learned you have to take a lot of them in order to avoid the biggest risk of all—the risk of failure. I've looked, but I've never found a good course of risk-free successes, and neither had Sid. So Sid picked up the check, I pulled up my socks, and we both said, "Let's go. We'll make it work."

We would have liked to wait and see what sort of executional idea we might come up with to fill with pictures the gaps that we had discovered in the song. But that was a luxury we couldn't afford. Now, of course, we would have to expand our Idea Family.

But would talented people want to join up? Was I organized in such a way that I could ferret out the right people for this kind of an assignment?

Up to now my role in the family had been that of Father who stayed on to be a creative executor. I would now have to assume a new role as a Judge. That meant, in all probability, abandoning the role of creator. With so many new people in the family, it would be hard to be both. Also, while I had created many of our TV executions for music, I knew the odds were against my coming up with a good one for "Buy the World a Coke"—I was, at this point, too close to its problems. And, finally I felt I might not be good enough. The idea had grown too big. The next step would take it beyond my limits.

CHAPTER ELEVEN

The Idea Channel

IN ORDER TO come up with an executional idea for a TV commercial based on "Buy the World" we were going to need all the help we could get, and luckily the systems were in place to tap a mother lode of it. What we were going to need first of all was a quick and responsible decision on whether or not to devote a lot of energy and talent trying to save what looked like a failed idea. To do that—and do it fast—we would need what I call an Idea Channel.

I didn't invent Idea Channels. They have existed in most young, on-the-move companies over the years. What I did was give them a name and articulate a reason why they are vital to all companies and most ideas.

But first some background.

We've talked about how everyday work in the mature company flows through regular channels and is monitored and managed by professional managers, and how those managers are ranked and rated on their skills at keeping the flow moving swiftly and efficiently. Such a company represents a type of organization that helps good managers-of-the-flow to flower. But it has no place in the garden for tall poppies.

"Tall poppies," by the way, are what the Australians call people who stand taller than their mates. In a "matey" society like Australia, tall poppies are frowned upon. While it is OK for ideas and their results to be outstanding in Australia, they must be the result of a group of mates, not of one individual.

Americans, however, admire tall poppies. After all, Paul Bunyan used a pine tree for a toothpick.

Our heroes have always been people who stood out and weren't afraid to lead. They created their own positive environments. If they were alive today, the classic American heroes would be savvy enough to understand Backer's Laws, but would still believe that they themselves were exceptions to the rules. And they would be. For one thing, they didn't worry about winning vs. losing. They wanted to execute an idea. And the fact that they wouldn't have lasted long in a bureaucracy that filtered their ideas through many different layers would have been a plus for them. Can you imagine Lindbergh working his way up through the ranks at McDonnell Douglas?

How do we fit our breed of tall poppies into orderly corporate gardens of today?

There's a maxim in the advertising business that goes, "Never set up a problem for which you don't have a solution." No question I have set up a lot of problems, some of which undoubtedly apply to your organization, whatever its purpose may be. It's now time for the solution.

The solution involves one of my more controversial theories. It's a theory about how to thwart Backer's Laws, bureaucratic bloat, and a host of other idea killers and create an atmosphere where good ideas are given their best shot. It's the theory of the value of an Idea Channel.

I know it is controversial because I tried it out once on some managers of major corporations at a conference of the American Association of Advertising Agencies.

I don't often accept speaking engagements. I believe I should put in my working hours helping my present clients, not trying to impress future ones. But when the invitation to participate in a conference comes from one of my agency's clients, I find it difficult to refuse. Which is why I found myself at this particular conference with a speech to present—the subject was given to me—on the first day, and a seat to occupy on a discussion panel the second day.

The speech went OK, no standing ovation, but then most of the audience knew they would be on the golf course twenty minutes after I finished speaking, so they had every right to save themselves. But my appearance on the panel the next day was a disaster.

The subject was, "What Can a Company Do to Get Better Advertising from Its Agency?"

In my own mind I recast the question to read, "How Can a Company Get Better Ideas from Both the Outside and the Inside?"

I knew the agency people on the panel could be counted on to replay the same broken records all of us in the advertising business have been playing since the mid-sixties.

"Give us more creative freedom!"

"Give us more time to think!"

"Trust us more and research less!"

"Let us interface with professional people whose specialty is communication!"

Et cetera, et cetera, et cetera.

I knew everyone in the room would listen to the broken record and nod—the young ones would nod in agreement, and the old hands would nod off to sleep. Why not? They had played poker until 3:00 A.M. the night before, and besides, they had heard all this many times.

The problem with the broken record as I see it now, and saw it then, is that it attacks the results of a faulty structure rather than the structure itself. It's like a big neighborhood group in New York complaining about the fact that a forty-story building is taking away all their light. They can ask for a system of reflecting mirrors, they can ask for shorter workdays so as to be outside in the few hours when the sun comes through to them, but all of this will get them nowhere. The powers that be will pretend to listen, of course, and do nothing about the complaints.

You can't cure the problems without attacking the structure itself. Either you take off twenty stories and build a second building, or live with the problem, stop whining, and don't go around running conferences that pose a question like "How can we get more light in our block?"

I was the last one on the panel to speak. I did not have a prepared text, just a few notes, which I conveniently lost after the meeting when the advertising trade magazines approached me and wanted to publish them.

The following is a pretty good recap, however, of what I said that caused the ruckus:

1. Ideas need their own channel in each company. They should not have to share a channel with sugar prices, product liability suits, or the annual report. They need a dedicated Idea Channel.
2. The Idea Channel should not take its flood of ideas to a dam that tries to generate power or profits with them instantly.
3. Instead, the Idea Channel should lead to a large reservoir capable of holding any and all ideas that might come along, no matter how big and dangerous they might seem at first.
4. The reservoir that holds the ideas is perfectly round—like a round table that has no head and no seat that can be designated as more important than another.
5. Around the reservoir of ideas there are spots where Judges can sit to sip and judge the water. The Judges should come, ideally, from all walks of life in The Company. Some may sit in big

corner offices where they spend 80 percent of their time, and some in cubicles. But around the reservoir they are all given the same space.

6. Although all the spaces at any round table are equal, at this round table one person is more equal than the rest—he or she is the Power Who Can Say Yes.

The Power Who Can Say Yes can be anyone who is high enough up in the company hierarchy to give the ultimate go-ahead to an idea. Without the presence of a Power Who Can Say Yes in an idea meeting, that meeting can only be neutral or negative, because it can only be attended by those who can say "no" or "let's change this" or "I'll rubber-stamp it and buck it on down the flow." Since the first two are decisive actions, they tend to justify a job. Something changes when you kill an idea or revamp it. Merely letting it pass down the river won't get you noticed by anyone. So guess which of the three are most used and abused?

If you want ideas to flourish in your company, *never allow an idea meeting to take place—other than a technical one—without a Power Who Can Say Yes being present.*

For what they're worth, here are Backer's four rules for how the ideal Power Who Can Say Yes runs a meeting around a reservoir of ideas.

1. The Power Who Can Say Yes recognizes the fact that although the Judges around the idea reservoir are treated equally, they are not, by any means, all of equal ability.
2. The Power Who Can Say Yes keeps a form sheet—mental or physical—on each of the Judges, much as a professional horseplayer does on every horse at the track.
3. The Power Who Can Say Yes runs the reservoir operation as a meritocracy, rewarding the winners with money and an array of titles that are different from the ordinary ones. He also bets on them to win in the future.
4. The Power Who Can Say Yes understands very well that he is asking his people to play different roles from the ones they ordinarily play. He believes, however, that anyone who cannot chew gum and skip rope at the same time should seek employment elsewhere.

When I outlined my theory of an Idea Channel at the meeting, responses from various managers of the companies present started with low grunts of amazement and ended in growls of high dudgeon. I can sum them up with what one very senior manager of one of the world's biggest marketers of food and beverage producers said to me:

"What you are asking us to do is ridiculous! We're not going to reorganize our entire company around advertising!"

I tried to point out that the question we were supposed to answer was "*How* do we get better advertising from our agency?" not "*Should* we (make the changes necessary to) get better advertising from our agency?" And I hadn't asked the question, the governing board of the conference had.

Also, companies like his had been asking the same question for many years and it was becoming embarrassing and boring to sit around and debate the same subject over and over again.

I realize now that in mentally changing the word "advertising" to "ideas" I had not only broadened the subject but also made it much more important without telling anyone. Also, there were then, and still are, certain companies, like Procter & Gamble, that already had separate channels for advertising. But these channels were 100 percent linear, never circular, and the power to say yes was vested more in procedures and research scores than in human judges. Although not exactly what I had in mind, this system could at least guarantee a clear channel for an idea, and if the numbers come in right all the way along, could give a go-ahead to take an idea to maturity.

However, when procedures do the judging instead of people, the organization fails to develop good human Judges, and sooner or later the lack of them begins to hurt. The company tends to become set in its ways and insensitive to new drumbeats and rhythms that inevitably creep into the marketplace. Its basic ideas will be less daring and its executions ordinary and predictable.

I realize now that I was not as articulate nor as well prepared as I should have been to "market" the concept of an Idea Channel. I was simply explaining an idea as opposed to marketing it. I had not taken time to lay out the needs it might fulfill, and I had not invited my audience or fellow panelists to stop and consider the relationship of size of need to inconvenience of execution before they fired back at me.

But the proceeding chapters, plus this one, try to accomplish what I failed to do back then. If by now you are willing to accept the theory that ideas are different from the rest of what flows through the company channels for a variety of reasons (one of which is that the flow of ideas is never constant or even predictable), and if you will also accept the theory that the best, most professional idea Judges possess a combination of native talent and skills honed by working with many of the thoughts outlined in this book—*and* if you will go along with the statement that any organization today needs to foster ideas that can keep it ahead of competition—then it is worth your while to think about an Idea Channel and to learn about how whoever has the power to say yes in your organization might set one up.

Let me say it right now: *You don't have to reorganize the company.* What you do have to do is *reorganize your concept of homo sapiens.*

We all have a tendency to think of a fellow worker as one person, when he or she is really a combination. He may be a dynamic head of sales during working hours and a collector of roadside graphics on weekends. He may have fifty people reporting to him (most likely through three or four lieutenants), but at home he still has to take out the garbage. He could be a scratch golfer, but a lousy driver.

How good is he at judging ideas for promotions? For advertising? For new products? For start-up situations? For training programs? For new business opportunities? No one will ever find out while he sits at the edge of the flow distanced by his precious margins of turf, shielded by a platoon of lieutenants, and protected from close scrutiny by a supposedly fragile ego.

Maybe he's a natural who should be brought along to help judge ideas in areas beyond his. On the other hand, some young maverick loading cases of the company's product into a Safeway Store pipeline could have more native talent, more energy, and more interest in learning about judging ideas, and could develop in the future into a much more valuable Judge and Uncle of ideas if he could sit at the edge of an Idea Reservoir on the receiving end of an Idea Channel.

The only way the Power Who Can Say Yes will ever be able to see him in action close up will be to sit him along with a number of others at a round table on which lay some raw, unfiltered basic or executional ideas, and let him go to work. To do that means setting up an Idea Channel.

And that means setting up and setting forth a clear company policy regarding ideas. It should go something like this:

1. Every idea that comes into this company—from inside or out—will be put into a channel that leads directly to a team of Judges who have one or more persons among them with the Power to Say Yes.
2. Before an idea gets into an Idea Channel, however, it must meet the following standards: (a) the basic idea must fulfill a basic need or want, and the executions must be organic to the basic idea; (b) it must be considered legal by the company's legal staff; (c) it must be considered technologically feasible by the company's technical people; (d) it must be accompanied by a written document containing all its possible negatives, such as "not budgeted for," "does not show target audience," "will take nine months to produce," "won't stand out on the shelves," "is not Frank Rich's cup of tea," "voters aren't interested in these issues," "will not sit well with minority voters," "will reduce contributions from big business," and so on. (This list of negatives should, ideally, be started by the original Idea Family itself and completed by any and all specialists whose territory the idea touches.)

When and if the above conditions are met, every idea in the company will get a clean shot at being put into an Idea Reservoir at the end of some Idea Channel. That means it never, and I mean *never*, is exposed to a judging session peopled by those who are only empowered to say no. Also, when it arrives at the judging session, it should be company policy to insist that it be accompanied by at least one member of the original Idea Family.

At this point you might not feel my passion for all this is justified. But it is. Let me explain.

My career was founded on ideas that reached maturity. For some I was an Uncle. For many I was a Father. For others I was a Judge. But all of them, at least all the big ones that made a major difference in my career, had the advantage of getting into some sort of an Idea Channel. So it is perfectly understandable that I am a staunch and vocal advocate of giving ideas that kind of a break. But equally important is the fact that some of the best brainchildren I ever Fathered, or played Uncle to, never graduated because they were asked to survive a line of territories peopled by flow monitors under the influence of Backer's Laws who had no track record of real by him because they contributed more, not because the others contributed less.

He is articulate. His opinions are rendered clearly and backed up by clear rationales, if necessary. And he never saves them for "after the meeting." If he changes his mind later on, he calls a new meeting with everyone present and explains his new actions and the reasons for them.

He is a good listener as well as an articulate proponent of his or someone else's thoughts. And he is not afraid to take a stand.

He would like to be a purist, but probably feels he has to be a pragmatist in order to survive. He knows that in an imperfect world outside pressures sometimes sway opinions about the values of a given idea. However, the good Idea Family man discusses these pressures with his family. He does not permit himself the luxury of hidden agendas.

He can conceptualize as well as or better than anyone on his team and he uses all of that special talent to help them, not to make them feel small.

Ultimately he can lose himself in an idea and an Idea Family, which means he is sufficiently secure to check his stripes at the door. Then the rest of his family will lose their awe of his position and say what they think, even if it means disagreeing with him—which he encourages them to do because he knows that more people in his position have been brought down by yes-men than by naysayers. So if he can be a shirt-sleeve member of the team, then the others will too, and if he can't do that, he will never have a family team that keeps its eye on the ball, only on each other.

Ike Herbert had many of the above characteristics. He would walk into a meeting, check his stripes at the door, and immediately lock in with a fierce intensity on the idea to be discussed and judged. When his opinions were negative that intensity could be so strong it occasionally obscured his explanations and insight as to why he felt the way he did. It also tended to discourage dissent from the timid. I think, as years went by and Ike's titles became more awesome, this characteristic caused him to lose from others what he so valued from us—good old honest dissent. He didn't want yes-men, but I think years later that's what he got.

Anyway, we realized that Ike welcomed dissent—in fact, counted on it to help steer him. You just had to develop a sense of timing about when to disagree, i.e., not while the storm was raging, but when the sun came out, which it always did eventually.

success with ideas in their past and no evidence of talent that would indicate a probability of success in the future. We discussed "Getting There in Life is Half the Fun" (for Buick) in an earlier chapter. It wasn't a brilliant brainchild, but it was half a step ahead of its time and deserved better treatment than it got.

In the 1960s the Coca-Cola Company had a fully functioning Idea Channel. At the end of it sat a Power Who Could Say Yes, flanked by a group of marketing professionals. It was a small group, actually, just three in number, which meant that there was plenty of turf to go around and no one was covetous of the others' responsibilities outside the Idea Channel. It was not, however, the classic Idea Channel described previously, because all voting members were there courtesy of their title (e.g., product manager), rather than having been chosen purely on their ability as Idea Judges. Also, there were no raw talents being looked over by the Power Who Could Say Yes. No one from the hinterlands was being groomed to be a certified Idea Judge in the future.

Doyle Dane Bernbach once did a campaign for "the Perfect Scotch," and to make their point they created "the Perfect Football Player," and "the Perfect Baseball Player." To do that, they took the hands of one player, heart of another, the speed of another, and so forth, and put them all together. The fact that the Perfect Athlete never existed did not reinforce their claim that the Perfect Scotch did. But it made for charming visuals.

I never met the perfect Power Who Can Say Yes, who could run the judging sessions at the end of an Idea Channel without a glitch, any more than I have ever seen the perfect athlete. But I'll share with you my list of the desired characteristics for the main man at the round table. (The same characteristics apply, of course, to the main woman as well.)

First and foremost he should be a true Idea Family man. That means a person whose ego gets boosted when the idea wins, instead of when he wins. He has a sense of humor and can laugh at himself, easily, which allows him to laugh at others as well. But he does not use the judging sessions as platforms that help him to shine at the expense of others. He never plays "gotcha" with members of his Idea Family and what he does take seriously is not himself, but his family.

He understands that family gatherings are not competitions where one wins because the others lose. Everybody wins or everybody loses. Most Valuable Players will be recognized and rewarded

And after a decision was reached, Ike saw to it that any acrimony that had grown up in the meeting was left behind in the room after the session was over. And outside the meeting room all decisions were represented as team decisions, and Ike was part of the team.

Criticizing big advertising campaigns is an American pastime. For most advertising that criticism comes from consumers. But Coca-Cola advertising has another body of critics, the hundreds of bottlers who, as I have said, contribute big money to the advertising fund.

It's only natural that the people who pay the piper want to have a say in what he plays, so the pressures on the Ike Herberts of this world and their Idea Families are always greater than normal. We drank Coke during the meetings and martinis on the Delta flight back to New York, because no matter how the meeting had gone, good or bad, we knew it was inevitable that the "fit would hit the shan" soon—it always did.

Today it's common practice for the Judges to disappear and leave just the Fathers and Uncles to face the music. It's as if nobody approved those ideas—they just got on the air or into the movie theaters or into our system of laws all by themselves.

The Judges today may be lousy at judging, but their survival skills are magnificent.

Ike didn't duck when the blame was flying around. He was the man who said yes or no. It was his team that made the decisions and he would accept the blame. At the next family gathering we would all catch it—and I mean for real—but to the outside world, everyone at the end of the Idea Channel had been part of Ike's team, and he defended us.

And it was that openness, those family-style discussions, no matter how violent, that allowed us all to keep some sanity during those years. But they took their toll. Sid McAllister developed high blood pressure and retired on the spot. Al Scully, the head of the agency's art department, took early retirement some years later, and I left the entire scene.

Yet the body of work that came out of that Idea Channel was timeless—all sunshine and light and the good things that count in life. Negative advertising is easy. Whether it reflects our malaise of spirit or leads it, I don't know. But I hate it.

We didn't escape into negative advertising or into blaming someone else. But we did have a pressure release—the fact that all titles were left outside and grudges were left in the room at the end of the meeting.

People who present ideas to captains of industry tend to forget that captains of industry weren't born captains of industry. And they probably won't die captains of industry. And when they are faced with ideas that are intended to capture the hearts or minds of their maids and gardeners, the wise ones try to get down off their high horses and walk at ground level where their market is, whether they are marketing a song, a TV show, a motion picture, or a bottle of soda pop.

Many months before I brought back the idea that the real thing in soft drinks could act as a social catalyst to help various races, colors, and creeds get together and talk things over, I flew to Atlanta with a very different execution of "It's the Real Thing." This particular execution compared Coca-Cola to a number of real things that were very contemporary, but some of them, to put it kindly, were a bit trivial. Our thought was that Coca-Cola needed a healthy helping of "cool and contemporary" to balance the fact that it was rapidly approaching its ninetieth birthday. And the desired effect was that the product would seem more contemporary and "cool" for having compared itself to such real things as "in" clothing, new "in" social interests, and whatever else was "in" at the time.

I can't remember whether I was the Father or Uncle to the execution I brought down to Atlanta. It makes no difference because I was the body beyond which the buck was not supposed to go. Also, I had brought down a flock of Uncles and Godfathers to savor the sweet taste of the praise I was certain would be heaped upon our contemporary execution, so it mattered not who was the Father and who were the Uncles.

A meeting involving national exposure via television is always important. So the meeting in which we would unveil our contemporary execution for Coca-Cola was to be held in the agency's big board room.

Imagine, if you will, a birch-paneled room some thirty-five feet long and fifteen feet wide, pretty well filled with a twenty-five-foot table in matching wood and ten men. The six of us from the agency consisted of two relatively junior account men who were present to discuss the details of the commercial production that would ensue upon the certain sale of the commercial execution we were about to present. There was a senior account man who basically acted as the assistant to Sid McAllister, the doyen on the account.

The team that was scheduled to present the television commercial was Al Scully, who was directly responsible for all visuals on brand Coca-Cola, and me. I continue to go into all the background and detail involved in this meeting to emphasize that this was no low-level affair.

Sid McAllister did the welcome, the warm-up, and the review himself. Ordinarily these duties would be shared with the lesser lights present, but not today. Today we were presenting a whole new angle on "It's the Real Thing," one of the most successful advertising campaigns of the decade. The phrase "the Cola Wars" had not yet become part of America's everyday parlance, but the wars were on nonetheless. And now the elite troops were assembled and ready to charge.

When everyone was seated, more or less comfortably, facing the ever-present cork wall, Sidney B. McAllister strode to the center of it and waited until the usual buzz of interoffice gossip was replaced by silence.

Then he began. No one from the Coca-Cola Company had seen what we were about to present. It had no hidden enemies or friends. It had not been mellowed or filtered. It was raw.

Halfway through Sid's remarks I began to sweat. I realized that Al Scully and I had done exactly what I have been advising you never to do. We had created an execution of an idea without going back and reviewing the basic idea itself. We had thought we knew it perfectly. We had lived and dreamed it over eighteen months now. And our executions of it surrounded us everyday in all media—TV, radio, billboards, magazines, and even a lighted sign over Broadway. And yet somehow we had been so sure of ourselves, or so preoccupied with the supposed genius of our executions, that we had forgotten the idea behind the line "It's the Real Thing." We had executed what it said, but left out what it meant.

Executions—I will say it again—are like the clothes that make your brainchild presentable. The brainchild is the main idea, but the execution, like a suit of clothes, will benefit from a style or idea of its own. For instance, a child in the 1990s who has seen *Dances with Wolves* might prefer an Indian costume to a cowboy outfit.

I have always felt it is a good idea to talk about the executional idea before presenting it. In the confusion of presentation the executional idea can easily get lost. In other words, I would talk about *Dances with Wolves* and the idea of dressing the child in an Indian costume before actually showing some buckskin and leather fringe, which the audience might think are what fur trappers wear. If you tell them its going to be an Indian suit before they decide it's a trapper's suit, you're much better off.

Today, however, our executional idea did not fit our brainchild. It was as if Al and I had ordered the outfit from a catalogue that mailed us the wrong size. But at least our execution (unlike many executions) did have an idea behind it, so I proceeded to present it.

"Teenagers today," I said, "have a list of real things that adults have perhaps not recognized."

I could see Ike Herbert begin to frown. And I could hear Al behind me begin to reshuffle the storyboards. "What's taking him so long?" I kept asking myself.

"So today," I continued, "We are going to compare Coca-Cola in a very humorous manner with contemporary hairstyles and clothing." Ike began to lean forward. Was he showing interest or was he preparing to do battle?

"Oh, I don't mean we are going to compare Coke to Elvis's bumps and grinds, though they are 'the real thing' . . ."

I had just worn out my welcome. Al stepped in. "Noooo," he interrupted, "just his hairstyle." No laughter. So Al began to skim through the pictures, dwelling on the less radical ones—like real leather cowboy boots and real Ovation guitars.

We were dying, and we knew it. But we—at least I—didn't have the sense to give in. It's a sixth sense I usually lack. Though I never push ideas I don't believe in, today the limb we were out on seemed too long for us to start crawling back.

Ike had started sucking in long before Al finished, and the rest of his team were shaking their heads. But he waited before he let the air come out. Then he spoke, and, mercifully, released the last few cubic feet of air before he did.

What made Ike Herbert's Idea Channel work so well was that he did not look at us as a hierarchy of advertising executives (though technically that's who we were), but as his own Idea Family—the gang at the end of his Idea Channel. And that's how we saw ourselves as well. We had all checked our stripes at the door. At the end of our presentation, Ike waited for his turn to speak. There was no formal order. Whoever assembled his thoughts first could go. Today, Ike was ready first. And his reaction was put in words of a gang member, not a senior executive of a Fortune 500 Company.

He could have said, "A lot of good thinking has obviously gone into this," and then killed the idea and all of us with it behind our backs. Or he could have said, "Obviously you don't understand what *we* mean by 'It's the Real Thing.' " Or then again, he could have said, "This is disgraceful. I'll get back to you later."

He could have destroyed our nerve in a dozen different ways—all standard devices. But had he been that sort of Power Who Can Say Yes, he would never have had a chance to wish that someone could keep company with the whole world over a bottle of Coke—and go on to bigger things in the Coca-Cola Company.

What he said was, "Have you guys been smoking pot?"

Ours had been a bad executional idea because it violated the spirit of the basic idea in an attempt to imitate youthful cynicism. A system of flow monitors in a bureaucracy might have sat on it for months and actually passed it on down the line guessing that this was what their peers were looking for, but in an Idea Channel the verdict was swift, precise, and right. We could have dissented, had we felt we deserved a yes instead of a no. But we knew we didn't and so we didn't waste any more time.

And no time was wasted later that year when we approached Ike Herbert with our new idea of executing "Buy the World" as a TV commercial. The answer was yes. Coca-Cola would reserve a slot in the summer schedule, a hunk of the year's commercial budget for it, based on our continued faith in the idea. How big a hunk? We could only guess and we all guessed wrong.

I cannot overstate how important Idea Channels are to the health of America's companies. They are not meant to be "push-overs" for idea people, and I chose an example of a moment in time when an Idea Channel was anything but a pushover. But peopled with those who have the talent and know-how, they give good ideas a chance to reach their fullest potential. Idea Channels might have changed the course of this country's history many times. I understand, for instance, that Michael Dukakis had no regular Idea Channel, and neither did Jimmy Carter.

Put one in your group, political party, or company and learn how to spot the people who should be at the table. *The Idea Channel fits Backer's definition of a good idea.*

CHAPTER TWELVE

Organizing to Create

"BUY THE WORLD" at this point needed an Idea Channel presided over by a quick-thinking Power Who Can Say Yes. But that wasn't all it had to have. In order to extend its execution into the world of television it would be necessary to extend its Idea Family. Doing that is always tricky, especially when time is short.

No matter what stage an idea is in—whether it must be brought in out of the blue or developed further—putting together an Idea Family to do the job is the most difficult of all the procedures we go through in the care and feeding of ideas. And adding Uncles and Aunts who must contribute fresh executional ideas to extend those already in place is the trickiest undertaking of all.

If an idea is going to serve the needs or desires of a large number of people it will, sooner or later, have to go through some sort of a formal system. The basic idea may have been the result of an informal or even an unconscious system in the mind of an artist or writer. And the execution may have been the result of a system no more formal than a typewriter, a tape recorder, or a palette of paints and square of canvas. But after that execution has gone as far as its Father or Mother can take it, a formal system must take over. The system may be made up of an editor and a publisher, an organized art gallery, or a producer, director, cameraman, and crew backed by a financial institution. Whatever the formal system, no big idea can escape it on its way to reaching its public, and many have to face it sooner rather than later.

Up to now, "Buy the World" had been the child of an informal system, and its family all hailed from the same area of expertise—we were music men. However you wanted it—lyrics, music, or both together—each of us alone could supply it. Sure, we had different backgrounds, and our strengths and weaknesses were not all the same, but ultimately any one of us was capable of "doing it all." So we were neither linear in an organization nor formal in how we viewed out titles and areas of responsibility as we approached our joint efforts. When push came to shove, I was the guy who had to say "yes" or "no," but that responsibility and position of authority was mostly forgotten when our sleeves were rolled up and our pencils sharpened.

But now the situation had changed. Sid McAllister and I had decided that "Buy the World" must be executed for television, and the client had agreed to give us our chance. We would have to extend our informal Idea Family, and my brainchild would have to hang together in a more formalized system—or fall apart.

I pointed out earlier that putting together an Idea Family to execute a basic idea is one of the more difficult assignments in the care and feeding of ideas. But adding family to create a second or third form after an idea has already been executed in one form is even trickier. It might be instructive to look at some of the various systems that have been set up by creative organizations in an effort to keep a supply of finished ideas flowing constantly.

I don't pretend to be an expert in systems, merely a student of them, so you won't emerge from my guided tour ready to set one up and run it yourself. The best I can do for you is give you a few general lessons from a short history of idea-generating systems, plus a couple of movie titles.

The movie titles are *The Guns of Navarone* and *The Magnificent Seven*. Rent them once in a while. I'm serious. They are both about pulling disparate—and desperate—people together into some kind of a family in order to execute an idea. And they are both good, exciting adventure movies, in case you've forgotten.

The history lesson is simply a look back at various systems used in the past by certain American businesses—particularly advertising agencies, motion picture studios, and music companies—to harness and focus human resources for the task of developing executions for ideas.

I have found it helpful to think about how, what, and why those systems did and didn't produce. A short detour through them will provide some insights for the day when you will be called upon to organize some friends, a few business associates, an advertising/marketing group, or an entire company in order to get something done that calls for "organizing to create" an execution of a good basic idea.

The way I see it, there have been five basic methods that idea-generating businesses have used to get the job done:

1. The Stable (Creators Anonymous)
2. Brainstorming
3. A Meritocracy of Ideas
4. Ideas from Boxes
5. A Meritocracy of Executors (The Creative Star System)

I'll start with The Stable, or Creators Anonymous, because it seems to me that approach is what Hollywood, popular music, and Madison Avenue all tried first when their businesses became so big they had to be institutionalized. What happened was the guys who owned the outfits began to look at them as if they were manufacturing companies mass-producing—as opposed to creating—communications for entertainment or advertising purposes. They set up a process that was not unlike an assembly line, and they looked on the people in the line as anonymous craftsmen rather than creative artists.

It became de rigueur to have the craftsmen pass a partially finished script down the line for someone else to work on without the two ever meeting one another. The same was true of the development of basic ideas. Many different writers or script doctors would have their hands in the process without any system of formal collaboration being in place. So it's not really stretching a point to say a script or any execution of a basic idea was manufactured like an automobile. One person bolted in the engine, another down the line put in the upholstered seats, and on it went until the last worker attached the door handles. The theory that a single individual could father an idea, assemble a family who liked and appreciated his brainchild, and with their help parent the idea to the healthiest maturity possible was foreign to the concept of the assembly line. Even when the basic idea came from someone at the top like Sam Goldwyn in Hollywood or Ray Rubicam on Madison Avenue, the assembly-line mentality of salaried writers who received few if any individual credits probably tended to blunt some of the sharpest and most original basic ideas.

I think it is fair to say that whenever the demand for a type of communication suddenly grows so big that the area becomes enormously profitable overnight there is a tendency for the guys who will profit the most to resort to Creators Anonymous. We know, for instance, that when many of the Old Masters became popular they employed large studios of students and journeyman painters to work on some of their paintings. And the practice continued on into the late 1800s whenever the demand for an artist's work exceeded supply.

In America the demand for new motion pictures began to exceed the supply some ten years after Al Jolson made *The Jazz Singer* and introduced real sound to the medium. In popular music, the coming of rock and roll, combined with the increasing affluence of young people, produced a demand for a huge volume of the new product and an explosion of profits that publishers and recording companies had never before experienced. Up to that time they had been the middlemen between star songwriters, big-band leaders, and the public. With the coming of rock they became the creators of stars, and the stars had to have material of a kind the publishers neither understood nor appreciated. But they understood and appreciated the money, and for a few years in the early fifties, anyone with a rough demo of a few rock-and-roll songs and the energy and ability to sell themselves was given a small cubicle in the Brill Building and turned loose to crank out the new music.

Neil Diamond tells of getting so bored in that assembly line that he began to write nonsense songs like "Porcupine Pie." Ellie Greenwich and Jeff Barry didn't have the time, energy, and perhaps in those days even the know-how to finish some of their songs. The publisher wanted them anyway. The assembly had quotas to fill. So Jeff and Ellie began to fill in the gaps in their songs with nonsense syllables—like "Do Wah Diddy Diddy"—and the publishers took them to the record companies anyway. Inferior goods? That's not how the kids perceived them—they loved the semifinished songs, perhaps more so because their parents hated them—and the Greenwich/Barry team hit the top of the charts month after month.

Early on, it was the singers who were the stars, not the writers. In the long run, however, Dickey Doo of Dickey Doo and the Don'ts ended up tending bar in New Jersey, while Diamond and Barry and Greenwich are still writing and are still stars, although not as glittering as they once were. They were pulled out of the anonymity of the stable by the strength of what they wrote. But they all started in a stable as Creators Anonymous.

Using a large stable of unidentified writers became popular in the advertising business with the advent of television. Since nobody was a TV writer, anyone who wanted to be one was. The obvious place to recruit TV writers was from the ranks of those who were writing print advertisements. Print writers presented the largest group in the agency's creative department, and they were also the most respected. Radio was—and still is—a major medium for advertisers, but a freelance music man named Ginger Johnson had taken much of the responsibility for creating radio advertising away from the agency creative department when he brought the jingle into full flower by putting the words "Pepsi-Cola hits the spot/Twelve full ounces, that's a lot" to an auld Scottish tune ("Do'ye ken John Peel/ With his coat of gray").

Most of the jingles that were created subsequently were done by freelance tunesmiths who put rhyme and rhythm to a list of product claims handed to them by the agency. And when the public domain tunes were all used up, original ones had to be created and that moved the jingle even further from the agencies, since original music called for special talents that—except in rare instances—did not exist in the advertising agencies.

And the pure radio writers who remained (and who understood that the medium represented theater of the mind), were never happy writing for television.

Small wonder, then, that many of the early TV commercials were written by print writers. The scripts were nothing more than magazine ads handed down—and down is the correct adverb for the way TV art directors were looked upon in the late forties and early fifties.

Luckily for all concerned, there were not enough print copywriters to go around. The workload in print had not diminished, and suddenly here were all these work orders for TV scripts and no one with the time to write them. Enter The Stable. It was an anonymous mixture of kids in love with the medium, bored print writers in search of an escape from the confines of quarter-page ads, would-be movie writers, novelists, poets, and songwriters. Among that last group was yours truly.

What was going on in the ad business was like what was happening in the music business as rock and roll hit. There were no experts. Everybody was given a chance but not an identity. That would come later when the public took its rightful position and began to sit in the judge's chair.

What came after Creators Anonymous in each business varied. But what came next in advertising was called "brainstorming."

Brainstorming involves putting a group of, say, eight to twelve people together, giving them an area to think in, and then encouraging them to let any and all ideas they may have on the subject just hang on out. Nothing you suggest in a brainstorming session is supposed to be laughed at. No criticism is allowed at all. And everyone is supposed to be equal, regardless of title. This reduces inhibitions, say the devotees of brainstorming, and people go really "far out" with their thoughts. You just come out with something, and maybe it lies there or maybe someone else takes off from it and goes further. Either way, everyone's a hero and feels good about his or her contribution.

There is a designated scribe in the brainstorming session who records all ideas—with or without name attribution. The ideas are then typed up and reviewed by the senior management involved in the session (so everybody wasn't equal after all). Management culls the list down to what it deems is worth pursuing and puts it back into the flow for more senior review.

I have been in many brainstorming sessions set up to develop new products, new advertising, or new marketing approaches. And I have been in writer's sessions for TV shows or songs. But I have never seen a single really good idea—basic or executional—that came out of a brainstorming session and grew to maturity. I don't mean to say they were never of any merit. Sometimes they were. The problem is they were always orphans. By the time they got written down, improved upon, and added to, they had lost whatever parents they might have had. And orphan ideas seldom make it to their destinations.

I don't mean to imply that all brainstorming is a total waste of time. It is often productive to put a group of people from different disciplines (engineers, marketers, designers, etc.) in one room to discuss problems, and then find some joint solutions by consensus. Today, the Japanese seem to have done very well on a diet of consensus-building, and political organizations large and small also need to build a consensus for action—or inaction. And since all group endeavors tend to involve politics after a while, consensus-building is important in all of our industries that involve ideas and groups. But consensus-building meetings are best used to judge ideas—not to capture a basic idea and execute it. You run the ideas up the flagpole and, as they used to say, see who salutes.

Informal meetings called under the heading of "let's get together and kick around some ideas" can fall into feckless brainstorming sessions if no one brings an idea to the table. But they can be productive consensus-building meetings if everyone does bring an idea and an open mind to the session. Then what happens is an idea starts with a Father or Mother, and he or she gathers active Uncles and Aunts. The rest of the people in the room happily become second and third Cousins who are delighted to attend the graduation ceremonies if the brainchild gets to college.

I was a junior writer at Young & Rubicam Advertising at the time brainstorming became popular. But Young & Rubicam refused to try brainstorming. I thought they were wrong, of course. I was in my late twenties, and at that age anything new seems better than anything else.

But Y&R had evolved along lines that were different from the other agencies. It saw itself as a place where raw talent got molded into finished talent, not by the standard training courses of the day—or of this day for that matter—but by having the talent work for and with a group of master craftsmen.

I once asked Bill Colihan, the general manager of the Y&R creative department, why he had not instituted brainstorming at the agency. Bill was a genial, even-tempered Irishman. He stood tall and handsome, and had a deep voice that rose a major third pitch when he answered my question. Obviously it was one he had been asked before, probably many times, and it touched a sore point. I think his answer is worth remembering. It has stood me in good stead many times, and will be a help to you when you need to come up with or organize ideas.

"My boy," he said, "putting two second-rate talents together does not add up to one first-rate talent. And putting a room full of second-rate talents together won't add up to one first-rate talent either."

Over the years I have added the following corollary to Bill Colihan's theory:

When hunting for basic ideas, having more than two tends to

scare the firefly away. When creating executional ideas, three is company, four is a gang, and five is a crowd.

The reason is simply that if more than two people give birth to a basic idea, you end up with a three- or four-parent family, and that leads to a confused child or a neglected one. Further on down the line when creating executions, three seems to be the maximum number of minds that can "think alike," although a "gang of four" has, on occasion, proved to be an exception to the rule. I think the reason for this is that an execution goes forward in a creative session like a relay team—only one person can carry the baton at any given moment. Each line, each phrase, each idea for the plot comes from one person at a time, and the partner or partners become momentary Judges. They say yes or no and the baton is handed off to them. But more than two Judges become a Jury—it dampens the process. Also, there are too many hands reaching for the single baton. The single mind working alone never has that problem, of course.

What Y&R did was establish a system built around a "meritocracy of ideas." This system would eventually evolve—I'm tempted to say degenerate—into today's "meritocracy of executors" or "the creative star system," which emphasizes style over substance and covers up tired or even nonexistent basic ideas with the excitement of big expensive productions, new camera work, anything-goes special effects, rap delivery, new product sizes, new financial setups and cover-ups, etc. In effect, this system asks the public and the stockholders to get nourishment from style alone. Unfortunately, as we all know, styles must go *out* of style in order to make room for what is *in* style, which is what makes clothing designers rich and why more people have seen "Polo" as a shirt than as a game and why Ralph Lauren is a bigger name than all the star polo players combined.

But from the late fifties through the sixties, in all forms of popular communication, the idea—basic plus execution—was the thing. That's why most of the advertising classics came from that era, at least in my analysis.

Y&R carried their system of providing a meritocracy for ideas well past the creative department. They realized that for an advertising agency ideas only pay off it they are properly executed and properly published. That insight holds true for all forms of ideas, of course. Y&R had a unique system for seeing to it that good ideas were able to gather the families needed to see them through graduation. They simply made the entire team responsible for getting the best idea published in the right media, not just the creative Fathers and Mothers and Uncles and Aunts, but everyone connected to the endeavor—account people, media people, research people. They were all held responsible. And judgment day came once a year at the account review, which took a look at what and where the group had actually published in the preceding twelve months.

All businesses have performance reviews, but they consist mostly of financial reviews—if your division makes or exceeds its numbers, you are a hero. The other reviews tend to consist of "vision plans," which involve what the group plans to do in the future. But reviews of this type mostly limit their view of a company, a division, or a group to how much profit it has produced since the last review or plans to produce by the next review. The group is graded as a money generator, not an idea generator, so the review sessions are held with the senior flow monitors. The ideas that might move the company forward in the future don't stand a chance in this type of review any more than they do under the day-to-day flow monitor system.

What those ideas need, of course, is a review conducted like those at the end of an Idea Channel. Everyone involved is either part of an Idea Family or a Judge with a good track record. The ultimate Power Who Can Say Yes is there, of course, but the rest of those present, whether Idea Family members or Judges, come from all areas of the company and all levels.

At this point, the ideas have already been executed. They are out there working—or not working, as the case may be. They were given a go-ahead months ago. Now the review board examines the ideas for success in relation to their size, their longevity, and, oh yes, their potential to generate profits in the future. But they are still presented as ideas, and written up, not in red or black ink, but—figuratively—in green to signify that they are seeds that everyone in the Idea Family sees as having sprouted. What is especially productive about this type of review is that it maximizes everyone's desire to win and to shake the corporate tree instead of merely sitting under its branches waiting to collect the fruits of someone else's daring shake. To put it another way, it minimizes the negative pull of Backer's Laws by letting the company know that in this review the rewards go to those who played the game—not to some select group of spectators. Maybe your team lost this year. But the ultimate losers are those who joined no team. They are left outside the meeting—invisible people down the hall. What makes the system work in the end is that it produces a single-minded desire on everyone's part to analyze, isolate, and ultimately be a part of the team that fields the best ideas.

Young & Rubicam's belief that the idea should be all-important, and that not only its Parents but its entire family should be the heroes of the day, did not sweep the agency business at that time, nor indeed the rest of the communications industry. The advertising agency of Doyle Dane Bernbach was founded on a strong belief in the Meritocracy of Ideas, and became very successful. But before the majority of communications firms followed suit, a new breed of management began to take over the corner offices—the Technocrats.

During the mid-seventies, as the founders and guiding forces behind the major Hollywood studios, the recording companies, the advertising agencies, and many other of America's most vibrant and innovative manufacturing/marketing companies stepped aside, what was left was a layer of Technocrats. And they ushered in the Age of the Organization, an organization that divided up the system for generating and marketing ideas into little boxes, all very neat and tidy sitting on an organization chart, but enervating to ideas.

I had lived happily in a Stable, flourished in a Meritocracy of Ideas, been spared brainstorming by wiser heads than mine, and now suddenly found myself in a Box manufactured by an organization set up by Technocrats. The Boxes were called "Collaboratives," and they were run by triumvirates, one person each from the three primary agency disciplines: creative, research, and client contact. Each collaborative was like a small, insular agency, only not really free to act like one.

I was lucky, and luck beats smart every time, in my opinion. I had the good fortune to be in the good graces of most of my clients at the moment when the reorganization took place and was able to pick and choose most of the members of Collaborative D, as we were called. Six months earlier or later my stock might have been off twelve points or so and I would not have been in such a strong negotiating position.

As it was, I could see to it that Collaborative D ended up with the gang from *The Guns of Navarone*, sprinkled with many of the outlaws from *The Magnificent Seven*. To Collaborative D, rules were there to be broken for the same reason mountains are to be climbed—because they are there. Ideas were our goal, but we saw them as being a locked in a fortress and surrounded by the enemy—

an enemy composed of top management, client, budgets, and in fact almost everyone who wasn't a member of Collaborative D. And getting to the quarry, surrounding it, defending it, and ultimately bringing it home was everybody's job.

Outside of our own walls we were still being judged by how well we maintained client relationships and the color of our bottom line, but within we were an old-fashioned Meritocracy of Ideas, and we judged ideas by how well they maintained the relationship of our products with our *real* clients—the millions of people in our markets.

Some two years after the arrival of the neat little boxes and tight management control from the top of the mountain, everyone began to realize that while all boxes look the same on a chart, they are not the same in real life. As George Orwell might have put it, some boxes were more equal than others. Bill Colihan could have told everyone why: no matter how many people you put in a box—three, four, ten, or twenty—if they are not first-rate talents, they won't add up to one. "You can add people like numbers," he might have said, "but adding quality takes a different kind of math."

The result was that the walls between the boxes were no longer consciously maintained and began to deteriorate with age. They were built of pretty flimsy material to begin with, and at the end of two years the inmates of Collaborative D escaped and took over the town in the dead of night. The ideas that had begun to come out of D had set up such strong bonds of friendship with millions of consumers that no one was willing to argue with them. There was no palace revolt, no bad blood spilt or left flowing. The Meritocracy of Ideas had simply proven itself yet again to be a better system. So for a period of four or five years those in the agency who came up with the basic ideas and created the executions, plus those who Godfathered them to their destinations, were rewarded—not as handsomely as they should have been, but certainly better than before.

And it was this system that was in place when "Buy the World" came along. It wasn't exactly the old Y&R system where the top creative and account people decided what ideas had merit, though their opinions certainly carried weight. It was more democratic in deciding what basic ideas and early executions should be cared for and fed. Junior and mid-level people were more free to say, "That stinks," and not to join the Idea Family of an idea they didn't espouse. "Buy the World" would need a "Magnificent Three or Four" but I knew I could never order anyone to join up. It would have to be an all-volunteer army. And if the system took it to heart, "Buy the World" would still have to travel the many twists and turns every advertising idea must go through on the way to its ultimate judge: not the client, but the many millions who make up our Soda Pop Culture.

CHAPTER THIRTEEN

The Very First United Chorus of the World

F OR MOST OF you, the preceding pages represent theory, not practice. You won't get the chance, as I did, to organize an idea department from the ground up. But what you will have to do sometime is take what is given and reshape it within whatever limits are prescribed. But with those boundaries you can often effect changes and take advantage of what each of the systems discussed in the previous chapter may offer—especially if you understand the disadvantages of each.

When I decided that "Buy the World a Coke" needed a TV execution, I had the authority to assemble and organize a large group of talented people any way I wanted to, as far as the agency was concerned. However, in the advertising business there are always two bosses—the agency and the client. I have always tried to make those two authorities understand that the ultimate boss should be the public. But as in most businesses, bottom lines and personal egos tend to obscure that fact, and, day in day out, the public gets more lip service than real attention.

Since clients like to feel that there is a full-time group of talented people living and breathing their business twenty-four hours a day, I presented my groups on the organization charts that were circulated inside and outside the agency as a set of neat boxes connected to each other by strong lines of authority. In reality, however, I kept the walls around the boxes low. People were encouraged to visit their neighbor's backyards, and if I felt local turf was being defended unreasonably, I was free to step in and criticize. Lowering the walls allowed me to keep some major talents who would never have been happy confined in tight boxes.

As I pointed out in the previous chapter, what I had done was put together a hybrid organization, one that combined some of the freedoms of the Y&R stable of roaming writers with the efficiencies of the box or group system. My roaming writers were, however, more senior than the Y&R ones—and my boxes looked more formal on paper than they were in practice. To be 100 percent accurate the lines around the boxes should have been in gray ink, not black. But let's face it, most of my clients were smart enough to realize they were not getting the full attention of everyone promised by the organization charts. They mostly had some sort of Idea Channel that judged the advertising on its own merits and not by the number of bodies or hours involved with the delivery system, so I could always stay a step or two ahead of disaster.

In order to dramatize the fact that we were a meritocracy and not a bureaucracy, I kept titles functional. Joe Jones "in charge of . . ." was the type of title that got respect. I realized that in order to get a bank loan for a house or an apartment you need company stationery with titles like Senior Group Creative Director. So titles that made the bearer seem extra secure and important were passed out to be embossed on stationery. But what counted at home, as opposed to at the bank, was "in charge of," "responsible for," or "creator of."

However, the system was a royal pain for the guy at the top—me—to administer. In the quest for quality, how many walls do you breach? And after they are breached, how much time does it take to patch up the bruised egos that have resulted?

No system is perfect, but this one produced some of the most effective and famous campaigns of the era—or any era for that matter. It's worthwhile to stop here and examine why.

The seventies were a time—the last time, actually—when the majority of American companies were still seeing the future as more than just tomorrow, next week, or next quarter. They were looking at least three years ahead.

They seemed to have what the Japanese have today—"patient money," money to build with for the long term. So basic ideas that answered some timeless, or at least some long-term, needs or desires of a large number of people were in demand, and these basic ideas called for many different executions to keep them relevant and fresh as time went by. How many ways, for instance, can one tap into the basic human desire for what's "real"?

When I originally took "It's the Real Thing" down Ike Herbert's Idea Channel, I did not see it as lasting on and off for nearly fifteen years. I explained to Ike and his team of judges that many years had passed since Pepsi had hit the scene as a cheap imitation of Coca-Cola. I thought Coke ought to take a year or maybe eighteen months and set the record straight. I never envisioned at that meeting a time when groups of us would see real things in "Country Sunshine" and "Hello Summertime," for instance, or all the things we in this country have to look up to, which are summarized in the line and the music of "Look Up, America." And furthest of all from my thoughts at that time was the executional idea that Coca-Cola could play a role in one of the most universal of real things, the desire to communicate with others all over the world. The same can be said when I presented a simple execution that tapped into a beer drinker's basic desire for a diet beer that he can drink without fear of derision. Was I thinking that Miller Lite's "Tastes Great, Less Filling" would ever be kept so relevant and fresh for nearly twenty years that in its last years it would still be voted the American male's favorite advertising? Of course not. All I knew was that I had the best system one can put together for such an assignment, and it was staffed by the best people I could find to come up with the fresh, perceptive insights into basic needs or desires that some of us would get in the wee hours of the night. The desire for recognition of one's self-worth, exemplified by "Because I'm Worth It" for L'Oreal, or "Now Comes Millertime" for Miller High Life, could never have been explored and given their long lives either without the organization we are talking about. The same holds true for "Here's to Good Friends," for Lowenbrau Beer and "Tab, What a Beautiful Drink for Beautiful People."

When you talk about organizing to create, it's obvious that you first have to decide exactly what you want to create. If what you want is to fully explore big basic ideas, then a system of boxes drawn in pale gray lines plus Idea Channels ready and waiting will beat out all the classic bureaucratic organizations that are so prevalent today.

So, as I say, it was a system that produced winners in the Idea Olympics. But it also produced severe chest pains in the guy responsible for keeping all the tigers on their stools, and led me to rethink where I was going in the years ahead.

Although I had kept the walls thin and low, I had never before completely flattened all of them and turned a series of backyards into one gigantic playing field. But that is what I decided to do for "Buy the World a Coke." In a formal system of tight groups in tight boxes the shock would have been too great. The various egos involved would have been shattered. But in this case the action was merely one step beyond how we operated day to day. The boss—myself—was going "a bit far out" this time, but was not "out of line."

The late, great Jack Tinker—who founded Jack Tinker and Partners, one of the important agencies of the 1960s, told me once that one of the differences between creative people and everyone else in the advertising business lies in their field of loyalty. "Everyone else," Jack said, "is loyal either to their company or themselves. But true creative people are loyal first and foremost to their craft."

Jack was speaking in the years when writing for advertising, motion pictures, and theater too, was more often referred to as a craft than an art, as it is today. Anyway, he was right about creative people.

Today some of Jack's opinions are out of date. The organization man—loyal to the company above and beyond home, hearth, and vacation time—is now a one-man minority. As the company has begun to desert him in order to protect its bottom line, he has become more loyal to numero uno.

But the good creative executor is still primarily loyal to his craft, and I know that when you ask talented executional people to join an Idea Family the first question they still ask themselves is, "How good is the basic idea?" Other people may go along with it because it is a politically astute move or because doing that is part of their job—but good and true idea types will consistently act as Jack Tinker said they would. They will be loyal to their craft first, themselves second, and their company third.

It was by no means a foregone conclusion, then, that a further group of Uncles and Aunts could be found to adopt my baby. I had the authority to assemble the prospects, nothing more. The fact that I felt the idea and its execution thus far were fabulous would certainly be a factor in its favor, because, based on my past record, my judgment was respected. But it would not be a deciding factor. Each person in the large group I would assemble would ultimately decide for himself or herself.

As a piece of music and lyrics the song was applauded by all, but as a piece of advertising many of the craftsmen met it the same way the public had—with polite apathy.

Several teams sparked to the idea, however, and worked hard to come up with a TV execution, and several came up with what seemed like excellent ideas. For instance, someone, I think it was Phil Messina, came up with the idea of a worldwide "block party" staged as if people from all over the world lived in a mythical town and sat down at a table so long it stretched for an entire block, and ate various ethnic foods together, washed down, of course, with Coca-Cola. It was a charming thought, and would someday make for very involving scenes when we wrote a song that fitted it, called

"Getting this World Together," and produced it as a television commercial. But that particular executional idea just didn't seem to grow organically from "Buy the World."

Somebody once said, "There are three things everybody thinks they can do better than anyone else—write a hit song, be President of the United States, and manage the New York Yankees." To that list I'd like to add "judge TV commercials."

Everyone's an expert, including my very bright wife, the capable editor of this book, and, of course, your mother-in-law. But for me, it's always been more fun to create advertising communications than to judge them. So I was not looking forward to the next couple of weeks and my role as the Power Who Could Say Yes—or No.

Time was short, and as it began to run out, I found myself with two TV finalists. They both came from TV art directors, which was to be expected since the assignment was 100 percent visual. But in both cases the art directors said they had bounced ideas back and forth with someone else—a writer and a film producer in one case, and another art director in the other. This was a smart move, considering that "Buy the World's" original Idea Family had all come from the music end of the business.

I have always believed that ideas—like vegetables—are best when they are fresh. So you have to keep the Idea Channel open at all times. That means, among other things, that the deliverers of ideas must have easy access to the Judges. Which means the Judges—whose duties always extend way beyond judging—must give judging top priority. I try to make it clear to people with ideas that they should feel free to barge in to my office at any time with an idea they have thought through sufficiently to put their names on—unless the office door is closed, which it seldom is. I, in turn, know I must have the right to assemble my judging team at a moment's notice as well. So the following two scenarios represent standard dramas.

I was hurriedly called out of my office to see some rough storyboards that were not completely assembled and therefore difficult to transport. The only fellow Judge handy was Al Scully, so I asked him to come along. The art director explained his concept with enthusiasm and conviction. Although a bit disjointed (art directors are seldom linear thinkers and are almost always better with pictures than with words), it was sound and went something like this:

> There are many different situations where people of different ages, races, and nationalities are thrown together much as they were in Shannon Airport. For instance, young people biking or hiking through Europe or the Americas; travelers on buses and trains as well as planes. There are backyards all over the world where new neighbors are moving in from other nations and getting acquainted with each other over the back fence with some conversation and maybe a Coke. Schools and sports are widely varied in race and creed. Holiday gatherings and block parties bring new people together. And in all of these Coke can—and does—play a part naturally and effectively. And the scenes of all this can be shot as a series of short vignettes so that they are each pictorially interesting and fun to watch.

Anytime someone is presenting an executional idea to you it is always advisable to stop and reflect on whether or not that person can "bring off" the execution they are promising. No matter what the executional stage—beginning, middle, or end—the whole train can be derailed by whoever momentarily controls the engine of execution, be they designers, directors, editors, or entrepreneurs.

In this scenario I didn't have to worry about those promises being delivered. The scenes would have been shot as billed, resulting in pictures that were warm and appealing—with pictorial integrity maintained for the original idea, the viewer's eye, and the product, Coca-Cola itself.

I was close to buying the idea, but something kept gnawing at me. Something wasn't right, but I couldn't figure out what it was. Al was enthusiastic at first. He gave it better than "a pair of jacks," but not a royal flush.

At this point what would you have said?

A day later another idea appeared, and it clarified what was not right about the first one.

I was sitting in my office trying to figure out how to square a group of salary raises with company policy, when I looked up and saw, standing directly in front of me, a young art director named Harvey Gabor. Harvey had a habit of presenting with one hand resting on the palm of the other and rocking forwards and backwards ever so slightly as he talked. And at this stage of his development as an advertising man he was not yet sufficiently advanced to organize his thoughts in a manner that made them easy to track. They were, like most good executional ideas, instinctive. But these instincts should ideally have been exposed to the scrutiny of logic and reason before facing the Judges. However, I had confidence in Harvey's instincts, so when he came at me with the intensity of a pit bull, I didn't assume a defensive position.

"If there was such a thing as a United Chorus of the World, what would it look like?"

How's that for an opener?

Harvey had a New York accent that stretched from the tip of Manhattan clear through the Bronx, and somehow the idea of him promoting a United Chorus of the World sounded like a setup. So I made him repeat the question.

"If there's such a thing as a United Chorus of the World, who would be in it and what would they look like?"

Remember, this is 1971. The idea of singers from all corners of the globe coming together to sing a single wish song for the world had never happened before and would not again until 1985, when "We Are the World" was recorded.

"I'm serious, it's for your Coke song," Harvey continued. "I see it being sung by a sort of world chorus made up of someone from every country."

LONG SILENCE.

"They should be young," I said, "because young people seem to care the most today about whether or not the world has a home."

"But they shouldn't be dressed up in similar duds like a chorus that sings together a lot," Harvey replied.

"They should be in limbo," I said.

Harvey disagreed here. "I see them on a green mountainside somewhere. It's like they are singing on a spot that's so perfect it isn't real, but it is. It isn't a set."

I didn't argue—because all at once I felt that Harvey's idea was the executional idea we had been searching for. I gathered the rest of the judging team to check my opinions. Why was this one "The One"?

Think back to the definition of a good executional idea: "A rendering in words, symbols, sounds, colors, shapes, forms, or any combination thereof, of an abstract answer to a perceived desire or need."

The basic abstract idea that a bottle of pop named Coca-Cola could act in a small way as a social catalyst was no longer abstract by the time the idea got to TV. The lyrics of the song had laid that out pretty clearly.

What Harvey had done was render in pictures the one abstraction still left unexplained, the abstract idea contained in the song itself—who was the "I" who was wishing all those good things for the world?

> Only one person walked away from the Plaza last night with two gold medals. He was Harvey Gabor, a McCann-Erickson art director, who won for the frequently honored "Hilltop" commercial ("I'd like to buy the world a Coke") for Coca-Cola, as well as for a spot on the thoroughbred for the New York Racing Association.
>
> Coke was the client also for the other win for McCann, with Don Tortoriello, an art director, winning for a nostalgic, antilitter commercial.
>
> *The New York Times*
> *September 8, 1972*

So Harvey's idea passed the test. But did Harvey?

The last time, in fact the only time, he had attempted a shoot of this magnitude it had been an unmitigated disaster and Ike Herbert had asked all of us, including myself, off the Coca-Cola account. I had stayed in the background and run the creative side of the account from the shadows until Ike had calmed down and then, little by little, reintroduced the old team.

Like this idea, the previous one had been good. But Harvey hadn't brought it off. In an attempt to show the pleasing and relaxing effect of a bottle of Coca-Cola, he had assembled in a barren desert gulch a group of well-known Hollywood villains, and had seen to it that a white-coated waiter served them all ice-cold Coke. They became, of course, a more congenial crowd, but the overall effect of "Mean People," as the commercial was called, was too surreal for the audience of the day.

Having the first United Chorus of the World sing about wanting to build the world a home and keep it company over a Coke was a brilliant executional idea. Al Scully loved it. So did I.

The idealism of the sixties had not yet been superseded by the rampant materialism of the late seventies and eighties, and heavy metal had not yet crept into pop music. The basic idea was right for the times and Harvey's execution was right for the basic idea and the song.

And yet we hesitated.

Harvey, who was in my eyes and in the eyes of the client a proven failure at this style of execution, was now, undaunted, asking us to trust him to assemble another group, a United Chorus of the World, at a location we would see only in Polaroid snaps, and pull off a totally different but even more abstract idea.

No wonder we hesitated. When big ideas fail, they fail bigger than small ones, and as Backer's Laws say, they can be very dangerous to the health of your career.

In actual fact, a creative director who was more interested in style than substance would probably have fired Harvey after "Mean People," and in the short term he might have been right. But in the long term, he and his company and his clients would have missed having the highest profile, most awarded, and best-selling commercial of the decade. And, perhaps even more important, they wouldn't have been the ones to launch the first United Chorus of the World.

Still, there was no question about the fact that for both Harvey and "Buy the World a Coke" bringing off the "United Chorus of the World" would represent their last chance.

Luckily for both, Harvey had learned something from his previous debacle. He had learned the value of an Idea Family, and he had already enlisted several Uncles for his executional idea—Al Scully, now head of the art department, and Phil Messina, a very talented and experienced film editor whom I had hired as a producer some years earlier. Phil represented what I thought was a very creative "hire." My reasoning was that feature film editors, when allowed by Hollywood producers to expand their duties, had made superb feature film directors—John Ford being a prime example—so why wouldn't an editor of commercials make a superb producer/director as well?

Agency art directors like Howard Zieff were already making the jump into directing commercials and feature films, too. So both Phil and Harvey were candidates to be directors—and both had ambitions to be one—which would make for a pair of Uncles whose backgrounds were perfect for each other but whose ambitions were not.

Harvey and Phil had learned reluctantly that they each needed someone else, at least for the time being, to help their executions come off. They hated that fact—but Al Scully had made them see the truth of it.

Many of the best executional teams in any form of communication do not represent marriages made in heaven, and Gabor and Messina were certainly no exception. Al and I told ourselves they could pull it off, however. But would we have mortgaged our homes to prove our point? No.

It was time to recheck our judgment one last time, cross our fingers, and keep the faith.

CHAPTER FOURTEEN

Separating the Basic Idea from the Execution

HOW CAN YOU be sure you have made the right decision when you chose an executional idea? I have already hinted at some procedures for judging, but there is no 100 percent surefire method for avoiding mistakes.

The "Buy the World" family had decided to go with an executional idea that involved the First United Chorus of the World. We were going to put it in an Idea Channel and surround it with enthusiasm. But still we were far from sure. What we did know was that we had examined our execution the right way. Mentally, each one of us had gone back to the beginning and retraced the idea from the basic idea to the lyrics to the recording. We had gone through a process that I would like to take you through once again, but with a different idea this time around. This is the biology chapter of this book. I will attempt to dissect an idea that I had no more to do with than you, the reader, and yet we all judged it at a distance. I will try to put you into the shoes of those who first bought the idea and those who later managed or mismanaged it. It is not an advertising idea this time, but a propaganda idea.

Many people confuse advertising and propaganda. Webster's separates them as follows. To advertise is "to call public attention to especially by emphasizing desirable qualities so as to arouse a desire to buy or patronize." In a broader sense, Webster's says, to advertise is to "make something known to: notify." But along Madison Avenue the first definition is the more accurate one. Propaganda, although it has acquired negative overtones over the years, can be positive or negative. Webster's defines propaganda as "the spreading of ideas, information, or rumor for the purpose of *helping or injuring* [italics added] an institution, a cause, or a person"; or "ideas, facts, or allegations spread deliberately to further one's cause or to damage an opposing cause."

The way I look at advertising and propaganda is that they are like half brothers with the same mother but different fathers. They both spring from the same source—a desire to persuade someone to think or feel a certain way and act accordingly. But what inspires the desire is different in the two. An advertisement starts with something finite—a product or service that consists of a measurable number and quantity of ingredients, parts, pieces of capital, or numbers of people. What the advertisement does, or tries to do, is connect all of these to an infinite and unmeasurable set of needs or desires in a human being. Propaganda, on the other hand, starts with the infinite—as Webster's says, "an institution, a cause, or a person." And propaganda attempts to make this infinite understandable and involving by synthesizing it into concrete images like Smokey the Bear, Michael Dukakis riding in a tank, or Willie Horton.

The careers of politicians and their advisers are dependent on their skills at propaganda. But the thirty- and sixty-second paid-for television spot, as opposed to the free sound-bite, TV debate, or newspaper editorial, is a form of communication in which the advertising man gets more experience in a year than the politician gets in a lifetime. The result is that neither the political adviser nor the agency man is really skilled at propaganda that utilizes thirty-second TV spots. And when the results are disappointing, each blames the other, each claims they don't need the other. But, actually, what they should do is join together and form an Idea Family.

This is the story of a piece of propaganda created by a skilled practitioner of advertising for use primarily in a thirty- and sixty-second television spot format. It had, as you will see, a basic idea and executions organic to that basic idea. It was, however, destined to be judged by people whose background was propaganda and whose experience in separating basic ideas from executions of this type was very limited.

In late 1985 and early 1986, the American Association of Advertising Agencies began pulling together a collection of agencies to do pro bono work for the Partnership for a Drug-Free America. Ordinarily a single agency will work on a given project, such as preventing forest fires or encouraging people to vote, but because of the enormity of the drug problem, any and all who wanted to pitch in and work on the problem were welcome.

The agency creative people may have been well versed in the thirty- or sixty-second formats demanded by TV stations, but they approached the issue with no more practical experience than a public relations expert, a journalist, or a psychologist specializing in drug addiction. Nonetheless, when the ball was put into the agencies' court, they responded with a great deal of energy and skill. Actual addicts were put in front of cameras while they told their heart-wrenching stories, which were edited down to thirty or sixty seconds. Similar situations were also re-created, written, and produced by many of America's most skillful advertising agencies and aired free by the media.

Former drug addicts were brought into schools to give high school students firsthand accounts of the horrors of prison sentences handed out for drug abuse, and their stories, too, were edited for thirty- or sixty-second lengths. Some TV commercials used highly memorable graphic depictions—for instance, comparing a drug user's brain under the influence of drugs to an egg frying in a very hot skillet.

At my agency, Backer Spielvogel Bates, we did a series of spots addressed to the large percentage of people who feel they are immune to the temptations of drugs for any number of reasons ranging from inner strength to the quality of their lives and neighborhoods. The spots showed ordinary people shooting up on heroin while an announcer said, "Statistics show that one out of every five people who try heroin become addicted. But that doesn't concern you. *Or does it?*" Just before the "*or does it*" was spoken, the camera showed that those who have injected themselves in clandestine corners of a public or private washroom are now stepping out into the sunshine to reveal themselves as airline pilots, school bus drivers, etc. In other words, they have jobs that touch the lives of all of us.

We figured the rest of the agencies would be scaring the hell out of those who had to live day to day with the problem. We would wipe the smug expressions off the faces of those who up to now had felt they were above the problem. Drugs are everybody's business, and we wanted to ensure that everyone understood that.

All this is a simple way of saying that the AAAA and the Partnership for a Drug-Free America did a superb job. They harnessed an important segment of America's communications specialists, and all the country's media channels, and helped motivate them to do their very best in every way. Advertising agencies, for instance, not only did their creative work pro bono, they also footed the bills for production costs on the commercials and print ads they wrote. And production houses, in many instances, offered their services at cost.

However, one agency, Needham Harper, took a very different creative tack from the rest. Its creative director, Bob Cox, was reviewing a stack of storyboards, most of which showed drug pushers pushing drugs at preteens, when he got a glimpse of a firefly. The storyboards were all ending with lines that attempted to sum up the dangers and horrors of drugs. Finally Bob came to one board that showed the silhouette of someone in a car traveling parallel to a young boy on foot. The camera looked over the shoulder of the guy in the passenger's seat as he was pushing drugs at the defenseless kid on the sidewalk. The kid didn't seem to know how to handle the situation, and as the spot ended it left him there on the sidewalk, confused and tentative. The line at the end of the spot talked about the dangers of accepting the pusher's offer. It was a good execution, Bob felt, but like the others he had been reviewing, it was an execution of a basic idea that other agencies were working on already, i.e., answering a need or desire that said people of all ages had to continually be educated and reeducated on the dangers of drugs.

Something flashed inside Cox's head, or gut, or subconscious, as he stared at the execution of the drug pusher safely ensconced in his automobile and the confused kid protected by no sheet metal, and seemingly with no inner resources to call upon. A little light went on for a moment—a firefly—and it illuminated a different need from what everyone else had seen. It was the need for an *answer*; for some *solution* to the problem, not merely a delineation of it. And the audience to whom he was talking, the kids on the street, had an even greater need for that answer than the general TV audience might have.

The airwaves were picturing daily the horrible scenarios of drug addicts, the tenacity of drug pushers, the distress of those close to the addicted, the crimes—and ultimately the deaths—that result. Faced with all that, Cox and the perceptive people around him began to believe that the entire program might be too much for preteens to handle. And television, being a nonselective medium—especially scattershot pro bono television—was in a sense demanding that the young kids handle everything it was showing.

The questions posed by adults in a twelve-year-old's world are more of the "answer yes or no variety" than what life asks of an adult. "Have you done your homework?" "No." "Did you wash the car?" "Yes." "Did you have a good time at the prom?" "Yes." So, if your idea is to give people in the yes or no stage of life a verbal solution to a problem, an execution that advocates a simple yes or no should most certainly be considered. And Bob Cox found himself saying to his creative executors—"Why can't we end that spot with a simple 'Just Say No to Drugs'? Why can't we end all the spots that way?"

And that's how "Just Say No to Drugs" came about. It aimed to provide an answer for young people who might come in contact with the reality of drugs and would most certainly be exposed from time to time to dramatizations of that reality on television. And faced with all the above, came a basic idea that said, "What these kids need is a something that helps them handle the horror; like a solution to the problem itself." And creative director Cox chose a solution that spoke their language.

Classic advertising always offers a solution when it brings up a problem. In fact, that genre is called problem-solution advertising. But the "Drug-Free America" campaigns were offering no antidote to the poison of fear they were arousing nightly, and for a pretty good reason. No practical solution had been offered to Drug-Free America by those creating their communications. Again, this is not a criticism of those involved. None of us saw the need for solution-type advertising until it was illuminated by Bob Cox.

What happened next was that Nancy Reagan appeared at the

agency to see the thirty-second and sixty-second spots. I don't know whether or not Mrs. Reagan was ever shown what the other agencies were thinking, but she liked what she saw at Needham Harper. At least we know she liked the line that came at the end of the pieces of communication showing the problem, as dramatized by drug pushers trying to push drugs on twelve- and thirteen-year-olds, and ending with the solution in the form of the line that Mrs. Reagan was to decide she should adopt for her own, "Just Say No to Drugs."

The world of ideas has always turned on four types of decisions:

1. The "No Decision."
2. The "Postponed Decision."
3. The "Thoughtful Decision."
4. The "Instant Decision."

"Agonizing" and "Painful" decisions are subcategories of all the above.

The "No Decision" and the "Postponed Decision" we have already discussed. They flourish in a bureaucracy and are pretty well eliminated by Idea Channels and Powers Who Can Say Yes. The "Thoughtful Decision" is what this chapter hopes to promote more of, but lately I have been forced to the conclusion that in today's world of instants—instant coffee, tea, mashed potatoes, cash machines, replays, etc.,—the "Instant Decision" is winning out over the "Thoughtful Decision" just as, on the evening news, sound bites have replaced substantive reporting.

I have a theory about Instant Decisions. My theory is:

INSTANT DECISIONS FAVOR THE EXECUTION OVER THE BASIC IDEA.

Those of us who knew that once seem to have forgotten it now. We have forgotten how to separate executions from basic ideas and the fact that it takes time to make good, thoughtful "go" or "no go" decisions when judging the hundreds of ideas we must accept or reject every year in order to make a little headway against the daily currents of our lives. And those of us who never knew, who never had a clue about style vs. substance, are reveling in our newfound expertise as Judges. A good example of this—one that will illustrate the point clearly—is what happened next to "Just Say No."

What "Just Say No" got was an Instant Decision, judging by how the line was managed from then on. Mrs. Reagan and/or her advisers must have judged "Just Say No" to be a basic idea when it was really an execution of a basic idea; an execution *aimed to communicate to preteenagers*. The basic idea was "help young people find an answer to the pressure of the drug pusher." If Mrs. Reagan's team had taken the time to think about the line "Just Say No," they might have said to themselves, "Hey, maybe this is a good execution for youngsters, but isn't it a bit simplistic for a twenty-year-old whose peer group is already into drugs and whose temptations are being provided not by pushers but by pals?"

If they had taken that kind of time, they might not have been swayed by the execution alone. They might have then said to themselves, "What this is all about is giving people some *answers*. 'Just Say No' is *one* answer, and a good one when aimed at one age-group. What we should do is provide answers for many different age-groups, income levels, sexes, and psychological profiles. And the answers should come from those who have been there—who have been in the same situations as the target group is in every day, so the advice given is advice that is based on experience with what has worked." (Actually, this is what *is* being done with some of the drug messages being written today, but nine years elapsed while a good basic idea was buried.)

What happened to "Just Say No," however, was that Mrs. Reagan became part of its execution. She was hardly an experienced adviser to any large target group, yet she began advising everyone watching TV to "just say no to drugs" as if it were as simple as that. And her audience began to snicker, regardless of party affiliation. Because what they were seeing all of a sudden was a sixty-something millionairess taking over as the main executional element in some general audience TV spots, and telling everyone from ten-year-olds to headwaiters and rock singers how to ward off drug pushers. Her heart was in the right place, but she was mutilating the basic idea with executions that were both too simplistic and too sophisticated at the same time. She had decided in favor of an execution without regard to basic idea, either because she didn't know how to separate one from the other or because she didn't take the time.

If tomorrow, or next month, someone brings you an execution of anything from a town plan to a marketing strategy to a script for a play they want you to back, take the time to strip away all the executional elements and expose the basic idea—provided there is one—and ask yourself, "Is it a good basic idea?" If it is, then ask yourself if the execution furthers the basic idea and has some fresh insights about how to do that. In other words, if you eschew instant decisions and go with thoughtful ones in the right way, I guarantee you will have more successes with ideas than you had in the past, or to put it negatively, you will have fewer failures.

The very thoughtful publishers of this book won't let me offer the above as a "money-back guarantee" but it's still one that has some value. It is backed by thirty years of experience in the school of trial and error—and believe me, there were plenty of errors. Learn to separate the basic idea from the execution—walk around each and give it a thoughtful decision. Going about it that way has another advantage. It leaves you with more faith in the correctness of your decision than when you merely shoot from the hip and fall for an execution. And keeping the faith is a necessary duty of all Idea Families if they hope to give their brainchild a long, happy, and successful life.

CHAPTER FIFTEEN

Maintaining Big Ideas

HOW LONG SHOULD a basic idea last? If you understand and agree with my definition of a basic idea, the answer is easy. It should last as long as the need or desire exists. And if it is a big idea, obviously the number of people who continue to have the need or desire that the basic idea originally illuminated is important. By not understanding how to separate basic ideas from executional ones, organizations all over America allow many basic ideas to die because the executions have become tired, dated, or just plain obsolete.

We already discussed the idea of giving people an answer to a drug pusher and how that basic idea was allowed to die before it really got started. The idea of a "people's car" as pioneered (arguably) by Henry Ford and revisited by Volkswagen is another that was allowed to die because in this case, the executions become obsolete (or in the case of the Bug, the cars were revealed as more dangerous in head-on crashes, because there was no engine in the front to help absorb the force of impact). Today we have many automobile models that the people can afford, but none are truly organic to the basic idea of "the People's Car," a car that represents first and foremost "basic transportation"—functional, affordable, and unconcerned with styling for style's sake. In other words, "the Levi's jeans of cars." The basic idea died because it wasn't maintained as a separate entity. It sounds simple to do that, but it isn't.

I'm sure there is an entire book to be written—with each chapter by a separate insider—about good basic ideas that were well executed at the outset and yet have been allowed to die in this country. Notice I say "good" basic ideas that were "well executed."

Here is what my chapter would be if that book were to be compiled. My area of insider expertise, obviously, is advertising, so this is a story of what I thought was a good basic idea that was well executed at the beginning and yet was allowed to die. Like everyone else in an idea business, I have a long list of ill-treated campaigns that I think would qualify. But my saying they were "good" represents a judgment that is suspect because of my bias. You can't let the cow judge her own cream, as they say. So I'm going to let someone else say the campaign was good, and I'll tell you what happened to it. The basic idea was partly wrapped up in a newly created executional word—Millertime. Twenty years after it first appeared, Joanne Lipman noted in her *Wall Street Journal* advertising column that "Millertime went on to become one of the most successful campaigns in advertising history." So how come it died? Because the need or want no longer exists? You decide.

When Philip Morris bought the Miller Brewing Company in 1970, Miller High Life Beer was advertising "Miller Makes It Right" on top of its basic identification, "The Champagne of Bottled Beer." Although the executions, with Al Hirt blowing his trumpet, were aimed at the middle class, the overall effect of the line plus the claim was to make the beer decidedly snooty. Snooties, however, were (and still are) very light beer drinkers. At that time they were part of a group that made up 15 percent of the market. Blue-collar workers were the heavy drinkers; they drank 85 percent of all beer. So it did not take an MBA to figure out why Miller was selling some five million barrels of beer a year, while Anheuser-Busch was selling twenty-two million, Schlitz fifteen million, Pabst ten million, etc. High Life in its clear bottle had built a franchise by being special. But it was now "too special."

I am a great believer in having a skilled moderator talk with groups of heavy users of the products in whatever category I must write about—beer, soft drinks, soup, television sets, hamburgers, or inexpensive automobiles. And at that time I had in my creative group a very skilled moderator—Dr. Winston White, a former professor of psychology at Harvard—and I depended on him and his focus-group sessions a great deal. When he and I began to learn about beer we had a convenient, ready source of heavy beer drinkers just across the street from the agency. A new high-rise building was going up in our front yard, and for a few bucks, a platter of burgers, and a six-pack of beer, the men who were setting the steel were happy to doff their hard hats after work and step over to our place to discuss beer with Dr. White while my creative team monitored the sessions through a one-way glass window.

It was evident from the sessions that Miller High Life was a beer no self-respecting blue-collar worker would be seen with, not because the beer was bad (they felt it was as good as the competition) but because its advertising and the "look" of its clear glass bottle seemed to support a class system that left them out completely.

The standard communications approach employed by politicians, propagandists, and marketers in situations like this is to say, "We're your kind of folks!" And the standard response is, "Oh yeah? Where have you been all my life?"

If you've got the time,
Music and Lyrics of the Miller Theme

If you have the money, the time, and very little competition, you can sometimes get away with the outrageous reversals and retractions you have to go through in order to execute a sudden shift in position, but doing it always looks easier in a big boardroom than it does when you mentally put yourself next to a steelworker and watch him react to your message on TV. But it became abundantly clear when we listened to our hard-hatted groups that they appreciated any

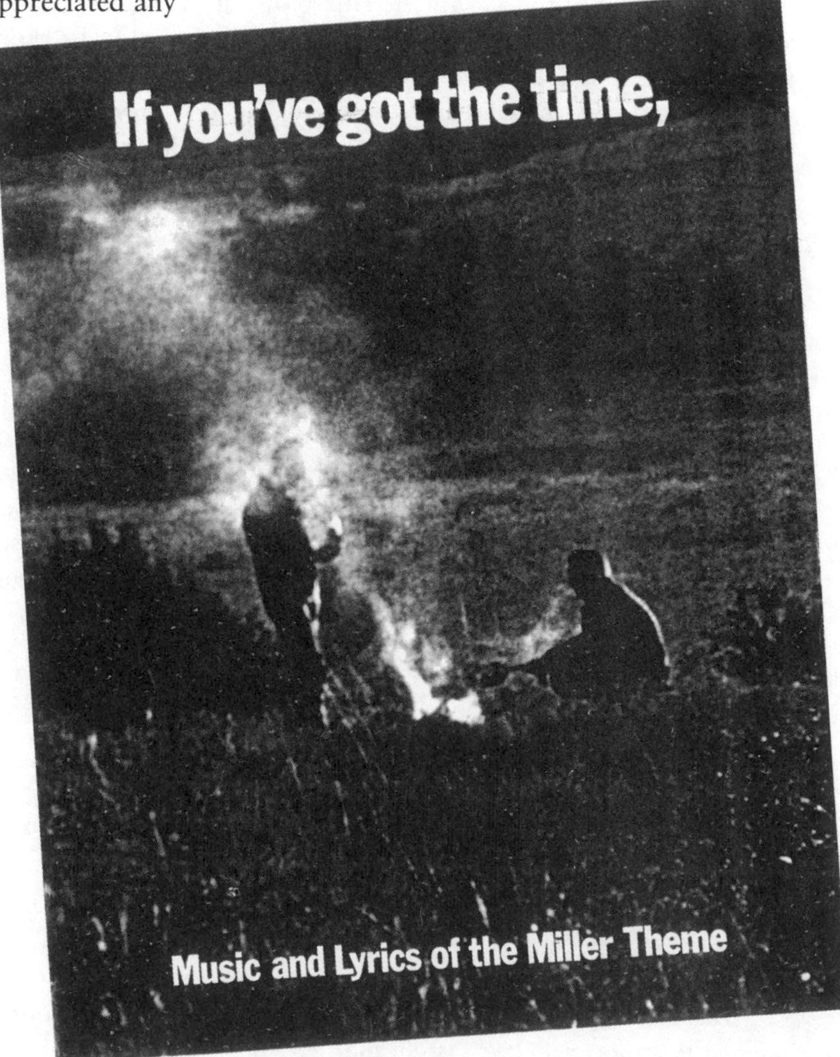

communication that saw the world through their eyes. And very little of what was out there did that.

The hard hats seemed to see life as a continuous effort by the Haves to minimize the contributions, and therefore the wages, of the Have Nots. They never whined, however, they merely bitched. They didn't really expect to have their contributions acknowledged, nor to have their rights to time off and vacations delineated except in their union contracts. But they seemed to have a buried need or desire to have some of those things brought to light above and beyond what some lawyers put on a sheet of paper.

Obviously, I decided

not to try to say, "We're your kind of beer." Instead, I fell back on a common sense maxim we all know but seldom follow. Years later I would make it one of the seven points of our advertising philosophy at Backer & Spielvogel and it would help us grow ourselves and our clients. It is simply, "People like people who like them."

I didn't want to "sell" the steelworker my beer; I wanted to say to him, "We are running TV ads that applaud what you have done to build this country and recognize the fact that you have earned the right to the best bottle of beer you can find." I wanted our advertising to project him as a kind of folk hero. And when it came time for him to relax—that time was defined, when the campaign started, as weekends—we saw those moments as well-earned moments, moments where he, as I say, had *earned the right* to the best.

Every element of the executions was geared to that basic idea—pat him on the back and help him feel good about himself and keep recognizing that one reason they worked was to *earn* "time to relax."

I wrote a cross between a jingle and a song using a rural chord progression I had heard many times in the Carolina back country. The song was later played and sung by a saloon piano player whom I had often heard playing in an Atlanta bar at night while I was visiting the Coca-Cola Company by day. Johnny Mack had never done a commercial before, and he sounded like he hadn't, which was all to the good. He sounded like what he was—a singer/piano player who had sung in a hundred bars from coast to coast for as long as he could remember. He sounded like he represented a beer that frequented bars and saloons, not country clubs.

The song he would finally sing opened and closed with the words, "If you've got the time, we've got the beer."

The words were catchy, they came from the vernacular, but *they were not a succinct outgrowth of the basic idea.* I knew they didn't synthesize the idea. Nonetheless, we had a deadline to meet, and they were the best I could do in the time allotted, which was very tight.

The Miller Brewing Company, having been recently sold, was in a quandary. No one at the brewery seemed to know who was going to go and who would stay. The COO and marketing director—a man named "Cush" Cushenberry—liked the music a lot when he heard it in a hotel room. I can't remember where the hotel was, although I spun the tape. If I remember right, *I* played and sang on the tape as well. At that point we had neither the time nor the budget for Johnny Mack. Anyway, that was the only sale I can remember having to make, which was lucky, since my singing is pretty bad and might have killed the idea.

The TV pictures I showed Cush were symbolic of "going with the flow" on weekends—they showed a leaf floating down a stream, for instance. They looked like many of the Infiniti commercials that would come years later—only we showed the product at the end.

In the months that followed, a fabulous Idea Family formed around the campaign. They came mostly from Philip Morris. I didn't choose them, the campaign did. Also, I expanded the executors at the agency, and enlisted the help of Bob Lenz, a talented art director at the agency and later on a very successful creative director and partner at Backer & Spielvogel. Together we changed the symbolic pictures a lot for the better. We both saw them as heroic portraits, and agreed to go for scenes so beautiful that you could blow up a frame from any one of them and hang it on your wall. And Bob Meury (in my opinion one of the best all around copywriters in the business) gave the copy a touch of poetry. The guys from Philip Morris—George Weissman, John Murphy, Jack Landry, Larry Williams, and Cliff Wilmot—constituted a family of Judges with a philosophy that's gone out of fashion today: "If it's got the right roots, let's help grow it."

In the sense that they had not been the first ones to approve the work, they could have felt it was not their campaign, but Cush Cushenberry's. Yet they recognized the strengths in its basic idea and couldn't care less about territory of origin. And in the end they made it their campaign by helping it grow to a height where the *Wall Street Journal* would later single it out as one of the all-time best.

They examined every element. We talked. They examined again. We talked again and again. It was a big, sprawling, brawling Idea Family at the end of an Idea Channel. It was too big to be formalized, but never separated by layers or walls. We wore no stripes. We had a basic idea about how to talk to heavy beer drinkers. Nothing more, but nothing less.

Best of all, we had an Idea Family that could recognize a basic idea, conceptualize it, and see a future for it. And why not? These Philip Morris guys had helped grow a tattooed "Marlboro Man" into a "Marlboro Country" cowboy. If you knew their win/loss record as a team, you'd bet them pretty heavy in the office football pool.

What we all figured out was: (a) We didn't need to narrow our appeal to weekends. Blue-collar workers see every night after work as "time to relax." (b) If you're going to create a new American hero you have to show him in some way. And (c) lyrics like "If you've got the time, we've got the beer," and "When it's time to relax, one beer stands clear" are all very nice, but they're not tight. We needed to tighten the executions so they could live on billboards and point-of-sale material.

We all came to those conclusions together. Keep the roots—the basic idea and many of the elements of the executions, like the music—but prune off all the deadwood so the tree can grow straight from its roots. And let's all of us—and I mean each and every one of us—grow it when it's ready.

I have always found that writing long copy is the best way to get to short copy. So I began to write little essays about blue-collar workers drinking beer after work, and I soon realized my essays were all about those golden hours between "quittin' time and bedtime." And one afternoon, in one such essay, I found I had named that time "Millertime."

Except for one very rocky moment, Millertime was the most enjoyable basic idea plus execution I have ever marketed—it was so damn BIG.

I started out by marketing it to the Philip Morris Judges as the next Marlboro Country. I said, "You guys have carved out a piece of territory—the Old West as idealized in countless movies and TV series—and used it to illustrate the rich, straightforward taste of your cigarette to the romantic, independent spirits among your customers. And like a smart cattle boss, you've branded it with your brand—Marlboro Country. I want to do the same thing—but not with a piece of idealized territory that hardly exists today, but with a piece of *real time*. This idea can be better than Marlboro Country," I said, "because it exists. 'Quittin' time to bedtime' happens every evening to every 'folk hero' who works to build this country. If we can brand it, and give it meaning, it will give our beer a way to stay relevant every day of the week."

It was an easy sale to the Judges in the Idea Family. But in the confusion that was rampant out at the brewery because of all the shifting responsibilities, we nearly lost the whole campaign. Someone, I am not sure who, got the idea of presenting Millertime to the entire white-collar work force out at the brewery—the sales force, the back room, the brewmasters, the market staff, etc. So we gathered in the main cafeteria of the Miller Building, long since replaced, and there we found an endless sea of faces—maybe seventy-five, maybe more.

I went through the music. They liked it. And the new idea for the TV staging that Bob Lenz and I had worked out—shoot every scene as if a frame from it would win a photography contest, and make the men in each scene heroic by shooting them as idealized symbols instead of sweaty groundhogs—and they liked that too.

Then came the M word—"Millertime."

It was too much for some of them. Many of these guys were salesmen who lived daily in the competitive world of beer. There was an uncomfortable shuffling sound coming from the audience. I couldn't figure out why. Finally from the back of the room, came a question, "Why aren't you saying, 'Miller High Life Time'?"

I was stunned. Everyone seemed to agree with that voice from the back of the room. I was changing the name of their beer. The bar call was "High Life" as often as "Miller." I looked over at Cliff Wilmot. He had no answer, but seeing him there inspired one in me and it saved the newly minted word we needed to grow the campaign.

"For the same reason Cliff there doesn't say 'Come to Marlboro Flip Top Box Country.' "

And then I got out of there fast before one of those many territorial czars poked a hole in my logic.

Label that meeting "Growing Pains."

Millertime grew, and grew Miller High Life from some five million barrels to twenty-two million in less than ten years. Moreover, the spread between Miller High Life and Budweiser narrowed during those years from approximately seventeen million barrels to six million.

In middle-class circles the cocktail hour was renamed Millertime, and in real beer circles, "quitting time" became "Millertime." I don't mean to imply that every time someone referred to Millertime it lead to his drinking High Life. But it helped.

High Life today is back down to around five million barrels. It's convenient to say "Millertime" ran out of steam. Convenient, but not true. At least not in my obviously biased opinion.

As America's blue-collar labor force began to shrink, the number of our typical heroes shrank, but not the number of guys who said, "Thank God it's quittin' time." As the beer world turned, beer drinkers relaxed more actively than in the past. They partied and boogied instead of sitting around. But they were still people who liked people who patted them on the back and delineated their rights to "time to relax." The basic idea was still as valid as ever.

High Life sales were destined to fall, no matter what we said in our advertising. We were all practicing fratricide. Younger brother Miller Lite was eating High Life's lunch every day and growing stronger while older brother was becoming malnourished. Also, August Busch had held a three-day meeting of his top brass in Busch Gardens near Williamsburg, and they spent hour after hour studying Millertime.

They didn't have to prove that Budweiser was a working man's beer. It already was. So they could take a less heroic view of the beer drinker—make him a bit younger and more accessible. And they had the bucks to outspend Miller nearly two to one. What they did not have was Millertime.

However, what *we* did not have by then was the original Idea Family in their old jobs. Most of them had moved up and on. They would look in from time to time, but on a day-to-day basis we had become institutionalized, and the new family was more interested in maintaining the flow of Millertime executions than the basic idea. Backer's Laws were beginning to take effect. We had layers of maintainers who checked the films for "juiciness" and "consistency." All of which was important, but not when it takes priority over the fact that the execution itself has become boring and old-fashioned. Not the basic idea, but the executions.

Bob Lenz and I could see the end in sight long before the sales decline started. There had to be a slippage. But there didn't have to be stoppage.

You don't have to be a political poll taker to know when you're boring the public. Your public will tell you in a half-dozen focus groups or less. Millertime had become predictable. Our cowboys with their hard hats were wearing out their welcomes. But the basic idea of Millertime was as valid as ever.

We needed some executions that made new people feel good about themselves and in fresh ways. We secured some experimental money to show them a new breed of hero with a new beat and tune to the music—his own beat, country rock. It was similar to what I had done on Coke years before, only the basic idea here was vastly different.

I had enlisted the aid of Jimmy Buffett, and together we wrote some new music with a new, less serious attitude, but still recognizing the importance of quittin' time—that is, Millertime. I had figured if Jimmy could immortalize the Margarita with his song "Margaritaville," he could also be a big help in revitalizing Miller Beer with Millertime. And he was. The spots were not a major departure in my eyes, nor in Bob Lenz's. But in Milwaukee they were. I took them out to the brewery without Bob because he was on a well-earned vacation, and, anyway, I thought they would sail through accompanied by bells and whistles.

The first filterer said, "The sunset shots don't match. There are clouds in the second scene and not in the first."

"But there will be dissolves in between," I said. "Time has elapsed between those scenes. These were rough cuts." The second layers picked up where the first had left off: "The production values are sloppy." The fact that the weather had changed from one shooting day to the next was apparent to them. It had also been reported by the company representative on the shoot.

I saved what I thought was the big basic question for the top layer. "Don't you find the new, livelier music and the more relaxed shooting style a fresh break from the past?"

"Shoot it over," they said. "The sunsets don't match."

I called Bob the next day in Europe. "It's the end," I told him. "Millertime is going to become 'When it's time to be bored.' These guys think their job is to maintain the integrity of the executions by paying attention to tiny details of production rather than to the executional ideas themselves. We are in the hands of maintenance men." Bureaucracy and Backer's Laws were killing us.

"I've been telling you that for six months now," Bob said. And he had. I had just thought they couldn't conceptualize and would understand when they saw a new execution. I was both right and wrong. Two years later sales went flat and then started to slip. For us the roof caved in. Millertime was blamed of course. "Too old-fashioned"—true. "Run out of steam"—true. "Bud's stolen our idea"—partly true.

But we had put our brand name on the hours when a beer means the most. We still had that. And we still knew that the need or desire addressed by our basic idea was still valid. The fact that Bud had learned that from us did not have to scare us off our basic idea. But it did.

The original Idea Family was gone. The original way of working was no more. A maintenance man's mentality had replaced a grower's outlook. The Idea Channel had disappeared, blocked by the boulders of bureaucracy. There was no one to talk to without going through three or four layers of maintenance men. And on and off they were indulging themselves by taking other agencies into their Idea Family at some level or another.

The Judges all wanted to take the standard way out: "Let's show young party animals. The drinkers we want are now young party animals."

I don't mind being "uncreative," but I hate being unsound. And I was. I took the obvious and easy way out, too. I turned Millertime into 100 percent Party Time. What a lie that represented.

Here we had been telling the working man that we recognized his contribution and we saluted his right to enjoy his free time however he pleased. If he wanted to party in that time, fine. That was his right. And in our executions we could show him partying from time to time. But always we had to salute him first.

Our basic idea was to be the beer that appreciates what the little guy does to make the big things happen. Men will like the beer that likes them best. So Millertime was time for a person to feel better about himself and his rights, better than he ever did before we created his beer campaign. Millertime was never supposed to be party time. Later on, Spuds McKenzie was Party Time. But Millertime was much bigger than that.

Tom Griffith and I wrote a very happy piece of music for Millertime as Party Time. America loved it. The marketing director of Miller told us everyone that year at the Fort Lauderdale spring break was singing our song. But they were drinking Bud.

The new bureaucrats at the brewery loved the idea because it was appropriately greedy; it was aimed at everybody. It told the consumer, "You don't have to work, or be hassled, or earn your beer in any way. All you have to do is like to party and boogie." The beer for party lovers may be a basic idea if you have earned some right to say it. But it wasn't the basic idea behind "Millertime," and we had no validity in our new message.

I sat up on the stage of a huge auditorium in Texas that year in a big convention of our beer distributors. I was at an upright piano and I played and sang the new song. "Welcome to Millertime, it's all yours and it's all mine. Bring your thirsty self right here—you've got the time, we've got the beer for what you have in mind. Welcome to Millertime." No reward for the consumer—just sixteen happy measures of come-on and brag and boast and greed from us.

Bob Lenz's TV spots—wall-to-wall parties devoid of real conviction—were as entertaining as those things can get without resorting to tits-and-ass and a host of MTV film effects. They too met with great enthusiasm.

By the standards of the day, it was good advertising—certainly as good as, or better than, most of the beer advertising on the air then and now. Typically, it represented a good execution of somebody else's tired basic idea. But Bob and I both felt really guilty.

For me the guilt came not so much from betraying the old Idea Family, because in my view the company had betrayed Bob and me and all the other Uncles and Godfathers who had grown the campaign. They had disbanded the Idea Channel and had split us up and separated us from them with territories manned by flow monitors and maintenance men who had no track records of growing ideas or maintaining them—and as I have said, maintaining them is even trickier than growing them.

What I felt guilty about was that I had betrayed the original idea. And I knew it could have been the biggest and longest lasting one I ever had. I couldn't have saved it, but I still feel guilty. I had sacrificed it in order to keep the account for a few more years.

"Wise business decision," as they say. But a lousy creative one.

Maintaining a basic idea takes a system of Idea Channels that lead to people who understand the value of the basic idea. Organizational changes, bureaucracy, and Backer's Laws are all enemies to maintaining the basic idea.

Put them all together and you're destined to live from execution to execution, from fad to fad, and from style to style.

CHAPTER SIXTEEN

Ideas vs. Money

WE HAD REAFFIRMED our faith in the basic idea of "Buy the World a Coke," and we had walked around the execution as carefully as we knew how. It was time to act.

The commercial was carefully storyboarded and taken to the client in Atlanta. There we knew it would have a great many advantages. It would be in an Idea Channel, not a bureaucracy. It would be given a proper hearing and the decision, whatever it might be, would be a thoughtful one. It would, however, have two major disadvantages: first the execution was "far-out," and second, it was much more costly than past commercials for Coke.

We were realists about the costs of executional ideas in advertising. And we knew, as you should, that money problems can cause rifts in Idea Families just as they do in real families.

Up to now we had been a tight-knit Idea Family. The Uncles, Godfathers, and Surrogate Cousins who were the Judges had not lost faith in the basic idea nor the execution as far as it went. Our goals were still the same—to broaden the already wide appeal of a world-famous product, and for that goal we were all willing to put our reputations, and to some extent our careers, on the line. But now we were about to become a family divided by perhaps the world's best divider of families—money.

"Put Your Money Where Your Mouth Is" conjures up an ugly image, but it says exactly what it means to say. Up to now we had been talking. Although talk is not cheap when a number of salaried professionals have been working on any idea in any field, there can never be a realistic price attached to an idea project. Time sheets are only an indicator. They are never accurate reflections of the energy and the quality of the energy that the Fathers and Uncles have expended, merely the hours spent at the office. And now we needed to convert our hours and our energies into hard dollars—the client's dollars.

Executors get excited about the quality of their executions

without regard to their cost. Architects, film directors, and campaign managers are famous for going over budget. And there is no hard and fast rule that I know of to guide the executors on how much they can reasonably ask for, or the judges on how much to give. Backer's Fiscal Policy is:

THE SIZE OF THE BUDGET FOR EXECUTIONAL IDEAS SHOULD BEAR SOME RELATIONSHIP TO THE SIZE OF THE BASIC IDEA.

In short, if you're aiming to fill a need or desire felt by millions of people, the Judges should be prepared to unzip their money belts if the executional idea happens to be costly. But the people wearing the money belts don't always agree with me.

On top of the fact that our executional idea would be expensive, it was also risky. "A United Chorus of the World singing about a bottle of pop? C'mon guys, Let's get back down to earth. We're in the business of selling a product, not entertaining." They could have said any or all of the above before we ever got into the question of costs. And we anticipated comments of this type. So we did our homework, and marketed the execution well.

Marketing an idea, as opposed to merely selling it, involves a great deal of what I have been talking about in previous chapters. You pull apart the basic idea and the execution. Wherever possible, you bring in facts such as the number of people who feel the need or desire your basic idea is attempting to satisfy. You develop the fact that the execution is not only organic to the basic idea but also involving and rewarding to its audience. Also, since originality and freshness in the executional ideas can be a help in these instances, a quick review of what has been done in similar areas by similar products is useful. I guess the best way I can describe the difference between marketing and selling is to say that salesmen try to make a point; marketers try to prove it.

We did all the above and more. We explained how "Buy the World" broadened the spectrum of the product. We reviewed competition past and present. We talked about how well it fit into the times in which we were living. And our efforts were rewarded—but only up to a point. The client was willing to take a chance on the commercial, but not for what we said it would cost. The budget raised the hair on the back of their necks and produced a firm growl, which, when translated by Sid McAllister, meant, "Get the costs down."

On one hand they had a point. The budget we proposed was the highest in the history of Coca-Cola advertising up to that time. But how do you cut down the costs of an execution like that?

The idea was not a United Chorus of Half the World, and the location had to be both out of this world, yet in it. It could not be the Jolly Green Giant's papier-mâché valley. The chorus had to be on location, sing on location, and that meant live sound to be recorded in "nowhere land." And the hundreds of singers in the Chorus had to sing together, which meant lots of rehearsal time. And, since they were looking right at camera, if there was any lip synching to be done, it would have to be perfect. The logistics screamed "money" at every line in the budget. There was just no place to cut and still deliver the idea. We had hit an impasse. Our baby was never going to graduate from college and get to go to work.

When money splits Idea Families, the fault line invariably runs right smack between the Creators and the Judges. Up to money-time our interests had run parallel, toward the welfare of the project. But now an inevitable suspicion began to creep in.

Do you remember the fable of the fox that got his tail cut off in a trap? He backed himself up against a large tree and called for a gathering of all the other foxes. And when they were assembled he began a brilliant diatribe against tails—they got dirty, they slowed a fox down when hounds were after him, they got caught in branches and briars—in short, they were excess baggage, so let's all cut off our tails. But while he was speaking, a young fox, a veritable cub, had managed to step between the old fox and the tree and noticed that the old fox's tail was already cut off. At which point the cub squealed out excitedly, "But you have already lost your tail!"—which, of course, wiped out the validity of the diatribe against tails.

We, the Fathers and Uncles in the Idea Family, were asking the Judges for money to produce the execution, but we had already lost our tails. We had already spent time and considerable energy creating the executions, and since time is money, we had, in a sense, spent our own budget already and we were now asking the others to start spending theirs. Our views could hardly be seen as unbiased.

In the eyes of fond Parents and Uncles, nothing is ever too good or too costly for their baby. So our Idea Family had to come up with one more idea. We all realized that to lose momentum now was to lose the idea itself. It is always possible to find some money that hasn't been spent on some other commercials the client has produced and try to move it to a new budget. But that takes a lot of negotiating and meanwhile time goes by. Then one day you wake up and the world is no longer thinking about peace and love, but something else. Shakespeare has provided us with all the advice we need at these moments: "There is a tide in the affairs of men, which, taken at the flood, leads on to fortune." And that thought holds for all ideas. We knew we had to either fold our tents or go camp in them. So Sid, as the guy in charge of the account at the agency, gave the signal to march on, but without the clients' authorization.

Advertising agencies go out on a limb every day with their recommendations. They risk their reputations with the client and occasionally the account itself. But very seldom do they go so far as to pay for a commercial that the client likes but considers too costly. Paying for one that is not liked in storyboard form in order to show the client what it will look like when finished is done more often, but even that is to be avoided. Because the moment you pay for a finished commercial in any category you find yourself being asked for a repeat performance the next time, and before long you are giving your client the chance to work with finished commercials every time.

Everyone would rather judge a finish instead of a prototype. But no agency's profit margin is such that it can allow its people to continually do commercials on spec and let the clients choose the ones they like best. The temptation to work that way is ever-present because it avoids confrontation, but it gives the accounting department real cause for fits, and rightly so.

Sid wasn't exactly putting his career on the line when he gave the word to proceed, but he was sure getting close enough to make us all nervous. Little did he—or any of us—know that in a few months he would be stepping over the line, not by inches but by miles. Before that happened, however, Sid had a basic idea of his own.

In the abstract, the need was simply to convince Ike Herbert there could be such a thing as a piece of film worth—in today's money—$20,000 a second. Sid felt that if he could get Ike closer to the pull of the idea, by showing him some pieces of footage along with a few token cuts in the budget to prove "we had listened," then a signature would be forthcoming.

It was a risky execution—an out-and-out gamble on the enthusiasm a few film rushes would generate.

As it turned out, that gamble would fail, but in the end luck would prevail. (Remember, it's better to be lucky than smart.) In the interim, a new member would be added to the judging team, a man named K. V. Dey, Jr. Ike had moved up to marketing director of all Coca-Cola beverages, and K.V. took over Ike's old job as brand manager of Coca-Cola.

When it comes to approval of advertising and advertising budgets, final authority varies from company to company. In some companies—bureaucracies mostly—it lies with a board. With Coca-Cola and its Idea Channels, the Power Who Could Say Yes always existed, but after K.V. arrived we were never sure whether K.V. had been given that unofficial title officially or not.

At this writing, Dey is president and CEO of the Ligget Group. He has had a distinguished career in the business of marketing. All of us admired him, but to this day I don't know what the K or the V stands for. He wanted to be called K.V., so why not? He had not been with the Coca-Cola Company long, and his background was less in advertising than in general marketing and certainly did not include commercials with this kind of price tag on them, or this kind of emotional message, either. So he was willing to play the role of an observer more than an active participant in the later judging sessions, since he had not been privy to the earlier ones.

In his new role, K.V. quickly realized what most of us learn too late in our careers. You can't be an expert in everything, but you can try to be an expert in the most important thing—people. In the end all businesses are people businesses. When the rough cuts of "Buy the World" were finally assembled and brought to Atlanta, I'm not certain K.V. understood exactly what we had, for they were very crude, the sound had not been mixed, and there were no words on the end.

Al and I were both enthusiastic and tried to explain the technical imperfections, but I think it was Sid's enthusiasm that persuaded K.V. The film lacked color, good sound, and cohesion, and Al's and my enthusiasm was that of Uncle and Father. But Sid was a Godfather, a bridge respected by both sides of the family for its solidity. And in the end, I suspect that K.V. bought Sid's opinion of "Buy the World," not his own, not Al's, and not mine.

But what mattered was that K.V. signed the budget estimate at that time. I don't think he had the authority to sign for the amount of money already spent or to be spent in finishing costs without the boss initialing his decision. K.V. said he would take it on himself to handle that with Ike Herbert. So in the end he joined Sid and the rest of us out on that limb.

My understanding is that Ike never did sign the estimate, and maybe he didn't have to. But I do know that shortly after the commercial was finished and hit pay dirt, K.V. left the Coca-Cola Company. Was it Backer's Law at work again, or just coincidence? All I know is that it is one more example of the fact that the care and feeding of ideas tends to be more difficult when they are big. A cat owner may get a scratch or two, but lion tamers can get their arms chewed off.

But, to go back, Sid issued the go-ahead without a signed estimate. We were frankly excited and optimistic, but also a bit scared. We knew we had a big cat to feed and care for and we were proceeding without official financial backing from the client—not even a verbal go-ahead. If I had known what we were in for, whether I would have voted to go ahead, I don't know. When you are in your sixties it's hard to figure out what you would have done at forty. I can only say that today I would—unfortunately—be less likely to vote for a risk of that magnitude than I was back then.

But we bashed on and in a few short weeks the big cat we were so carefully feeding got loose and we were holding on to its tail.

I'd like to take a minute here to defend ourselves. We were not a bunch of featherbrains being wafted along by a slight breeze. And yet what we were about to do cannot be explained by your basic, everyday human motivations such as the desire for money, power, or security. We were in the grip of something much less logical—the Pull of an Idea. It's very difficult to explain, much less justify, but I will try to do both in the chapter that follows. For now, all I can say is we were a family fractionated by ideas vs. money. We all agreed with the fact that the idea was worth pursuing—but how much was it worth?

The Pull of an Idea has got to be pretty strong to overcome the pull of financial prudence backed up by precedents.

CHAPTER SEVENTEEN

The Pull of Ideas

WHAT HAD HAPPENED to all of us bears out another theory of mine, that most people will develop stronger loyalties to an idea or to someone with an idea than to someone with money. The best way I can state it is:

MONEY GRABS BUT IDEAS PULL.

Ideas are a siren song. They are the beam of a lighthouse, only you never know when you first see the light if its beam is legitimate or the product of onshore wreckers. And even if the light is legit, following it is never without risks. So should you go wherever it takes you even though you are risking a portion of your credibility, your job, or even your career? Or will it silhouette you so clearly that you become a target for jealous people? I'll say it again,

IDEAS CAN BE DANGEROUS TO THE HEALTH OF YOUR CAREER.

And yet every time I catch one—my own or someone else's—and I ask myself, "Do I need the grief that could come from pursuing this?" I am reminded of a passage in Peter Shaffer's play *Equus*. The main character, an English psychiatrist named Martin Dysart, leads a life he finds depressingly normal and dull and is challenged by an emotionally disturbed patient whom he is trying to "normalize." Dysart begins to doubt whether he is really helping his patient. Is "dull and normal" better than being sick and free to "gallop"? His patient, Alan Strang, has been sneaking a horse out at night from a local riding establishment and—in a highly symbolic action—galloping the steed at midnight through the mists and thistles of a local wild meadow. Strang, totally naked, rides the horse bareback at a full gallop, and for a brief time knows the complete freedom of his hero, the American cowboy, while also reveling in a cowboy's danger and discomfort.

Dysart confesses to his cohort, Hesther, after Strang has been brought to him because he blinded a horse for no apparent reason, "All right, he's sick. He's full of misery and fear. He was dangerous, and could be again, though I doubt it. But that boy has known a passion more ferocious than I have felt in any second of my life. And let me tell you something: I envy it." "You can't," Hesther interjects. But Dysart continues, vehemently: "Don't you see? That's the Accusation! That's what his stare has been saying to me all this time. *'At least I galloped. When did you?'* . . . (simply) I'm jealous, Hesther. Jealous of Alan Strang."

There's no question in my mind that those who have never run with a big idea and felt the excitement of watching and helping it grow (all the while understanding full well the pain that will ensue if they're wrong in the mists of the meadow at night and take a bad fall) have missed an experience that is like no other.

So have those who galloped only partway there and then quit.

I look back and see the faces of the many talented people I have known who had fabulous ideas, both basic and executional, but galloped only halfway across the meadow and then gave up. I don't know where many of them are today. They are not in the mainstream of advertising/marketing, or I would hear about them.

But every time I start to feel sorry for people who never "galloped," or who hollered "whoa" too soon, I say to myself, "Hey, maybe they feel sorry for me, and others like me." Because, in order to stay in the running we had to, time and again, go with our Idea Families, instead of our normal families. And in many cases the families back home suffered, were stunted by lack of attention, or, as in my case, were postponed while I chased fireflies across the meadow.

I am not about to pass judgment on the merits of pursuing ideas on into the night to wherever they may lead. The ratio of risk to reward varies for every individual. From time to time I enjoy asking leaders in industry and politics as well as in the entertainment and marketing/advertising worlds who were pulled along by the spell of one or more ideas, "Was it all worth it? When the fat lady finally sang your song, was the applause and gratitude of your public worth the private anguish of the real family back home, the one you abandoned for the Idea Family?" And here is my favorite story about someone who felt the pull of an idea to such an extent that he changed his address, his business, his personal life, and his goal and yielded to the pull.

In the fall of 1970 someone who had advised me in financial matters for many years brought me a movie script. His field of expertise was not investing in motion pictures, or entertainment of any sort, but he had gotten involved in this project through a special set of circumstances. He had given the author of the movie some financial advice that had not turned out successfully, and consequently had offered to help with this project to compensate for the other that had not worked out. The reason he brought me the script was that it was written by someone in the music business whom I knew slightly and respected highly, a man named Joe Brooks.

I have said earlier in this book that instant decisions lead to an overemphasis on executions. And, unfortunately for me, an instant decision is exactly what I gave Joe Brooks's script. "No way," I said. "It's banal, pedestrian, and boring," and it was—to me. What I had not taken the time to figure out was that the script was not written for forty-year-old males. The idea behind it, which, as I say, I never bothered to separate from the execution, was a big basic idea—because it answered a big need.

The script attempted to see the world through the eyes of teenage girls—teenage *girls*, not *boys*. The views of teenage boys had been represented many times already in feature-length motion pictures—adventure movies, buddy movies, sports movies. But the sensitivities of the teenage girl growing up in a male-dominated society had never before been given their proper place in a feature.

Never mind that the script was hardly destined to win an Oscar. What I should have seen was the brilliance of the idea behind it—and the song behind it, "You Light Up My Life." I missed the idea behind that, too—the fact that it could put a teenager on a firm, old-fashioned pedestal.

In spite of the fact that my financial adviser said, "Bill, I don't pretend to know music or entertainment, but I know people—and this guy Brooks strikes me as someone who won't give up till the film is produced," I kept my money in my pocket. I just felt that someone from the jingle business would never be able to crack Hollywood as a producer/author/songwriter. What I really underestimated was the pull of Joe's idea and his ability to use that pull on others.

The buildup of the Pull of an Idea, the kind of pull that was to be needed later on, had started in 1969 when Vittorio De Sica called Joe Brooks and asked him to write the score for a movie to be called *The Garden of the Finzi-Continis*. Vittorio had heard the lush scoring Joe had done for some American Airlines commercials and felt that kind of musical thinking would be appropriate for *Finzi-Continis*. The movie won an Oscar, and as Vittorio walked up to get his award the band played Joe's theme. Joe, watching at home, was bitten and bitten hard by the movie bug.

The score for a documentary called *Marjoe* followed, and then the score, complete with songs, for *The Lords of Flatbush*. *The Lords of Flatbush* was a launching pad for Henry Winkler, Sylvester Stallone, and others. It was also what launched Joe. He had had a taste—now he wanted to eat the whole thing.

He'd never written a script for a full-length motion picture. He had helped doctor scripts for sixty-second commercials, but that's about as far as his past experience could take him. So he borrowed some experience from Woody Allen, who once reportedly said, "Eighty percent of making a film is getting up in the morning and writing it."

For three months he devoted every morning to writing his script—armed with Woody's advice and something else—a thorough understanding of the nature of basic ideas.

Narrowing one's search for a basic idea to a target audience, and further defining that audience in terms of demographics, is always a good place to start. Instead of wandering around an entire prairie looking for fireflies, you can confine your search to an area—an apple orchard, for instance—where you know the territory. Of course there is always a question you must ask yourself when defining an idea in terms of a target audience, and that is, "How big is that audience?"

Obviously, you don't want to sit down and write a full-length movie script for an audience of left-handed croquet players.

Joe looked into various target audiences for motion pictures and discovered that the biggest single group of moviegoers is made up of teenage girls. So Joe got up each morning to write a movie that attempted to see the world through the eyes of a dues-paying member of the biggest single movie going group of all, a teenage girl. Not only was his target audience a huge one, it was, amazingly, a neglected one as well. No matter what you are looking to accomplish with your ideas—whether you want to get elected to public office, become the head of your company, or make a mint with a hit movie, a target group that is both large *and* neglected is the ideal spot on which to focus.

Joe believed that his group wished desperately for songs and stories that expressed what they wanted to believe—that they could escape the realities of their everyday lives and enter the glamorous world of "stardom." It could be as a movie actress, an entertainer, a songwriter, or anyone who lives in the glitter world. And, of course, a necessary ingredient to making that escape complete was love. You had to meet someone you have dreamed about, and he has to fall in love with you. The result may not exactly be art as defined by people who go around defining art, but if it makes adolescence a bit easier for a few hours, I say it is an idea worth pursuing. A sophomoric idea, to be sure, but just right for an audience still in high school.

Since the corner of the entertainment world that Joe knew best was music, he decided to execute his basic idea in the form of a love story about a teenage girl trying to make it big in the music world. As a songwriter? A singer? A club act? Joe wasn't exactly certain when he started, and it took him nearly five months to finish his love story set in the world of music. And then he set out to raise as much money as he could.

His budget was, to put it delicately, flexible. Which means he would later shape the script to fit what he could raise. But as presented to prospective investors at the outset, the operation appeared to be buttoned up.

Joe, however, was not able to raise nearly the amount he set out to get. He felt he needed $1,200,000. He raised $400,000. But he was in the grip of the idea's pull, so he chose to ignore the unwritten rules of investing in entertainment properties and put up $250,000 of his own money.

If you talk to the pros, they will tell you that putting up your own dough is a foolish move. The professional producer/writer doesn't believe in investing his own money in ideas that he or she is pushing, and I can understand both sides in the argument. To move an idea to maturity takes a lot of time. In today's world, it takes the time of a whole Idea Family. And since time is money, you can argue that the Parents, Uncles, and Aunts of any big idea have already invested pretty heavily in it by the time it needs hard cash. Since most prudent—or at least conservative—investors seek a balanced portfolio, putting cash into an idea that one has already invested in heavily in time and energy can unbalance an investment strategy. On the other hand, real money will always talk louder than words. So if you want to make sure that investors hear your idea, nothing gets their attention like the knowledge that the Father or the Idea Family is putting a portion of their paychecks in the pot. Joe went even further than that. Joe subordinated his standard payments for writer/producer to the investors' monies. In other words, they would be paid first, not last, as is the custom in the entertainment world.

But with all of that show of faith he still had to take off for Hollywood with less than $650,000.

He had no one with him—no staff, no assistant, no family, no friends, and no member of an Idea Family. His keys to the kingdom consisted of a script (by an unknown author, himself), $650,000 (raised by an unknown producer, himself), a ton of faith in his basic idea, and a philosophy that went, "You never know what people will do until you first expose them to the pull of an idea and then *ask*."

And he started doing just that.

Joe had recently seen and liked the movie *One Flew over the Cuckoo's Nest*, and in the credits he saw the name Lynzee Klingman listed as one of the editors. To Joe it sounded like the name of someone who just might be susceptible to the pull of a good idea. Besides, you gotta start somewhere. So he called and introduced himself to Lynzee over the phone, but not as the famous creator of many musical ad campaigns. As who then? As a producer with a great script based on a great idea that someday soon was going to be a film that would need a great editor. And he had chosen her.

Could they talk? In person?

Somehow, somewhere during the talk Joe asked the big question. Would she edit the film for money that doesn't exist now, but will exist in the future? "Yes."

You never know unless you let the idea talk first and then you ask.

So Joe began asking for the names of all the good cameramen, crew members, casting directors, and others whom Lynzee knew around town. Plus the names of people who might have some vacant office space just sitting there eager to be rented by an unknown writer/producer with a pocketful of promises.

The problems were mountain-high, but on a clear day everyone could feel the pull of the basic idea all the way to the start of shooting. So somehow or another the yeses kept coming in.

Without a doubt the people who had joined Joe Brooks's Idea Family were caught up by the pull of the idea and became intensely loyal to the project. And certainly not for the money. Because there was none. No matter how hard Joe drove them—some nights they went fourteen hours—there seemed to be no grumbling and no one said, "Take this job and shove it." (That particular statement had not yet been set to music.)

In film parlance, you would say the original script was completed in just thirty-six shooting days (all on weekends, because many members of the Idea Family were gainfully employed during the week). But then, when they were about to wrap up the job and go home, something happened that prompted Joe to change the script and ask for some extra days of shooting.

During the early weeks of filming Joe had been under pressure from BBDO Advertising Agency back in New York to work on a new campaign for their client, Pepsi-Cola. At first, Joe had flatly rejected the idea of splitting his time, but as the weeks wore on, and he began to realize that he had Mondays through Thursdays pretty much free, and also that his cash flow was now flowing in the wrong direction—out, not in—he changed his mind. Finally he struck a deal with the gang at BBDO. He would help write and record the campaign for them if they would pay for him to ship out to Los Angeles his favorite group of singers, plus his support group of assistants. BBDO agreed to do what Joe was proposing.

The result was a big, classic—one might say old-fashioned—recording session. It had been a while since Joe had done one like that, and in the midst of it he saw all over again how exciting, glamorous, and visually absorbing a big session, one where everything happens at the same time instead of in steps, could be.

And suddenly he knew that the execution for his movie had gotten away from the basic idea. The story line, as he had written it, was about a teenage girl who longed to be a singer/songwriter, but whose father was a stand-up comic who wanted her to assist in his act and ultimately follow in his footsteps. And she was dutifully, if very reluctantly, trying to do just that.

As I have said already, ideas, especially ideas for executions, must be aware of the times in which they are to live. The high school girls for whom Joe was writing were about to be dubbed the "Me Generation." But they weren't aware of who they were right then and it would be another year or so before they would get enough confidence to take advantage of the title. In fact the Pepsi campaign on which Joe worked contained the instruction, "You be you and I'll be me."

Maybe it was that line that nudged him. Maybe it was a signal from the antenna that all good idea people develop for catching the vibes around them. Whatever it was, sometime during the recording of the Pepsi commercial called "Pepsi People Feeling Free," Joe knew his heroine had to politely but firmly reject Daddy and "be me."

He rewrote the script overnight to make the ending—where

she suddenly discovers herself—be a big, classic, recording session where she sings *her own song*. And the song he wrote for it was designed to be a song that would call for a big traditional session. It was a waltz-ballad with the kind of strong chord progressions that could happily use a full string section, brasses, the works.

The decision involved, of course, extra money and extra promises for the extra days of shooting. But when it was over, Joe had the execution that his idea called for—the story of a teenage girl who realizes her special dreams and along the way becomes "me."

After that it was easy, all downhill with a cheering crowd waiting at the bottom, right? Maybe in the movies, but not in real life.

In real life, as I have warned you throughout this book, you will have a problem getting people to recognize the worth of good basic ideas and to separate them from their executions. So the real story of *You Light Up My Life* is that no one would buy the finished movie. No one.

Lynzee Klingman—loyal to the end—had flown to New York and edited the film there. Why New York? Guess. Joe had been able to rent some editing rooms in the Big Apple for promises. He was long out of cash. He was close to bankruptcy, his personal life was in shreds, and he had let his jingle business dry up. So by the time he had gotten nos from all the major film studios—United Artists, Columbia, Warner Bros., and Paramount—he was beginning to feel that the beam of the lighthouse he had followed had lured him onto the rocks.

He flew out to the annual Independent Film Distributors Convention—it was in Kansas City that year—and talked to all the minor studios. But to no avail. Nobody bit. He didn't even get a nibble. The trumpets he had been hearing in the background for over a year now playing "There's No Business Like Show Business," began to blow "Taps."

It was time to abandon ship or navigate under a new set of rules.

When Joe had been working on *The Lords of Flatbush* he had met the marketing director of Columbia Pictures, Norman Levy. Norman wasn't exactly a friend, more of an acquaintance, and one who was now politically out of the idea loop around Joe's film, since someone under him had already rejected *You Light Up My Life*. But, somehow, Joe prevailed on Levy to see him.

Joe knew, and so did Norman, that they were breaking the

rules of how you navigate in structured businesses—or at least they were bending them. In business today people-skills are considered more important than idea-skills. If the people under you reject an idea, you don't ordinarily override them. I have taken up the problems of territories earlier in this book, and I won't "beat those boundaries" again, except to say if you are the boss, make sure the people under you respect your decisions on ideas enough to allow you to get up an ad hoc Idea Channel from time to time. Evidently, Norman Levy was that kind of boss. And Joe made that kind of presentation.

As he had done all along, he let the strength of his basic idea be the pull. And a pull it was, highlighted by desk-pounding and screams of anguish. Yet it was totally different because Joe did not ask Norman to screen *You Light Up My Life*. He was merely asking Levy to screen the basic idea and feel its pull.

What Joe had done was to cut a would-be trailer for the film. Many trailers for films today do not reveal the film's idea. Or perhaps there is no idea to reveal. Today's trailers are usually a series of video sight-bites that consist of the big scenes of sex and violence, or maybe a few of the gags that spice the comedy.

Joe's film trailer traced the idea, with the big song underneath it all to remind everyone that it was a romance.

But let's face it. Doing what he did was not all pure genius. Practicality played a part as well. For $500,000, give or take a few, and $500,000 in promises, you don't end up with a lot of big scenes. Joe had only one—the recording session. But his film was based on an idea that filled a void in the lives of a big slice of the film audience pie, and he played that idea for all it was worth. And Levy thought it was worth something, worth a try. Not a big try, not a spotlight at the end of the tunnel, but more like a penlight. He offered to put the film in two test markets, Seattle and Houston.

You might well say, "What kind of a marketing director would give a go-head for a film release—even a very limited one—without screening the entire film?"

Doing it that way may be a bit unusual, but it is certainly not unheard of. People who feel the pull of ideas on an everyday basis—marketing directors, heads of studios, A&R people in record companies—learn very quickly to separate the basic idea from the execution and to rely most heavily on the basic.

Take Ray Stark, for instance, one of Hollywood's most durable and successful producers. Ray is not only famous for his string of hits (including the musicals *Funny Girl* and *Annie)*, but also for the fact that he often pays substantial sums for books he never reads.

According to legend, when Ray was negotiating with Gore Vidal for the rights to Vidal's novel *Burr*, Gore turned him down. He didn't want to sell the fruits of his talent and labor to someone who couldn't even be bothered to read his words, much less digest them. But Ray wanted the book. He understood Gore's basic slant on *Burr*. He saw it as a basic idea, felt its pull, and figured the execution would be changed anyway by the screenwriter or teams of writers.

One would expect that Ray would have said, "Okay, Gore, I'll read your masterpiece and then we'll talk about my offer." But according to the way insiders tell the story, Ray said something like: "I'll tell you what I'll do. I'll pay you twenty-five thousand dollars more for your book if I don't have to read it."

Gore accepted the offer. And that's fact, not fiction. However, Ray Stark is yet to make the movie.

Evidently, Norman Levy felt about Joe's idea the way Ray Stark felt about Gore Vidal's. Levy felt the pull of Joe's basic idea after seeing the trailer. Also, he had a pretty good hunch about the quality of the execution from the eight or ten scenes Joe had chosen to use.

At first Joe was on cloud nine. Then he realized how slim his chances were. He was to open in Seattle, which welcomes Californians only as tourists, with a film about Hollywood and its denizens. And he had tied the film to the kind of song that takes a bit of time to build—a slow waltz-ballad. But at least he was in the tunnel. Now it was up to luck and the Pull of the Idea.

When Joe hit Seattle he was tempted more than at any time during the production of *You Light Up My Life* to turn back out to sea. He had made contact with Columbia's regional sales manager for the Seattle area, who had been allotted a few advertising dollars for a radio campaign. The theater had an opening in eight days and if the movie didn't pull well above average, Joe's baby would be a goner. He had no star to hang on to, and no contacts to exploit in the media. But he had been told he had to draw a better-than-average crowd from get-go. This baby would be allowed no time to build slowly.

Joe had cut down the full song to sixty seconds for commercial purposes. And he had one last idea, it was not what I define as a big idea because it only satisfied one person's needs—Joe's. Joe's need was simply to have the title song be an overnight success so the radio commercials would be hooked on to a star—the song itself.

In every city there are disc jockey shows that play the records that are selling best locally. Joe resolved that for that week, "You Light Up My Life" would be the number-one-selling new release in Seattle.

How?

He visited every record store listed in the yellow pages and gave them each two hundred copies of "You Light Up My Life" (paid for out of what was left in his pocket), and then made sure someone came in and bought a big hunk of the two hundred.

Overnight, "You Light Up My Life" was the song sensation of local radio, and the commercial just played the song and ended with the words, "*You Light Up My Life*, now playing in your neighborhood, at the so-and-so theater." Opening night there was a line, and the lines never stopped.

Houston was the same story.

I'm sure you've guessed the ending of this small saga. You've guessed that the movie was a success. But you'll never guess how big a success it was.

I recently looked it up in *Variety*, the newspaper of the entertainment world. I found the end of Joe's story in the September 14, 1977, issue. On the page that listed the top-grossing movies for that week, the biggest money-earner was *Star Wars*. You'd expect that. The second top-grossing movie of that week was *You Light Up My Life*, the Joe Brooks movie that had come to me under the working title *Session*.

Further research revealed that the movie paid off its backers (this Backer was unfortunately not in that number) in one year. In the years since, it has returned over twelve times its original investment. And its original investment had been mostly in the form of promises, promises, promises, to an Idea Family held together by the pull of an idea.

CHAPTER EIGHTEEN

There Is Nothing So Powerful As an Idea Whose Time Has Come

IN THE MID-SEVENTIES I had presented a basic idea and some executions to the Campbell Soup Company. I have always felt soup to be one of the world's most romantic products. If products were people, soup would be a nurturing, caring mother, a very special one who has comforted mankind since the dawn of time.

But in America it seemed to me that soup was losing that romance, not just in our daily lives, but in our language. Soup was getting, as Rodney Dangerfield likes to put it, "no respect." People in trouble were "in the soup." Somebody had dropped a pair of overalls in Mrs. Murphy's chowder and we found that a worthy subject for laughter and a comic song. Even the words "soup kitchen" seemed to forget the warmth and love behind that institution, and remember only the long lines of poor people who stood in the soup lines during the Great Depression.

I wasn't sure I was right about all that, I just felt it in my gut. But a quick look at the downward sales curve of the entire product category, and Campbell's in particular, confirmed my suspicions.

Campbell's was, and still is, the dominant player in the category, but its lead was diminishing. Its soup advertising had been too disjointed over the past ten years, a broth tended by too many cooks: a bit of life-style one year, price value the next, uses and use-occasions here, specific flavors there. I wanted to give the product back its dignity.

In my opinion dignity implies importance and has to be earned, not just assumed. That goes for people and institutions as well as products. If you put something or someone on a pedestal without their having earned the right to be there, it doesn't come off as being important, just pompous, or dull and boring. Surrounding products with classical music and a sonorous voice won't help.

Real dignity has to be earned, and to my way of thinking the amount of it you have should be directly proportional to the contribution you make, or have made, to mankind—whether you are a product, a person, a political party, a religion, or a business of any kind. What soup has done for mankind since prehistoric times is provide a way to take nourishing, available, and affordable ingredients from the land, the sea, and the air, and blend them in a hundred tasty, digestible, and affordable combinations.

In doing so it provided elegant first courses, quick snacks, cold remedies, convenient lunches, great values, and a wide variety of tastes to tickle the most jaded palates. But each of those in and of itself served only a relatively small portion of the population. Emphasizing those virtues one by one may have represented good quarter-to-quarter marketing, but not the kind of big idea that was needed to arrest a fifteen-year slide in sales.

I went for the big one.

No, I didn't see soup as a catalyst for understanding between peoples of the world. Nothing as far-out as that. But I didn't see it in the traditional sense, either, as a liquid that precedes a meal, helps cure a cold, or provides internal heat when the weather outside is frightful.

To my way of thinking, what soup provided mankind with first and foremost was food that was nutritious, affordable, available, appetizing, and easy to prepare. It was good, not just in a relative sense, but possessed of a basic goodness. And because what was good for soup as a whole was extra good for Campbell's—since they had, and have, a lion's share of the soup market—the campaign I took down to the company's executives was "Soup Is Good Food." And the discipline I called for was to focus 100 percent on situations where food was needed; that meant no more elegant first courses, or delicate broths, or quickie snacks—we were not to be symbols of affluence, or casual belly stuffers (though we did recommend some tactical reminders on local radio where the weather got really foul). We were at all other times food, good food with all the pride and dignity those words implied. We had to reflect what we were in every piece of communication we prepared.

The executions I took down were wrapped in motherhood music; tune by Rod McBrien, one of New York's best tunesmiths, and lyrics by Al Lerman, who later became creative director of D'Arcy in St. Louis, and me. Bob Lenz, who later became a partner at Backer & Spielvogel, was the art director, so the Idea Family was loaded with people who had amassed some pretty impressive records and would continue to do so.

I was on cloud nine. I thought the campaign had everything. Although it lacked proof positive of soup's goodness, our research indicated that people were more than ready to accept the fact that soup was indeed good food. Their mothers had thought of it that way. Why shouldn't they?

The campaign, then, was more a reawakening than a restaging. Although I thought it had everything, its Idea Family lacked something—the ability to get its idea into an Idea Channel. One didn't exist at the Campbell Soup Company in those days. So when "Soup Is Good Food" made its way through the territories, we found that as far as new ideas were concerned this smooth, efficient, 100 percent mature company followed the motto of a first-rate antique shop: "Anything new can't be worth much."

When I toured the nearby soup plant, I discovered they were still making soup in the original kettles. Every layer worshipped the past—forget that contemporary mothers found the Campbell Kids too fat. We were not allowed to restyle them. Forget that the slogan "M'm! M'm, Good!" tended to narrow the claim of "good food" to "good-tasting food." Everywhere there were defenders of small pieces of turf, fearful of personal failure and totally unconcerned over the big failure that was occurring daily—the slide in soup sales. Throughout the territories they were victims of Backer's Laws at every level: filterers, sit-on-its, or just plain naysayers. They all understood you mustn't be caught failing, or shaking the corporate tree.

While they were making all the classic mistakes of negativism, I was making all the classic mistakes of being too positive—such as not listening, being in too much of a hurry, not hiding my disdain for their inability to conceptualize, and being 100 percent sure I was right. Instead of finding someone in the company to join my Idea Family, I snuck through all the territories and arrived at the top wounded and with a host of enemies behind me.

Top management bought "Soup Is Good Food," but reluctantly, I felt. I had had to push pretty hard. Nonetheless, they were pleasantly surprised by the finished commercials. Bob Lenz's TV executions were organic to the basic idea that soup was food, good food. They were warm, yet strong, because they had a single vision of the product, and were beautifully shot.

The campaign went on the air in a limited number of test markets, three if I remember correctly. And I went off the account.

My departure was more the client's decision than mine. I had overspent my goodwill account, and was foreclosed upon by numerous creditors at many levels.

There was now not one single blood relative of the campaign

available to walk the halls of the company, and answer the naysayers. So "Soup Is Good Food" was destined to fail.

I have found there is always one number in a series of research scores that isn't "better than average" and there is always one test market out of three that will show "no improvement in the first few months" of a new piece of advertising. All of that is perfectly normal, especially when the product has been around as long as Campbell's Soup. But it gives the "I-told-you-it-was-no-good" voices a chance to raise their warning a decibel or two. An Idea Family—especially when joined by some Judges at the company—can drown out these voices before they become a roar. But my brainchild was left an orphan at the company and didn't make it to high school, at least not that year.

These things happen in the world of ideas just as they do in most other worlds. You just pack up and go home with some new experiences to digest.

I thought "Soup Is Good Food" was a goner like so many other good ideas that couldn't get through the territorial filters of a mature company. But I was wrong. The campaign didn't die. It went underground and hung out in the back country of my mind until conditions changed.

The value of basic ideas varies over time. As I've pointed out with "Buy the World," the thought of people loving and understanding one another was uppermost in people's minds during the sixties. Had that basic idea become stuck for a year or more in a bureaucratic system of territories and filterers it would never have achieved what it did. But the tides of time flowed differently for "Soup Is Good Food."

Over the years, America's attention had become even more focused on how we eat. The importance of good food grew between 1975 and 1980.

So when "Soup Is Good Food" reemerged, its lucky star was all polished up. It was put into a test market—the West Coast Feed, which is California and much of Washington and Oregon—and performed so well in nine months that it became the national campaign within a year and Backer & Spielvogel became the Campbell's Soup agency.

In maturity, "Soup Is Good Food" became one of the more successful food campaigns of the eighties. It ran over five years and helped turn around the long slide in Campbell's Soup sales. And

The New York Times

Business

A Small Ad Agency

The New York Times / Don Hogan Charles

William M. Backer, left, and Carl Spielvogel

soon the CEO was referring to the entire company as "The Good Food Company."

But I am getting ahead of myself.

I would like to double back to 1980—some three years after my last visit to Campbell Place. A new advertising agency called Backer & Spielvogel has hit the roster of agencies since then, and for an agency that is less than two years old is doing extremely well. It is generating enough profits to pay the interest and some of the principal on its bank loans, and has begun to pay some salaries to its owners as well as to over fifty other professionals. Its advertising for Miller High Life, Miller Lite, and Lowenbrau beers is helping to sell a lot of beer and gain the agency a very special creative reputation.

But beer is all Backer & Spielvogel has. And no agency should try to live by beer alone, or any single product category for that matter. If it can broaden its base, it should.

Creative people want challenges in a variety of categories. Ac-

Sunday, June 21, 1981

Section 3

That's No Small Beer

Spielvogel and Backer quit top ad jobs and started anew with the Miller Beer plum. Now their shop leads in growth.

By LYDIA CHAVEZ

JUST when Madison Avenue had settled comfortably into the age of the superagency, something happened.

Carl Spielvogel, vice chairman of one of the world's largest advertising conglomerates, the Interpublic Group of Companies, was passed over for chairman in May 1979, and he left.

He hit tennis balls. He festered. He lunched with William M. Backer, who had recently turned in his vice chairman's title at McCann-Erickson, Interpublic's largest agency, because of what he termed "philosophical" differences with the front office.

Within weeks, the two were in business. Three weeks later, Bob Lenz, the creative director of McCann-Erickson's New York office, defected to the Gotham, where the new agency had set up offices.

In their old jobs, Mr. Spielvogel had managed the marketing side of the successful Miller Beer campaign and Mr. Backer the creative side. In August, the Miller account followed them to their new agency, although Mr. Spielvogel and Mr. Backer say they didn't know that would happen when they decided to leave. The giant Interpublic crown was left clearly askew, its creative team at McCann-Erickson spotty and its client roster minus more than $70 million in annual billings.

Backer & Spielvogel is the fastest growing agency in the history of the street. It finished last year 29th in the industry for domestic income and celebrated its second year this month by winning the $20 million Campbell's Soup account from Batten, Barton, Durstine & Osborn and topping $210 million in billings.

It has not stopped growing, but it says it wants to; and its six principals, all from McCann-Erickson or Interpublic, scoff that Madison Avenue's conventional wisdom about this being the era of the superagency is hogwash. (In the late 1970's, nearly half of the top 92 agencies disappeared through mergers in a rush toward bigness.)

"Clients are tired of big agencies," Mr. Spielvogel said. "They can go to a major agency and never see the top people."

In many ways, however, Backer & Spielvogel is a superagency in miniature. The two founders are not wonder boys who broke away from the stifling backrooms of a big agency and slowly made good. They are seasoned corporate executives with the clout and experience to attract blue-chip clients.

"They are big names in the business and that didn't hurt," William Knobler, an analyst with Sanford C. Bernstein, said.

Mr. Spielvogel, 52, is as solid in administration as his bow-tied partner is in the creative side. Mr. Backer, 53, participated in campaigns like the ones for Coca-Cola that set standards for the rest of the industry.

"Backer is extremely bright and creative, and Spielvogel is an ad man who knows how to count," said An-

Continued on Page 22

count people want diversity in their horizons, and careful financial officers know all too well that what goes up can come down. No category keeps rising forever. Also, owners of any business sleep better knowing they have their eggs in more than one basket.

Besides, Backer & Spielvogel needs to show the outside world they can market other products as well as they do beer. In short, we are all very hungry for some new business in a new category.

So two of the partners, Carl Spielvogel, the CEO, and Bob Holmen, our new COO, have instituted a Dial-a-Friend program. Once a week each partner in the agency has to make at least one new business call to someone he knows in a marketing company, arrange a lunch date, and tell his friend about Backer & Spielvogel. Everyone is doing their best to make the program work except yours truly.

I have a genuine talent for avoiding chores that I find distasteful, and I find new business calls ultra-distasteful because I am no good at them. I can't control my desire to say, "What you are running now is nothing but sizzle with no steak under it. You're wasting stockholders' money." Or, if I think what they are doing is good, I find myself saying, "Carl pushed me into making this call, but you don't need any help from me. You're doing fine." I am just too direct for new business calls. But I know I should be a better team player in our Dial-a-Friend program.

The agency is in temporary office space—we call it our Chapter 11 space because Carl has picked it up from a company that is going out of business and has filed for bankruptcy. Only we don't have all the space. We are sharing it with the personnel of the dying company and they are the most dispirited group of people you can imagine. We are occupying every other office in some of their rows of offices, none in other rows, and all in one row. We don't have full use of the conference room. We are entitled to it every other day. The company that is in Chapter 11 needs the room at least two days a week to negotiate with a small army of people—bankers, lawyers, and creditors, I presume. They don't speak to us much. Their frowns are as big as our smiles. It's as if we're living on a seesaw, going up while the guys on the other end are going down, and we feel for them.

Carl and Bob have large, important-looking offices to themselves, so if a client—or a future client—drops in and we can't get the conference room they have a place to meet.

I have a windowless cubicle down another hall where it's quiet and I can get some writing done. Bob Lenz and Bob Meury share an office, but it is spacious and contains several windows. No matter where we are none of us is complaining. We have come from sharing three rooms and a large closet in the old Gotham Hotel off Fifth Avenue. We are like sailors just off a destroyer escort. The dingiest room in town looks great to us.

We are campers in search of some new camping grounds, but we are happy campers, and we meet once a week to discuss the results of our new business calls.

On this particular day we are in Bob Holmen's office and everyone has reported except me and I am hemming and hawing about how I have been too busy to call anyone on my list, which includes Bill Williams, who has just been elevated beyond the soup division to become president and CEO of the entire Campbell Soup Company.

I keep saying I should strike Bill from my list because he and I had sort of a stormy relationship, although I admit it was a professional, not personal, problem.

While I am talking, and frankly not even convincing myself, Bob Holmen dials Campbell's headquarters, asks for Bill Williams, and hands the phone to me.

I'm knocked out by how cordial Bill sounds. He has heard of our new venture and would like to hear more about it. So the next day I am on a train to North Philadelphia and then by cab to Campbell Place on the outskirts of Camden, New Jersey, some twenty-five minutes from the train station. Most people get to Campbell Place from New York by automobile, but I don't like the New Jersey Turnpike and much prefer the train.

A lot of soup has been canned since Bill and I last talked. The advertising account has left my old firm, McCann-Erickson, and has returned to BBDO.

Bill fires a barrage of questions at me. Are we a boutique? No, we are a full-service agency. Why? Because no creative gut is so infallible that work should proceed without the checks and balances of some research. I think I'm good and my people are the best, but I can't look a client in the eye and say, "Lay thirty million dollars on this idea and don't bother to research some of its assumptions." In spite of rumors to the contrary I have a healthy respect for a client's money. And I have learned that no creative output is so consistently extraordinary that it can ignore the advantages of some insight plus superior media planning and buying. I am a believer in the advantages offered by a full-service agency. If a client knows how to take advantage of the know-how and skills offered, it represents the best value among all the choices offered to advertisers—and over the long term, it's far and away the best real bargain.

It's then Bill's turn to talk. And as he does some interesting new information begins to emerge. It seems that during the Kennedy administration some extensive health studies were done on large groups of people, mostly in West Virginia. Some people will say the politicians were looking for "pockets of malnutrition" to make speeches about when and if they ran out of new "pockets of poverty." All I say is that during my absence from the company, Congress has passed the Freedom of Information Act, and ordinary citizens are now allowed to review these health studies.

When for-profit companies conduct a detailed study (as opposed to a simple telephone poll or survey), a sample of several hundred people is considered sufficient. But when the government does a study, then money is of no consequence—except to us taxpayers—and the sample size is enormous. Government studies also tend to be far richer in the details covered than are studies that have to be funded by American business.

The results of these government health studies, then, were above criticism as far as sample size is concerned.

As Bill begins to talk about them, I get the feeling that soup, in general, emerges from them as Mother Magnificent—calorie for calorie, one of the best foods you can eat. It's also good diet food. Since you have to eat hot soup slowly, it helps dieters eat less. And—here comes the big one—people who eat soup three or more times a week tend to be just plain healthier, according to the study. Maybe they have healthier habits in other areas besides eating. The data are not conclusive there. But, for whatever reason, the soup group is healthier than any of the other groups in this huge study.

Bill doesn't go into details, but as he talks what I hear is that he has given an assignment to two major agencies—their names are immaterial at this point—to base an advertising campaign on the new information about soup.

I gather, further, that both of these agencies have come back to him saying the new information makes for lousy advertising. They have written a number of ads using the new facts about soup and the ads have researched badly. According to what they have told Bill, it seems that the public is no longer interested in the details of products; in fact, people find them dull, boring, and uninvolving.

Bill is obviously disappointed at what he has heard from the agencies.

"Have they given up on the assignment?" I ask.

"I've told them to keep trying, but you know how much good that will do," is Bill's answer.

"They're wrong," I find myself saying. "Just plain wrong."

Bill begins to dig into why I feel the way I do. He obviously agrees with me, but wants to be sure my reasons are professional, not merely pragmatic.

As I reply, it begins to dawn on me that I am, for the first time, at the end of an Idea Channel, the first one I have ever found at the Campbell Soup Company. I mean here I am having a one-on-one discussion about ideas—both basic and executional—with the ultimate Power Who Can Say Yes.

Later on, as we got into executing ads, researching them, and putting them into test markets, Bill would expand the judging team to include Herb Baum, who had recently joined the company, and a young man named Dan Santangelo. It was to be an extremely well-balanced team.

Bill had spent most of his business life with the company, rising through the production ranks, and being loyal almost to a fault. His gut feelings were heavily influenced by company ethos, and by what had worked and not worked in the past.

The fact that Campbell's tomato soup coursed through his veins, however, did not blind him from seeing the future. And all this was to the good when balanced by Herb Baum, who had arrived new to the company from a career with major advertising agencies.

To Bill's and Herb's backgrounds was added one that was heavily influenced by MBA thinking, i.e., that numbers are truth and goodness because numbers don't lie. Dan Santangelo had had virtually no hands-on experience in judging advertising ideas, but he was far and away the most daring of the three—emboldened by youth that is yet to feel the weight of failure and still possessed of keen enough hearing to hear the "clang, clang" of the warning signals ahead. His numbers predicted disaster within twenty years if the sales slide was not arrested.

So Bill Williams, the Power Who Could Say Yes, was the team's dedicated, thoroughly experienced company professional. Herb Baum, the man who would conceptualize and translate communications materials like storyboards and rough layouts, was thoroughly grounded in advertising and advertising agencies. And Dan Santangelo, the man who would carry the banner of urgency emblazoned with the words "We Cannot Sit on It," was absolutely secure in his ability to interpret what the numbers were saying and wise enough not to covet other bases that were already well covered by people who had been playing them for years with solid success.

It was a model team to have around a reservoir of ideas at the end of an Idea Channel. I have been a part of a few judging teams that equaled it. And the results of the ideas they helped to mature bear out my opinion.

My reasons for feeling that the new soup facts could be made persuasive to soup buyers evidently satisfied Bill. "I'd like to see you try doing some ads that use the information," he said. "Would you like to try?" Does a bear go in the woods?

I was almost speechless. Here I was, Mr. Difficult himself, being offered a second chance to work on Campbell's Soup, and all I could say was something dumb like "You bet."

There was no question that time and tides were flowing my way. The country was waking up to the importance of healthy eating, the facts were falling in place for soup, and there I was with an Idea Channel that made a mockery of Backer's Law of Corporate Gravity.

I began to realize, while Bill's give-and-take was proceeding, that there is another great advantage to Idea Channels. When you discuss ideas in open and informal sessions people are forced into a kind of group therapy. They tend to let their hair down. And the fact that the ideas are bigger than the people involved seems to minimize the politics of position, especially if all the important territories are present, have had their boundaries wiped out, and become one large territory with a reservoir of ideas in the center. What counts, then, is not outguessing another territory, or protecting one's own, but what sort

of insight you can add to the process of judging the ideas being presented by an Idea Family.

As Bill and I talked about the past, and how I saw my role at Backer & Spielvogel in the future, I started to make an apology, "I know from time to time I may have argued a bit too much, but—" Bill cut me off abruptly. "Maybe we need someone to argue with us," he said.

He and I never discussed the subject again. But at that moment I realized more than ever another disadvantage of the filter system when applied to ideas—it reduces the ability of the people at the top to help ideas.

When ideas arrive in front of a Power Who Can Say Yes all smoothed out, aged, and doctored to a point where they sound and look alike, the Power Who Can Say Yes is dragged into a meeting with many different layers present, each there to signify the fact that he has put his seal of approval on this turkey.

What if the Power Who Can Say Yes wants to say "No"? Or "Maybe"? Or at least ask some questions?

He may be both smart and savvy but his background may not include a lot of experience in the language of judging ideas, especially in this particular area. So he is inarticulate on the subject, and he knows it. And that makes him doubly shy and reluctant to say what is on his mind. On top of that, when he is faced with the Father of the idea, plus some Uncles, and maybe a professional Godfather or two, tacitly backed by level upon level of his own people, no wonder he finds himself resorting to a simple yes or no when he probably means neither. And he hasn't time to stop to analyze why he is in this situation.

He is there because the process leading up to the meeting is linear—and so is the meeting itself—and it all leads smack dab right to him. The idea gets to him shaped and stamped "a product of" every territory it has passed through, and he has had no chance for open and circular discussions where thoughts, not titles, are what counts. So, naturally he comes off as a patsy, a curmudgeon, or a total incompetent. Ideas in his or her company never seem to reach maturity in a shape that does the organization some genuine good.

After "Soup Is Good Food" had gone into test market, Bill began to open up in our informal idea sessions on some other subjects that he had evidently had on his mind for a number of years. One of them was the peripatetic nature of agency people. It came up because the reports from the field on the progress of the campaign in the test market were coming back stamped "thumbs up" and Bill began to realize that Backer & Spielvogel just might become his soup agency, and I began to realize that an Idea Channel has some pluses above and beyond its ability to judge ideas.

An idea—no matter how sound the basic idea and how inspired the execution—will often have problems above and beyond its intrinsic qualities. And these problems need to be sorted out with the Power Who Can Say Yes and his team in informal discussions. In these kinds of meetings, the people involved get to know each other as well as they know the idea itself, so they can develop the same degree of faith in each other that they have developed in the idea. Because once the idea has gotten its "yes," its family is going to be called upon for new and different executional skills plus a commitment to seeing that the idea reaches its ultimate goal and performs to its fullest potential.

Bill's problem was simply that he might soon be asked to move the Campbell Soup account from an old, established agency whose people he knew to a new one whose people he didn't know, other than myself. The long and informal discussions that he, Herb Baum, and I were able to have in the Idea Channel format, without getting bogged down in mainstream politics, were invaluable to the success of "Soup Is Good Food." Bill and Herb had developed full faith in that idea. It was the thought that Bill Backer, a relatively unknown player to them, would now be cast in a new all-important role that worried them. How could they be sure that I would stick around and see my brainchild through to graduation? "If I change to your agency," Bill finally blurted out in one informal discussion, "how can I be sure you won't just move on to some other agency or to some more important job in your agency? Every agency president I have talked to promises he'd stay in the picture after we gave him some business, and the only one who ever kept his word was David Ogilvy."

Without the relationship and the chance to build up some faith that an Idea Channel provides, you can never answer a question like that. But months later, when "Soup Is Good Food" had emerged as a clear winner, and Bill and Herb Baum came to my office to award America's "youngest major agency" with one of the country's most respected advertising accounts (we had moved out of our Chapter 11 space and were in very respectable quarters at 11 West Forty-second Street), I don't think either of them had the slightest doubt about whether or not I would stay in the picture. "As long as you are in the day-to-day picture, I will be too," I had promised. And I was. And thanks to our Idea Channel I was able to make them understand and believe that.

But, back at our first meeting, Bill is shifting the subject. He has spent a lifetime keeping costs down at Campbell's and he isn't about to change his spots now.

"What kind of a fee would you charge?" he asks.

Ordinarily this would not be my area. But I believe you never leave the party while the band is still playing, and this one was in full swing. So I repeat that we are not a boutique. We don't sell our work for other agencies to manage. We are in the business of creating ideas for our clients that will help them build their brands and their businesses. "We won't charge you a fee," I say, "just out-of-pocket expenses. If our work gets into a test market, we want full commission on the media and, obviously,"—here comes one of the most important "obviouslys" I have ever clarified—"if our work finally becomes *the* campaign for Campbell's we would expect to be *the* agency."

Bill looked out of the window and wrestled with this "obviously" for what seemed like a very long time, then he said simply, "OK."

There was nothing ever in writing that covered our conversation about our getting the account if our work succeeded. Just a handshake. But as events unfolded I never felt the need to confirm the handshake with words on paper. Bill represented a breed that was rare then and is nearly extinct today—a man of his word.

Anyway, I shake his hand and head for the door. Quickly. "Never snatch defeat from the jaws of victory" is a good maxim to follow in these situations. But Bill stops me with one last question. "How do you see using all the new facts about soup?"

The country is getting more health-conscious every day. New facts have emerged about soup specifically, and they point to it as an important part of a healthy diet. Added to all that is the fact that an Idea Channel has emerged at the Campbell Soup Company. Time, often an enemy of ideas, is turning out to be a friend of this one. And yet, I don't want to press my luck by reviving the memories of myself in the roles of Mr. Stubborn or Mr. Difficult.

Looking back now, I think Bill expected my answer. I honestly feel, in retrospect, he would have been disappointed in me if it had been otherwise. But at that moment I can't believe it is my voice I hear saying, "I see my people analyzing all these facts very carefully,

THE NEW YORK TIMES, TUESDAY, MAY 26, 1981

Advertising | Philip H. Dougherty

Edward Ozern

William M. Backer, left, and Carl Spielvogel flank an annual report depiction of their important client

Campbell Switching To B.& S.

BACKER & SPIELVOGEL has struck again.

The agency with the fastest growth record in the history of the business has now become the national agency for Campbell Soup's line of condensed soup, the good old red and white cans, the "Mm-mm, good" American institution.

Last fall, the Camden, N. J., soup giant assigned the young agency to handle the soup account for the 20 percent of the nation's population living along the West Coast. Campbell said at the time that if the Backer shop's results could top those of Batten, Barton, Durstine & Osborn, then either the B.& S. advertising would be transferred to B.B.D.O., its agency for 27 years, or Backer would get the business.

Well, Campbell obviously chose the latter course.

Campbell dominates the condensed soup business with a worldwide market share of 80 percent. Its problem was not in how to get the product into the home, it is already in most. It was in how to get people to eat it more often.

The B.& S. advertising theme has been based on nutrition and the line has been "Soup is good food."

Campbell also gave McCann-Erickson, one of the Interpublic Group of Companies, a four-year turn at the soup commercials. William M. Backer, president of the new agency, was creative chief of McCann at that time.

The total billings for the condensed soups are about $20 million and that includes some $5 million that Backer & Spielvogel already had.

So that would mean that the agency is billing at the rate of about $215 million, counting the $7 million it got a couple of weeks ago from Bon Jour International.

B.B.D.O. will continue to be a Campbell agency, handling the Chunky Soup and the Soup For One accounts, the export brands and new products. Campbell credits the agency with helping to develop and introduce Chunky, which it characterizes as one of its most successful new-product introductions.

In addition to the soup business, Campbell, the country's 69th-largest advertiser with 1979 advertising spending of $60.5 million, also includes among its holdings a restaurant operation, Pepperidge Farm, Swanson Frozen Foods, V-8, Franco-American, Godiva Chocolatier and Vlasic Foods.

Its agency roster includes Ogilvy & Mather; Needham, Harper & Steers and Lewis & Gilman.

And Backer & Spielvogel's clients include Miller beer, the first and the biggest; J&B Scotch, Seven-Up and the Savings and Loan Foundation.

and then I see us using them as back-ups for—'Soup Is Good Food.' "The lesson of all this is: Hold on to the ideas in which you have an abiding faith. Time can be kind to them.

Perhaps Victor Hugo put it best: "An invasion of armies can be resisted, but not an idea whose time has come." The trick is to know when that time has arrived and be ready with Idea Families and Idea Channels in place plus an abundant supply of the energy necessary to keep the faith.

CHAPTER NINETEEN

Keeping the Faith

MEANWHILE, FOR ME and for my Idea Family, it was now time to keep the faith. In a few of the preceding chapters I referred to keeping the faith in passing. It is a necessary part of the care and feeding of ideas. Now it's time to go into why it's so necessary and take a detour into the land of Ye of Little Faith.

Originally, of course, all faith in an idea comes from the Parents. They feel the pull, get swept up by it, and tempt Uncles and Godfathers into the circle of light where they can be mesmerized by the flame itself.

As long as an original Father can stay close to the center of the idea—as Joe Brooks did with *You Light Up My Life*—the energy that fuels the torch will be there to keep the flame burning, no matter how dark it gets or how harshly the winds blow.

But it can't always be the way Joe Brooks had it. In most instances where big ideas are involved, the Father has to let go of his torch somewhere along the line. Someone involved in the execution has to now be central supplier of the energy that the flame needs to stay big and bright. And often he or she has to pass that torch on to someone else in the chain of executions. And the further the flame gets from the original source of fuel, the more likely it is to be carried into the lands of Ye of Little Faith. And in order to stay lit there, the flame starts to call for extra energy just about the time the fuel supply is running low because the supply lines are stretched.

As I look back over thirty-five years of being closely involved with the various aspects of commercial film production—music, filming, editing, casting, and handling clients in all of these various steps, I can honestly say that "Buy the World a Coke" was the most star-crossed film shoot with which I have ever been connected. And consequently it demanded more faith from those further from the basic idea than any production I can recall before or since.

I wasn't at the actual shooting. I had really depleted the agency's resources by committing not only Harvey Gabor and Phil Messina to the shoot, but also Billy Davis—who, as I have said, was head of the agency's music department. We all felt that handling a combination of live sound and lip sync with a crowd of amateurs on an unknown hillside somewhere five hundred thousand miles away was a job for the most experienced musicians and technicians we had. So Al Scully, Sid McAllister, and I decided to stay home and play utility infielders, and also be in charge of keeping the supply lines open to carry energy to those who now had to carry the torch of faith in the idea.

Actually, my role at the shoot would have been a narrow one at best—confined to diplomacy and to making certain that Harvey's vision of the United Chorus of the World was what got on film. In film, as in everything else from music to developing new technology for a specific purpose, the addition of many new Uncles acts to blur the basic executional idea and therefore weaken faith in it. My role would have been to see that that didn't happen.

You might well ask this point, why the heck did we travel so far to find an idealized mountain or hillside in the first place? Why move the execution so far from the original flame and stretch the lines of faith perhaps to the breaking point? Between New England and North Carolina, there must be a hundred green hillsides that are not rocky or menacing and begging to be conquered by intrepid mountain climbers, and yet are far enough from habitation to seem surreal—and there are.

But we had a hidden agenda.

In order to calm everyone's justifiable jitters over such an expensive gamble, Sid had assured himself and all of the Idea Family that the chances were good that Coca-Cola Europe—which was a separate operation—would take a liking to the commercial and want to air it themselves. If they did, it was customary for them to pay a portion of the production costs. So the budget would automatically become bite-sized and Ike would eat it.

There was a hitch, however.

American talent demands residual payments every time a commercial is aired—even if it is run in France or Italy. A hundred or so residual payments for every airing would have turned off the Europeans from ever participating in the commercial in any way. European actors and singers do not receive such residuals. Hence the odyssey over the Atlantic.

The plane took off for London the last week of March 1971 with Phil Messina, Harvey Gabor, and Billy Davis aboard, along with production assistants from the agency. On another plane were the key personnel of the American Production Company, which was headquartered in California and organized around one of the most highly touted cameramen/directors, Haskell Wexler.

In order to amortize some of these costs, we had coupled the shoot for Coca-Cola with another shoot—this one for the New York Racing Association. The scripts for this commercial traced the romantic history of the thoroughbred—the breed of horse that dominates horse racing in most parts of the world. The story line involved the landing in England of the three Arabian stallions that when crossed with native British mares produced the ancestors of today's race horses.

While horses and castles were being cast and scouted for by one group, another was busily rounding up several thousand young people to represent a mythical group of singers—an unofficial United Chorus of the World. Sixty-five of these young people would appear singing in close-ups, so casting for them was a one-at-a-time job. All of this activity was organized by a British production house called, if you can believe it, Harpoon.

Haskell Wexler filmed the horses first, and that made sense. They were ready and so were their locations.

The weather smiled on the three days of horse shooting, at least by British standards. Only two of the three days were overcast, and the sun actually shone on one.

Since each scene depicted a different decade in the evolution of the thoroughbred, the fact that the weather changed in between made no difference. The dailies were beautiful, authentic, and exciting. And later they would cut together easily. The shoot was an unqualified success. Then came the shoot for Coca-Cola.

The location was to be the White Cliffs of Dover—what else? The United Chorus of the World was to consist of several thousand British schoolchildren who would be seen as background for the sixty-five "principals" who would be seen close up; the Chorus would be actually singing the song along with the New Seekers track that Billy Davis would be playing over loudspeakers. And he would be conducting so that all lips were moving in sync with each other. The principals, of course, would represent every nationality on earth. Our team had also assembled the support system needed for such a large cast—the food trucks, the makeup trucks, the toilets, the sound trucks, the generators to produce electricity on the White Cliffs of Dover, etc., etc.

The shoot was scheduled for April 8 and by the time that day arrived no stone had been left unturned, except one. Somebody had forgotten to tell the weatherman to order up sunshine. A cold front moved in, tentatively at first. It eventually liked what it found there, decided to stay, and even seemed to call for reinforcements.

The shoot was canceled.

The weather worsened daily.

Back in the offices of Harpoon Productions, chaos moved in. Canceling shoots of this magnitude involves a thousand details, most of which involve money. Union rules are different for commercial shoots than for feature films. Every move or change is generally more expensive for commercials, mostly because over the years the giant marketing companies such as Procter & Gamble, Coke, and Pepsi have not been as hard nosed at the union bargaining table as the film companies have. In fact, rather than soil their hands with such arm-twisting, they have tended to ask their agencies to do the negotiating for them, and the agencies have gone in as a divided army simply because their clients are in competition with one another.

The result of all this was that Phil Messina knew that one more cancellation would eat him alive. He had a "weather day" contingency that covered him for the first cancellation, but that was it. The next time he said "go," they had to go.

In the midst of all this gloom and doom, a producer on another Harpoon job arrived back in the offices from Italy. He was suntanned, he was happy, he was within budget. The weather outside of Rome where he had been shooting had been perfect. Phil and Harvey listened to his story with envy.

On the morning of the third day of the cold front, Phil called one of his Keepers of the Faith, Sid McAllister, back in Atlanta. It was 2:00 A.M. in Atlanta, but the question Phil posed was of a nature to wipe the sleep from anyone's eyes.

"It boils down to this, babe. We stay here until the weather clears as we run out of money paying daily expenses. Or . . . we pack up and move to Italy. Which do you think?"

"Do we have money in the contingency budget for a move to Italy?"

"Maybe a few dollars, babe. But we've used a lot of the contingency sitting around here. What we do have is enough for one full day's shoot."

"Have you found a production house in Italy that you have confidence in?"

"There's a producer here from Harpoon who recommends an outfit in Rome called Recta. It's headed by a man named Cesere."

"Ever heard of them yourself?"

"No, babe."

"Phil, you're telling me they gotta locate five thousand kids for background, sixty-five principals from thirty or forty different nations, find a very special location, and all we know about them is what we hear from Harpoon?"

"That's right."

SILENCE.

"But the sun is where they are, babe."

MORE SILENCE.

"Call me when you get to Rome, OK?"

"You can count on me, babe."

There was one expense Phil had incurred in England that the entire group believed they would not have to repeat in Rome—the expense of casting for the "head girl," the one who would sing in close-up at the opening of the commercial.

The Harpoon casting director had discovered a young folk-singer who looked the part, sang in the right key, and could either lip-sync to the New Seekers track or sing live on location and give Billy Davis the option of combining or using either track when he did his final mix back in America.

The folksinger wasn't a name on anyone's lips. She sang folk songs in small-towns pubs in the British Midlands. She had agreed happily to front the United Chorus of the World on the White Cliffs of Dover for a double daily fee. Phil had intended to fly her to Italy when the time came to start filming there. But when the time came, and the day was set and the rest of the casting completed, Phil called her only to discover she now had an *agent*; she was going to star in a Coke commercial, and the price, according to her new agent, would be the equivalent of $100,000 in today's money. Phil had the satisfaction of telling the agent what he could do with his price, but it was small consolation.

With the shoot already scheduled, the quest for a new lead singer had to begin all over again.

Recta and Phil finally located another folksinger. She wasn't as ideal as the first one, but she had a special light in her eyes and an enthusiasm that Phil thought was for the project ahead. Actually, it was because she was getting married two days after the scheduled shoot. But no one knew that until too late. If there were to be any pickup shots for close-ups, they couldn't be of her. She would be on her honeymoon in South Africa.

Recta had also found a hillside. It was not far from Rome, it was deserted (mostly) and available. It wasn't as green as Dover, but it would do. It would have to do.

Recta had also found a source of schoolkids for the background—not several thousand this time. With money running short, Phil and Cesere agreed that a United Chorus of the World would be amply represented by twelve hundred kids plus sixty-five principals.

Sunrise was due to come a little after 7:00 A.M. Haskell Wexler wanted to use the inspirational morning light for shooting his principals close up—the faces that hailed from the Orient to Ireland, from Nigeria to Nepal—the faces that would pictorialize what the words of their song were trying to say; those were the faces he wanted to shoot in the glow of sunrise, and rightly so. Later on in the day he would arrange the twelve hundred background young people in some sort of order, clamber aboard a helicopter camera plane and shoot "The Big Scene" from overhead. That would be the scene that would show the magnitude of the wish.

But it rained. It rained that morning for the first time in two weeks.

Everyone arrived in buses and stayed in them waiting, hoping, and praying. And around ten o'clock the rain stopped. The sun came out and everything was beautiful. But it began to get very hot very quickly. Haskell Wexler and Harvey Gabor started lining up the principals. The best of the light was gone and Haskell would have to shoot with the sun partially overhead. So be it. At least he had light.

While Haskell and Harvey were art directing the opening scenes—the ones with the principals—Phil decided to wander down the hillside to get a Coke. The heat and the pressure were both beginning to get to him and he thought a few minutes of peace and quiet with a cold Coke would settle his nerves and cool him down. There was a large Coca-Cola truck parked at the base of the hill to supply the product for the big scenes ahead, and Messina headed for it.

But before he reached the truck he got hit by one of those triple-whammy shock waves we all experience from time to time. They start with anger at yourself for being stupid or careless and getting something put over on you. Then the anger turns outward at whomsoever done you wrong. And finally a cold sweat takes over as you ask yourself, "What do I do now?" and tell yourself, "I am in trouble."

On the way to the Coca-Cola truck, Phil had to walk between the buses that had brought the "school kids" to the hillside. The buses had arrived at seven o'clock along with everyone else. It was now approaching eleven, and getting hotter by the minute. But the kids had not been let out. They were still locked inside.

Outside of the buses, in full view of the young people inside, were a number of fat "field marshals" sitting in folding camp chairs. Next to each of them was a large bucket filled with ice and bottles of Coke.

It was so hot inside the buses that the windows were beginning to steam up. But they were not so clouded as to obscure the view those inside got of the field marshals enjoying their ample supply of refreshment. The howls from inside the buses were in Italian, but to Phil the sense of rage and frustration was unmistakable. So were the violent actions that were rocking the big buses from within as if a hurricane were buffeting them from outside.

Lauds Coke's coup

To the Editor: Now, in the past, many products have taken hit songs and capitalized by re-wording them as their own jingles. Pepsi, Plymouth and several others come immediately to mind.

But not since "Come and ride with me, Lucille" (for Oldsmobile) can I personally note a product jingle which resulted as a hit song!

The benefit here is that no one can listen to the standard-length single version of "... teach the world to sing" (which has no reference to Coca-Cola) without thinking of Coke.

The "coup" may or may not have been planned. Coke's management and agency, however, struck a bonanza; and they are to be commended.

Charles W. Tomlinson Jr.,
Communications Consultant,
West Chester, Pa.

With a name like Messina you might expect that Phil spoke a little Italian, and he did—enough to ask the field marshal, What the devil is going on? Why are the people in the buses being treated that way? Not even being offered a visit to one of the latrines outside? Or an ice-cold Coke? The story that unfolded was more chilling than any Coke at the bottom of the hill.

It seems these were not children from regular schools. They were orphans who had had very few glimpses of the outside world. "And," the field marshal said with a smile, "they are animals. You have to treat them this way."

Phil ordered the marshals to turn them loose, but the marshals refused. They said they only took orders from Cesere. Phil began to yell at them, a stream of Italian and American curses. That demonstration at least produced some action. One of the field marshals hoisted his bulk from the folding camp chair and waddled off, but not to open the buses. Instead he went to find Cesere.

Meanwhile, back at the top of the hill, Wexler had finished shooting the close-ups. There was no way to be sure that the principals were singing in perfect sync with the New Seekers track that was played over loudspeakers. (Today you can assure perfection by putting the singers on videotape as you film them.) But Billy Davis was conducting vigorously and all the while he and Harvey were watching the lip sync. Even though not all of the principals spoke English well enough to pronounce every syllable of the lyrics—they had been recruited from embassies all over Rome—Billy was reasonably sure they were singing the correct words in sync with the New Seekers.

The hunt for Cesere proved to be unnecessary. By the time he was located Haskell Wexler had finished shooting the principals in close-up and medium shots, and was ready to board the helicopter for the overhead shot that would include everybody. The word came down that Haskell was ready, so "the animals" were let out of the buses. And Phil watched with horror at what happened next.

They emerged sweating and screaming. They didn't know why they were there or what they were supposed to do, and they cared less. The field marshals were yelling and cursing at the twelve hundred orphans, trying to get them rounded up like maverick steers.

Pushing and shoving seemed to make matters worse, so Phil suggested that one of the marshals try leading them to see if they would follow. And they did. Only the marshal led them up the hillside on the wrong route. He took them over the ground that was to lie in front of the chorus, instead of over the fields behind where they would be standing. The result was that the ground in front of the singers was trampled and scarred before the helicopter took off. Real was beginning to be substituted for surreal.

The helicopter was running and ready to take off, but the sound of its engines kept everyone from hearing any plans or orders. Recta's bullhorns were not loud enough. The kids had by now been crowded and shoved into a loose mob at the top of the hill and were yelling and throwing at the chopper the Coke bottles they had been given to hold as symbols of harmony and understanding between peoples.

In the midst of all this, Wexler took off hoping to get at least one shot. As he circled, the crowd ran out of Coke bottles to hurl at him and, ignoring the shrieks of the field marshals who were still trying to maintain some semblance of order, they stampeded, not helter-skelter in forty different directions, but almost as if they were a herd that had traveled many miles of prairie together. They performed their first uniform act of the day and charged down the hill to where the Coke truck was parked. They then began to rock it—trying to turn it over.

When the dailies were screened there was not one usable frame of footage from the helicopter.

There were a few scenes of the principals that might have been used for cut-ins. But most of them, especially those that involved the lead girl, had been taken with a zoom. And it seems that the zoom lens was faulty. All the shots that used it were out of focus.

So the spark, the little elusive firefly that I had managed to catch in Shannon Airport and that Roger, Billy, and I had turned into a beautiful brainchild (in our eyes at least) had managed, as it matured, to run afoul of the exact ills it hoped to eliminate—lack of harmony and lack of understanding between diverse peoples.

What if the field marshals had offered every orphan on the buses a bottle of Coke and tried to explain to them what they were there for and why? There was a truck full of Coke twenty yards away and plenty of ice around. It wouldn't have cost them a cent to bring every orphan a Coke and, as the lyrics asked, "keep them company."

Would it have worked? If not perfectly, certainly better than the way things had turned out. My simplistic, idealistic basic idea was at least better than "treat 'em like animals." But the fact of the matter is that the marshals had sat hoarding the goodies for themselves, and the United Chorus of the World never got to sing on film about love and sharing. At least not on that day.

And now the money was gone. And a day later so were Wexler and his producer partner. They cut out in the middle of the night, leaving a note for Phil in his hotel box.

The note said that Phil and Harvey had a better grasp of the commercials than anyone else, and they were therefore capable of directing the next shoot, if there was to be one. However, neither knew how to operate a camera. So they were back to square one. No, they were worse off than that. They were off the board. On square one they had at least had money. Now they had no money, no lead girl, and no cameraman. And they had no faith in Recta after the debacle on the hillside.

What they did have was one gigantic problem. They were in a foreign country with no facility to lean on and no money to buy one even if they could locate it. And they were running low on faith in each other and wondering whether the basic idea and the executional idea were worth the risk and the grief.

They were in the land of Ye of Little Faith—Wexler had lost his, and Cesere had never had enough to care. And though they were still carrying the torch, the flame was growing dimmer by the minute.

However, the three torch carriers had something a great many of those lack who are asked to carry faith in ideas far away from home. Phil, Harvey, and Billy knew where to find a new supply of fuel for the flame. And they were not too proud to admit they needed it.

Ovation
To impress his audien with the power of mass co munications, Richard K. Ma off, the advertising executi asked the members of the International Congress Nutrition in Mexico City l week to please rise for t "World's National Anthem
Then he played a recordi of "I'd like to buy the wor a Coke." Cola, cola üb alles.

It was time for another call to the Keepers of the Faith back in the U.S. of A.

CHAPTER TWENTY

"Make It Good"

PHIL MESSINA KNEW that faced with such a bleak financial picture, only Sid McAllister could give the go-ahead. So once again Phil called him in the early hours of the morning—before Harvey and Billy would reach Al and me.

The time is three in the morning. The phone rings in the bedroom of Sid McAllister's house in Atlanta, Georgia.

"Hello."

"Hello, Sid, babe, is that you?"

"Yeah, Phil, it's me. How'd the shoot go?"

"Horrible. The kids rioted."

"Yeah? So I guess you didn't get the chopper shot. Is that right? How about the rest of the footage?"

"Most of the rest is out of focus. The zoom lens wasn't working right."

"I see. And what about the shots that didn't use the zoom lens?"

"The pan shots are OK, but we'd need to reshoot some zoom shots with the lead girl."

"That sounds OK. Shouldn't cost too much. You could shoot her all by herself or with just one or two others."

"Yeah, babe, except she's gone to South Africa on her honeymoon."

"So we don't have much I can show the client."

"I'd say that's about right."

"Do we have *anything* I can show the client? The pan shots?"

"They all have the lead girl in them. We'd never be using them."

"Do we have any money left?"

"A few dollars, babe. I'm not going to pay for a lot of what went on out there."

"How's Wexler holding up? Will he work with us?"

"He cut out—left us a note in the middle of the night."

"Jesus, Phil. How about your Italian production company?"

"I never want to see 'em again."

"Yeah?"

"But I got a lead on a new one. It's called Roma. I think they could help us hold on to some of the principals we already cast."

"What about the cameraman?"

"Roma's got one."

"Yeah, what's his name?"

"You're gonna love this, babe. Giuseppe Retumo."

"Giuseppe Retumo. Jesus, Phil. I can't even pronounce it. If we do go ahead, who's gonna direct?"

"Me and Harvey."

"You *and* Harvey?"

"Yeah, but it'll really be me. Harvey can't speak Italian."

"Phil—"

"Yeah, babe?"

"Scully will want Harvey to frame the shots."

"Sure, babe, I know. So do we go ahead?"

"Well, I never saw the Coca-Cola Company pay anything for a blank piece of film—much less big bucks. But I've never seen them refuse to pay for film they thought was good, so Phil—"

"Yeah, babe."

"Make it good."

And "Make It Good" became the credo for the months ahead, and I've tried to make it mine throughout my career, but it's a hard credo to live up to 100 percent of the time.

I have always been uneasy with the word "great," but I never stopped to think about why until after "Buy the World" became a hit commercial and "I'd Like to Teach the World to Sing" became a hit song. Creative people—and their sponsors and backers—have always been very free with the word "great." They slather gobs of "great" lavishly and lovingly on contemporary icons of popular culture. But when the rains come down over the years, a lot of "great" washes away because there isn't anything under it.

Oscars and Emmys and Clios and Lions and even Nobel Prizes are all very well—but what they are bestowed upon cannot be judged "great" by panels that are voting today. "Good" they can pass out, even "best of the day." But it seems to me that Messrs. History, Perspective, and Time have to sit on any panel of judges that passes out "great."

I will take on the responsibility of awarding "good" or even "very good" or "best" in my own narrow field of advertising. I can set standards there, and by now you know most of them. You

Play Back

By BEN ALLEN

HIGH ON A WINDY HILL: What do you do with a thousand kids high on a hilltop outside Rome? You line 'em up, holding cokes and have 'em sing "I'd like to buy the world a coke and keep it company . . ." This brilliantly conceived commercial has to be one of the most dynamite spots ever seen on the tube. "We were over budget before we got one piece of footage in the can," says McCann's Bill Backer, Coke's ace creative director. "It had to be the toughest shoot ever. 10 whole weeks. But it was worth it. The client's reaction was instant love."

• • •

The idea started out as a radio commercial. Backer dreamed up the first line and together with McCann's music director, Billy Davis, they fashioned the rest of the lyric. The got The Seekers to record it and it was such a success they ran a contest at the agency to see who could come up with the best visual. Art Director Harvey Gabor came up with the United Chorus Of The World approach on top of the mountain which sent the Coke team out to comb the embassies of Rome to get the kids. Phil Messina produced and the result is super watching and super listening. (Must've had a super budget, too.)

• • •

may not agree with them, but to all who don't, I say, "publish yours."

My own business is full of people who pass out awards for creativity and can't even define that, much less set standards for what is good creativity. The same holds true for many other endeavors that involve ideas from filmmaking to educating to peacekeeping. We have millions of experts who know "great" but can't define "good."

When I was in college I flirted with trying to be a cartoonist, and the college humor magazine, the *Yale Record,* published some of my work. It was highly stylized and imitative of *The New Yorker*'s Peter Arno.

My roommate, Henry Koehler, a talented artist then, and in later years a very successful one, viewed my output with a jaundiced eye. He found out that my idol, Arno, had himself been a contributor to the *Record* in his undergraduate days at Yale, so Henry took it upon himself to pull out from the old *Record* files some examples of Arno's undergraduate work. The ability to poke fun at the foibles of the upper crust was already evident, but the drawings were basically straightforward. Henry showed them to me accompanied by a piece of advice. "Billy," he said, "before you try to stylize, you gotta learn how to draw."

Henry's advice holds for those who would be experts at "great" before they understand what's "good." Good I understand, and so did everyone else in the Idea Family of "Buy the World a Coke."

By the time Harvey and Billy called Al and me it was 10:00 A.M. New York time and they both knew that Sid had said "keep going." What they needed from us was some reassurance that the final result would be worth the effort. They were homesick and discouraged. Also, some tension had understandably begun to creep in between Harvey and Phil, whose areas of expertise overlapped in this project.

Idea Families are like other families in that sibling rivalry occurs quite frequently. But in Idea Families they tend to crop up for different reasons—the rivalry is not so much for parental affection as it is for executional territory. When someone contributes an executional idea to help a basic one reach maturity, he or she wants the contribution to remain pure and to emerge intact as envisioned. And that is only right and fair. But what happens in practice is that executional ideas often overlap. So executional duties cannot be separated by clearly delineated lines of authority, at least, not if the idea is going to reach full potential.

Phil's ability to think ahead to the editing room while filming on location was unbeatable on that team, or on any team anywhere for that matter. But it was Harvey's executional idea 100 percent that they were shooting, except that his executional idea depended on a piece of music and lyrics to which Billy Davis had made major contributions and understood much better than Harvey or Phil.

So where does one draw the lines of authority?

Ideas are more like batons than basketballs. Basketballs can be bounced around and tossed to someone else. But a baton in the hands of a crack relay team is jointly held by two team members for a few moments while the runners race alongside one another. In other words, to be consistently successful the handoff must be a mutual one.

You can toss a basketball over a backyard fence, but not a baton. That's why members of an Idea Family can't live in separate boxes or houses with backyards separated by fences. While working on an idea together they kind of have to live in the same organizational box or house and share the kitchen and the bathroom, so to speak. And that's what can lead to tensions.

Al and I were well aware of the tensions that existed. But we also knew this was the kind of Idea Family that every idea needs. They would put aside their differences, circle the wagons, and defend the child as long as they felt it was worth the effort to see it grow to maturity. What they needed was not the usual "I know it's rough and we really appreciate all you're doing," but rather a good helping of renewed faith in the idea. And Al and I did our best in that department. Al made his plea in one simple thought: "Harv—just get it on film. It'll be terrific. Don't worry that the extra production values won't be there. Just get it on film. It can't fail. And Phil—make sure it will cut. OK?"

My thoughts to Billy were even simpler: "Billy, just make sure whoever sings those opening lines comes off as someone who would have those kinds of values—and is the right age and can sing in that key. If you just do that the commercial will have the strongest opening of any commercial this year. I promise."

After that Al and I knew it was up to the ideas—basic and executional.

So Billy, Harvey, and Phil set out on what would be the last leg of their journey, knowing full well it promised to be strictly a "no-frills" trip.

God had to be in the very few details they could afford, and had better be blessing the ideas. All they had left to count on was a fresh approach to a lyric that had been judged incomplete by the public up to then, and a visual idea that attempted to fix the problem by singing the song with a mythical group in a surreal setting that would help it come off as a United Chorus of the World.

There would be no fancy cameraman with yards and yards of softly lit, inspirational "great" footage in his previous credits, no director with a director's card and a room full of awards for "great" work, no folksinger who would be asking for double or triple scale, and a few hundred less extras in the big scene.

But I have found that a small number of competent people, when working as a team, can make their own luck. And certainly the three Americans who were left were some of the best in their respective fields. They also had the benefit of some hindsight and of having met many new production people in Italy. They could begin to choose them now with firsthand instead of secondhand knowledge.

A young woman named Lisa, who had coordinated the casting of the principals and the location scouting for Recta, appeared to Phil and Harvey to know what she was doing. And she agreed to join the family, although assurances of future payments were made with fingers crossed.

With Lisa's help two other decisions were made that paid off. Roma was hired as a production company and they along with Lisa recommended someone who they said was a solid journeyman cameraman. "Guiseppe Retumo" was not exactly a household name on Madison Avenue, as Sid McAllister pointed out, but at least he was being recommended by competent professionals.

Also, Harvey, Phil, and Lisa decided that they had better find in the now-empty budget enough money for a costume designer. In looking at the out-of-focus footage that had been previously shot, they realized that the different faces and skin colors of the principals did not separate them one from another as clearly as a viewer might wish. In order to quickly establish them as being from diverse cultures and countries, the differences in native garb had to be pushed by a good, cheap, and very speedy costume designer. And Lisa led them to one.

But they still had no lead girl. And the shoot was scheduled for the day after tomorrow.

The following morning, while Phil was having breakfast with Lisa in Piazza Navona, a governess pushing a baby carriage across the piazza caught his eye. You already know what it was about the young governess that drew Phil's attention. You saw her singing the opening lines of the original Hilltop commercial or its revival in 1989. Phil saw in her—even at a distance—what the world would see later on. Here was someone whose attitude reflected exactly what the opening lines of the song were saying, a concern for the little people, those too small to have a house and care for themselves.

Phil asked Lisa to walk over and speak to the governess, so Lisa duly set off across the piazza. But even from where he was sitting, Phil could see that Lisa was getting nowhere, so he strolled over to join the conversation. As it turned out, the girl was not local, but English, very shy, and adamant about not wanting to appear in a Coca-Cola commercial—or any commercial for that matter.

Phil couldn't believe it. He wouldn't take no for an answer. He

▸ Marketing

Coke's New Ad—It's the Real Thing

I'd like to build the world a home and furnish it with love;
Grow apple trees and honey bees and snow white turtle doves.
I'd like to teach the world to sing in perfect harmony;
I'd like to buy the world a Coke and keep it company.
It's the real thing. What the world wants today is the real thing.

BY LYNN TAYLOR

Lynn Taylor

Unless you've had your head under a bushel basket for the last two months or absolutely never watch television, you probably will recognize the above lyrics as one of the hit songs of the season, which also just happens to be an ad for Coca-Cola Co.

We have been curious to find out about the commercial which shows young people gathered on a hillside in Italy singing the song together. Is it for real!

The company and McCann Ericson, Inc., the agency responsible for the ad, assure us that it is for real . . . well, almost.

Hot in Italy

Anyway, it was shot in Italy and not on a hillside in Brooklyn close to the agency's headquarters or in Atlanta, where Coca-Cola is based.

It was supposed to have been filmed on a hillside outside of London, but bad weather forced cancellation. The film site was switched to Rome, but the first rain in months forced postponement.

In the main portion of the commercial, about 40 young people ranging in age from 15 to 19 years are shown, Harvey Gabor, vice president and art director of McCann, told us. Some of them are children from the embassies in Rome; others are foreign students going to school in Rome.

The final view, taken from a helicopter, shows 500 students. No wonder that when the weather finally cleared up, it took 2½ days to shoot the commercial.

Some of the students are wearing their own native costumes; others had to be custom-made—a project in itself. Look closely and you may see some of the Coke bottles has lettering in the languages of the country the singer comes from. [By the way, Coke is sold in 130 countries.]

On a hillside in Italy Coca-Cola gathered together young people from many nations to make its latest commercial—which is on its way to becoming a classic.

Are they really singing!

Yes, they were singing when the film was made, but that's not the sound track you hear. It took several weeks of rehearsals in an auditorium to get the young paople to get the timing exactly right, especially difficult since many of them only spoke Italian or languages other than English, Gabor told us. The sound track is done by The New Seekers, London vocal group.

Appeal to Young People

The theme was chosen, specifically to appeal to young people who have developed a deep concern about the problems of the world. The song itself is fresh and has a little hope in it, Gabor said.

"The idea is to sell Coke . . . and to give a little joy at the same time."

The hillside, 25 minutes from Rome, was selected because the agency was looking for a place that had a pastoral, simple look.

"We were presenting a bit of fantasy," Gabor said, "almost a wish that the world was really like that."

The song appeals to people of all ages, Coca-Cola reports. Consumer response has been great with 90 per cent of the letters it receives requesting copies of the lyrics. One teacher who wrote in wants to write a play around the commercial's theme; a choral director requested sheet music, and some youngsters are composing additional stanzas to the music which was written by Bill Backer, Billy Davis and Cook and Greenaway, a songwriting team.

Copies Available

Copies of the handwritten score of the music are available upon request. Write to Consumer Services Manager, The Coca-Cola Co., P. O. Drawer 1734, Atlanta, Ga. 30301.

Is the campign a success! Coca-Cola is calling it the real thing and equates it with other commercial successes such as its own "Pause that Refreshes," the Volkswagen series of the late 1960s and the humorous Alka-Seltzer commercials.

had worked on the Coke account for over a year now. His files back in New York were stuffed with letters from people all over America—not professionals but amateurs—who wanted to do a commercial for Coca-Cola. He was well aware that you could probably scour a hundred piazzas, parks, squares, or plazas the world over and never run into someone who did not want to be in a Coke commercial. Somehow he had managed to find that one needle in the haystack, and doing so just reinforced the feelings that we had all begun to feel ever since Phil and Harvey were first rained out in England—the feelings that whispered, "This project is snakebit, star-crossed, hexed, forever doomed."

The girl, however, said she had a sister who would like to do the commercial, she was sure. But Phil was unconvinced about the sister. He and Harvey had by now looked over nearly a hundred candidates for the part since the first casting sessions in London, and had developed some pretty firm ideas about what characteristics were needed. And suddenly Phil realized that her kind of shyness was exactly what he needed, and he saw in this girl's reticence a projection of the same idealism that the song was trying to project. Anyone who appeared as if she might want to do this commercial shouldn't try, he decided. She would not be believable.

So, Phil and Lisa refused to take no for an answer, and they fell back on three different elements of persuasion that the Italians can combine better than any other people—food, wine, and song. The food was Italian, of course, and so was the wine. But the song was "I'd like to build the world a home and furnish it with love." They sang it on the terrace of a local restaurant all evening—until the young governess could sing it without their help—and then she finally said yes.

As in a dozen other instances that I have described in this book, the idea, basic and executional, had carried the day, or in this case the night.

So it was back to the hillside, this time with Phil and Harvey directing.

The results of that shoot are what you saw on the screen—except that the tight close-ups were not shot there. To save transportation time and money they were shot at a location closer to the center of Rome—an empty racetrack. Why not? The commercial had been a long shot ever since the day my plane had been forced to land at Shannon Airport.

CHAPTER TWENTY-ONE

The Idea Tower

EVERY PARENT, UNCLE, and aunt of an idea, no matter how democratic they may be, go through periods when they long for an idea world where they are all-powerful, unelected dictators with no one to answer to but the persons whose needs or desires the ideas are supposed to serve. They would then eliminate not just bureaucrats, flow monitors, money men, lawyers, critics, unfavorable reviewers, and review boards, but even the often-wise and helpful men at the end of an Idea Channel who can say yes. "My ideas must have absolute freedom to soar on gossamer wings and ride the currents of the times to glory; above criticism, above profits and losses, and/or government grants, even above the rat race for Oscars and Pulitzers. Let my public judge." That is how we all feel from time to time.

There are people who by virtue of wealth, corporate power, or years of unbroken successes find themselves occasionally in those kinds of beautiful situations—I call them "Idea Towers." They are like ivory towers, only from Idea Towers you feel you are in the perfect location from which to drop pearls of wisdom on the barnyard below, and on a clear day, which is every day in an Idea Tower, you always have a view of the destination you want for your latest inspiration. And that view is 100 percent unobstructed.

But living in Idea Towers represents a high-risk operation. When you're right, the public gets a winner like the Model T Ford, the first automobile a working man could afford. But when you're wrong, the result is an Edsel.

People like me, professional suppliers of ideas, almost never see the inside of an Idea Tower. But once in my life I did. I got to be Father, Uncle, Judge, and Jury, and to make a point, I want to go into how it happened and what resulted.

It started with a radio campaign I had written for Beech-Nut gum, "I'm Not Talkin' While the Flavor Lasts."

First Sailor: Hey, Columbus, we're getting to the edge of the earth. What do you say we turn back?

Columbus: I'm not talkin' while the flavor lasts.
Second Sailor: Whad'ya chewin'?
Columbus: Beech-Nut gum.
First Sailor: We could discover America by then!

Sounds pedestrian and dated today, but as far as I know it was the first of many fractured history campaigns that have been aired on radio and TV over the years. None, I might add, with much success.

My campaign won what few radio awards existed in those days. It also produced a weekly stack of mail from listeners who created their own commercials in the format of the campaign. It was a dream campaign in every respect but one—it didn't move Beech-Nut gum. Sales continued flat to down.

The campaign had been sold to the owner of the Beech-Nut Company, E. J. Noble, by a team of account executives. I had not been present at the meeting. E.J. was considered a mercurial tyrant by the agency, Young & Rubicam, and creative people didn't deal directly with him. (We were told he was too brusque for the tender egos of us writer/art director types.) But, I suspect, some of us might have rubbed E.J. the wrong way in the past.

Anyway, my campaign was doing a good job of selling its author, me, plus the agency, but not the product.

At Young & Rubicam, the wiser and grayer heads decided that some changes were definitely needed. And the change they decided on was a change in medium—from radio to television.

I disagreed.

I was happy to move to TV, but I felt my campaign had created a big enough stir on radio to prove itself. Whatever problems were inherent in the campaign would not be fixed by a change in medium. My gut kept telling me that the audience we should be talking to might not know enough history to realize we had fractured it.

But TV was judged to be the answer by my seniors, and the media department was told to come up with a recommendation.

What they came up with was the new *Dick Clark Saturday Night Show*. It had just gone on the air—on ABC—without a sponsor. I mean there was no advertising on it at all. None.

The show featured rock stars of the day lip-synching to their most recent hits amidst all the pyrotechnics that Dick Clark could muster without money. He had virtually no budget. But since an appearance on national TV could make or break a new recording, he got his talent for little more than their travel expenses, and he paid for their airline tickets with on-air plugs for the airlines.

Today, the production values of *The Dick Clark Saturday Night Show* would be viewed as too crude even for local TV. But back then, to its teenage audience, it was wonderful and wild.

I can still see the expressions on the faces of the account men when Bill Dollard from the media department brought up a reel of the first *Dick Clark Saturday Night Show*. It opened with a rock group—The Royal Teens—dressed in what had to be the shortest shorts ever seen on national television up to that time. They were cut very high up the thighs—like many of today's bathing suits. The group was singing, or rather lip synching (in those days no one knew the difference) outside the Little Theater on Forty-fourth Street west of Broadway. The group was surrounded by a huge mob of onlookers, and as its members sang they would head into the theater itself like Pied Pipers, wiggle through the lobby, and then down the aisle to the stage.

The lyrics they sang were "Who likes short shorts, we like short shorts"—what else?

The effect of all this on the audience was a harbinger of things to come as rock and roll began to split and then widen the gap between generations.

Elvis Presley, on *The Ed Sullivan Show,* was the rod that drew the most lightning (no pun intended), but week after week Dick Clark's parade of established and would-be rock stars, the first ever on national prime-time television, introduced the American teenager to more of the new music makers than any other show. Because this prime-time dash to freedom was clearly stamped "For Teenagers Only—Adults Twenty-one and Over Not Welcome," the kids embraced it like nothing else on TV.

But to the seniors at Young & Rubicam the show was clearly rated PG—Perfectly God-awful—and dangerous as well to respectable careers. They could envision themselves being cut down by E. J. Noble's sharp tongue like a row of spent tulips.

But I really liked "Short Shorts" (not the garments, but the song), and all the other hits of the day, such as "Great Balls of Fire," "Click Clack," "Party Doll" and a disc full of others that predate even today's popular collections of Golden Oldies. My course in music theory under the celebrated Paul Hindemith at Yale had never civilized my ear, and the first time "Let the Good Times Roll" came on my car radio I literally had to pull over to the side of the road. I was knocked out.

So when the smart money began to desert *The Dick Clark Show*, I jumped in and volunteered to be the fall guy who would take the 16 mm film—there was no tape at that time—to E. J. Noble and recommend he buy it. Why not? I could find work on other accounts much easier than they could. And I would walk in with some credentials, having been the writer of "I'm Not Talkin' While the Flavor Lasts."

Beech-Nut's offices were in Westchester, but the screening was to take place in E.J.'s apartment in the Waldorf Towers on Park Avenue.

Walking up Park Avenue, I remembered that Jack Greer, the head of the account, had told me that Noble had just purchased a large block of stock in ABC and I should try to slip in the obvious fact that Dick Clark would be representing a losing half hour unless the show secured a sponsor. Also, he could probably buy it at a very, very good price. In other words,"Heads you win, tails you don't lose." But we never got past "Short Shorts."

We never even got off Forty-fourth Street into the theater where in the months to come Jerry Lee Lewis would literally explode great balls of fire while pumping the piano wearing a leopard-skin coat, and Buddy Knox would start down one of the aisles in total darkness, singing "Somebody Touched Me in the Dark Last Night" and risk his life in the pandemonium that ensued as hundreds of kids tumbled from their seats in the pitch-black theater and scrambled to touch the singer himself. This was destined to be live TV like it was never before or would ever be again. But E.J. stopped at "Short Shorts." "I know what this is," he said.

Beads of perspiration had already gathered on Jack Greer's forehead as E.J went on. "Can you be on it this Friday?" he asked. Today was Tuesday.

"What do you mean, 'on it'?" I asked.

E.J. sounded impatient: "With commercials and a show opening that says Beech-Nut. If Beech-Nut is going to sponsor the show, I want people to know it. I want the whole show. I WANT TO OWN IT. Can you own it by this Friday?"

"Sure," I said. "We'll do the commercials live, but we'll need a production budget of—"

I can't remember what I quoted. Whatever the amount, it represented a totally uneducated guess. I had no idea what the commercials would involve, since they weren't written yet. I had never seen the show's facilities. I had no idea whether or not Dick would cooperate. Besides, as a writer, I had never dealt directly with production budgets, merely sat in meetings where they were discussed. So, I covered my butt and quoted what later turned out to be an amount that nearly equaled the entire production budget of the show itself. The result was that Beech-Nut would be not only the show's sponsor, but also sort of its coproducer with the power of my production budget.

E.J. never blinked. But Jack Greer certainly did. Anyway, we walked out with the show and the dough. Now we had to figure out what to do with both of them.

The next day, Wednesday, Bill Geeslin, the number-two account executive on the account, and I went over to the Little Theater to meet Dick Clark. On the way over, without realizing it, I started to cast myself in the role of Father, Uncle, Judge, and Jury, and began to live in an Idea Tower. I was not being sneaky. I was being pragmatic. Had there been time I would have checked through channels, but without the time to check with anyone, I simply tossed out the campaign everyone thought was going to continue—"I'm Not Talkin' While the Flavor Lasts"—and wrote a new one.

This was the era when "magic ingredients" ruled the kingdom of commercials. Every other product seemed to have a secret and/or magic ingredient with a scientific or code name like D-5 or Hexachlorophyll. So I decided to give Beech-Nut Gum a magic ingredient named "iffic" which when added to Beech-Nut's flavor made it "Flavor-iffic." Pretty corny, I agree. You'd probably give the basic idea—the promise of superior taste—a D minus or an F for originality. And the execution might rate a C or C minus. It was a piece of tongue-in-cheek shtick, a take-off of packaged goods advertising. Takeoffs of any kind of communications are always an easy way out and often catchy, but they are seldom as brilliant as their creators think they are. But you have to admit, Flavoriffic was directionally sound, since a little burst of flavor is what kids were looking for in gum.

But on the way to growing up, something was added to the execution. And history gives that addition a solid A. With it, Flavoriffic became a sow's ear that ended up in a silk purse factory.

Dick Clark sparked to Flavor-iffic. He got on the phone and called the guys who had put the words of "Short Shorts" to a traditional army marching chant and come up with a rock hit. Could they do the same thing for Beech-Nut gum and Flavor-iffic? Sure they could.

Next morning, Thursday, I was on a train bound for Philadelphia, where the "Short Shorts" team did their recording, to write and record "Who Likes Beech-Nut Spearmint Gum, We Like Beech-Nut Spearmint Gum. It's Flavor-iffic." Hardly the stuff of advertising legend, except for the addition of one word—Spearmint.

As I had left Dick the day before, he had mentioned that the kids really didn't like the traditional Beech-Nut gum in the yellow pack because its peppermint flavor was too strong for them. Young & Rubicam's research had uncovered the same antipeppermint bias. Spearmint and Juicy Fruit were the flavors of the younger generation. So I changed the advertised brand from Peppermint—the big brand—to Spearmint. Why not? When time and circumstances put you in an Idea Tower and you sit above all the systems of checks and balances and filters and egos, you can call 'em as you see 'em.

We were ready to record by three o'clock Thursday, only we had to wait for the building to empty at five. The echo chamber the gang was using was the building's elevator shaft; a fine echo chamber as long as no one wanted to use the elevator.

I arrived in New York with the recordings around three the next morning and played them for Dick Clark as soon as I could. Dick thought they would make a good show-opening billboard for Beech-Nut. So part of my assignment was accomplished. Next came the job of writing some commercials for the show, which was due to go into a run-through in a few hours.

What commenced between Dick and me would normally take months of research and many hours of meetings in any major advertising agency or marketing company, then or now. We positioned, or rather repositioned, an about-to-be nationally advertised product in fifteen minutes. We decided to say the gum was FOR TEENS ONLY, not figuratively, but literally. The positioning line we came up with was "Wrapped in Green, Made for a Teen."

"But you've narrowed the market!" "You've thrown away our traditional adult audience." "What about the preteens?" All the dumb questions that marketers ask, especially when they forget that in this country no one has to buy what you are selling, never had a chance to be asked. In a company conference room filled with bean counters, a market of fifty million looks five times better than a market of ten million. But out on the street it's different. Those numbers turn into people. And if the ten million number represents kids who like not only what you are selling but also the way you are selling it, and if each one is three times as likely to chew more gum than the adult who makes up the broader market, you begin to think less in terms of numbers and more in terms of individual people with their separate tastes in both chewing gum and life-style.

However, the one question that should have been asked wasn't. It was so obvious that no one bothered with it in the rush to get on the show. It was even more basic than Marketing 101, just everyday common sense: "Does the product exist in the markets where your advertising message is going?"

It wasn't until Friday morning when we were playing "Who Likes Beech-Nut Spearmint Gum?" that Bill Geeslin's assistant said, rather matter-of-factly, "Of course, you guys know that coast-to-coast Beech-Nut Spearmint has less than fifteen percent distribution."

Bill was ashen. I was numb. Suddenly my seat in the Idea Tower began to look more like a perch on the end of a long limb. But Dick was elated. "We'll introduce it like it was a new gum made especially for this show," he said. And that's how we wrote the commercials.

The show had to go on—and go on with Beech-Nut owning it. And it did. We renamed it *The Dick Clark Saturday Night Beech-Nut Show*, and it went on without a glitch, at least not one that anyone could or would notice. Dick introduced the gum as if he, personally, had commissioned the Beech-Nut Company to make this new gum just for his audience—nobody else. It was to be their private gum—like a club product, "made exclusively for the Dick Clark Club."

What we had done, in essence, was introduce a new gum to America.

So we hadn't alerted the sales force—so we had no point-of-sale items prepared and ready to ship, or publicity announcements typed for release. So what? Beech-Nut spearmint was not destined to be a model of push-marketing. It was to be a case study in pull-marketing like I've never been involved with before or since. Overnight we had a majority of our target audience on the prowl to find a product that didn't exist at their local gum counter.

Another target audience might walk away grumbling. This one actually cracked the glass on the display cases that failed to carry the gum—the one that was "wrapped in green and made just for teens." For a period of time, the entire output of Beech-Nut gum had to be devoted to spearmint. I was informed that within six months Wrigley's had registered a drop in share of market—the first in its history.

Meanwhile, Dick and I, with the help of the audience, cranked out commercial after commercial—some of them outrageous. And the only "judging" we ever got was on Monday morning after the show, when E.J.'s comments would be passed on to us.

We knew we were taking huge risks even then. Now, I wouldn't dare. Because what Dick would do for one commercial each night was to conduct live, on-air, unrehearsed discussions about gum and life with members of the audience. In order to let more teenagers see the show, and to keep their reactions fresh, Dick would completely change the audience between run-through and show, so there was no way to rehearse these conversations. Other commercials were done with the singers or Dick alone.

We never knew exactly how long a commercial would go, and some nights we exceeded our three minutes. When ABC objected, we did a whole show without any commercials to average out our times. Dick merely announced that Beech-Nut was donating its commercial time tonight to some singer so he or she could sing an extra song. The effect of all this was to build a momentum none of us had ever experienced.

We all know that nothing succeeds like success. And when it happens, everybody wants to crowd in on it and make their mark. But E. J. Noble and Young & Rubicam were both smart enough to know that "if it ain't broke, don't fix it."

Not only did we do the advertising, we did the promotions as well. We got out records with collector's labels on them, autographed by singers of the day. We had a "Beech-Nut Top Ten," we staged songs on lavish sets provided by the commercial budget, and we elicited cooperation from singers and managers that was unheard of even then.

We were a group that had hitched a ride on a rocket called rock and roll and ridden it to the top of an Idea Tower. But what a mixed bag we were. Dick was a former radio announcer from upstate New York who had recognized the music movement as it was starting to happen. What made him unique among all those who recognized it with him was that he never tried to be an adult teenager like Cousin Brucie or Alan Freed. Dick was someone who could see things from a teen's point of view and could and would take their side, but he never joined them. He represented what they wanted to be in a few years. He knew their music, their stars, and their thoughts. But he kept a small distance between him and them. He was always a little above and beyond and never allowed them the familiarity that could lead to contempt. In short, he was a very decent, very nice, slightly older brother. And what he engendered was a kind of special respect that would last for decades. I just watched, learned, and marveled.

I was the star-struck kid. Awed, however, not by the stars but by their songs. So much so that I was totally oblivious to the world around me.

Two years later accusations of "payola" would echo through the halls of popular music. I myself had seen favors being traded. There were agents and managers constantly wheeling and dealing with Dick's people. If someone wanted some extra production values devoted to his singer and was willing to pay for part of a set, instead of a drab curtain, that seemed fine by me. ABC had to know its budget wasn't paying for everything it was seeing.

I had moved on by the time most of the big DJs were wiped out by the payola scandals (Dick, I was happy to hear, came off squeaky-clean), and my opinions took the high ground at that time along with most everyone else's. Looking back, though, I'm not so sure. I think the stations teamed up with the press to make bigger headlines out of the whole payola system than were warranted, because the stations weren't in on the payouts. But they were never blind to them.

Today they've elevated payola to a higher level; they should rename it "powerola." We have traded Charlie Hustle with his fist full of twenties for Charlie Potatoes with his iron fists loaded with Corporate Power, or Charlie Chan, who buys the whole entertainment company while promising not to influence the song or the story. I'll take Charlie Hustle, thank you. He promoted new faces and grassroots record labels. And to my ear, he peddled a better brand of music, more original and less packaged.

The world of ideas is like the Kentucky Derby in that it costs money to get into the race and start. After that, if all goes according to the rules, the best horse, or best idea, will win.

There are far more records made each month than can be aired by disc jockeys, just as there are many more horses born each year than can fit into a Kentucky Derby. Someone along the way has to single out this or that one, keep the faith, and put up some money to get it started. After that the best recording or race horse should win.

The same holds true for many of the products sold in supermarkets. The manufacturer decides, "This one's a winner," and pays the supermarket chain something extra in price-offs or cash-backs in order to give its products a better showing than its competitors—or, in the case of new products, at least an equal showing. But in all those thousands of cases, which occur daily, the press never cries "foul."

Some of the mistakes we made in our Idea Tower make me wince today. We built promotions on singers without checking on their sexual habits, and occasionally we paid the price. We didn't set up an apparatus to secure the gains we had made at retail. But success papered over what we were doing wrong while we were doing most things right. And that's the problem with Idea Towers. They break the old countryman's rule that says, "You can't let the cow judge her own cream."

We were judging not only our own basic idea, but every extension of it all the way through promotional and marketing executions. So we were establishing our own set of priorities as to what was most important—and least important. We were like a music trio who seemed to have decided that nothing mattered but the melody. To heck with rhythm and harmony. Any sour licks that turned up we would simply ignore. And when suddenly we found ourselves playing in the Rainbow Room, we lacked a brass section, reeds, and the discipline of arrangements to bring our songs home.

All ideas need the protection of a small Idea Tower when they first sprout. They must have that first little group of Parents, Uncles, and Aunts to surround them with the warmth of understanding and enthusiasm and shield them from the burning winds of negativism while the roots are still shallow and the leaves are very tender. While an idea remains sheltered there, it is immune to the stunting effects of bureaucracy and the killing frosts of Backer's Laws.

But every big idea, by definition, has to someday face the mass audience for which it was executed. And if it isn't flanked by a big enough Idea Family, including Judges, it is courting disaster.

Beech-Nut didn't have the support system in place to take advantage of, and consolidate, our gains. So as time passed, our successes tended to shrivel while our failures grew like weeds around the feet of our successors. What good is doubling your share of anything if you are not prepared to hold on to what you have worked so hard to achieve?

I have rules, but not a theory, on the value of Idea Towers and when to step down from them into the real world. I can only list them in a few obvious, and probably corny, maxims:

- *When you need to move fast, travel light.*
- *The bigger the tour group, the slower the tour.*
- *The more apples you put in the barrel, the more chance you have of getting a rotten one.*

On the other hand:

- *To play hardball you need at least nine players, a manager, and someone to pay for the uniforms.*

And sooner or later, all big ideas have to play in the major leagues.

Ultimately, the whole Beech-Nut experience was too heady not to change each of us personally. Bill Geeslin seemed to burn out, and left the business when his Dick Clark stint was over. I bumped into Dick in the fall of 1991 at an introduction of a new electronic product that Backer Spielvogel Bates was advertising. Dick was hosting the event. After a few minutes of pleasantries he turned to me and—out of nowhere—said, "It's not fun like it used to be, is it, Bill?" Clearly Dick's *Saturday Night Beech-Nut Show* had left a small, empty feeling in him that has never gone away.

As for me, I had developed a hankering to go where I might write some of this new music myself—in another Idea Tower, of course. And when McCann-Erickson made me an offer of "freedom" on an account that used a lot of music, plus a salary that I couldn't refuse, I accepted. The money came at once. The freedom I had to earn all over again, as I had done on Beech-Nut, and I headed back to McCann full of enthusiasm for "total freedom."

Today, I think differently. I realize you should step down from an Idea Tower probably sooner than later, especially if you can step into an Idea Channel.

CHAPTER TWENTY-TWO

The Bigger the Idea, the Harder the Pull

EVERY CHAPTER IN this book had at the outset a reason for being, with one exception—this one. I knew I had to write the others if I was going to make certain points that I felt were important in the care and feeding of ideas. But this one was different. I found myself writing it, and didn't know why until I read it. Then I knew. I was explaining to myself, and to you, why anyone would spend some of the best years of his or her life doing what I did after I left Beech-Nut, Dick Clark, and the rock and roll years.

Writing about it has helped me understand why I did what I did. What happened, very simply, was that I got pulled into the magnetic sphere of an idea that was so big, and demonstrably so successful, that it was by then an institution.

When someone puts an idea in front of you and says, "How does that grab you?" what they have presented in all probability is a shallow execution that will get from you an instant decision. But big basic ideas seldom yank you out of your shoes in an instant, the way, for instance, an offer of money can do. Big ideas pique your interest, tug at your sleeve, and then the closer you get to them, the harder they pull. That's why I said earlier that money grabs but ideas pull. And big ideas pull the hardest of all, perhaps because they pull you out of yourself to where you leave your common sense and natural self-defense behind.

Joe Brooks got pulled in by an untried idea of his own and let it gradually pull in others. I got pulled in by a much bigger one. It wasn't mine. In fact, its origin was not man, but serendipity. Its eventual pull, however, was stronger than any idea of mine, or anyone else's that came along in the years that followed.

I offer the following not as an excuse for what I did, merely as an explanation. I could have totally wasted my opportunity years. Young people today who seem to plan each step and stop in their careers with linear logic and no emotion would never do what I did. But as I said early on, I've been lucky.

I hope as you read on you will get a better understanding of, and gain some sympathy for, the many zealots who, without realizing it at first, got inextricably caught up in the pull of an idea so big, so successful, and so long-running that it has become an institution. In my case, it was a soda pop, the final execution of which had happened when an Atlanta druggist—or his assistant—made a serendipitous mistake one day and mixed an existing brown tonic called Coca-Cola with soda water instead of the usual "branch water."

Putting me on the Coca-Cola account fresh from Beech-Nut is analogous to what happened to Tarzan in the British movie of his adventures—the one where Tarzan has to trade life in the treetops for the confines of a British house. I had been enjoying life in an Idea Tower, where I could see not only a line of ideas reaching maturity, but also a never-ending supply of Party Dolls of all ages in Short Shorts of every cut and color. And suddenly I found myself in Atlanta, Georgia, at that time the Beehive Hairdo Capital of the World.

It happened this way.

I went back to McCann-Erickson for money and cookies—specifically Nabisco Cookies and Crackers. Nabisco had missed me when I went to Young & Rubicam. I had written a great many commercials for their products, many of them musical. One of the musical commercials, "Little Girls Have Pretty Curls," was being credited with putting Oreo ahead of Hydrox, which had been up to that time America's number-one chocolate sandwich cookie. Among Nabisco's plans for the future were sequels to some of my commercials, among them the one for Oreo.

But at McCann, the National Biscuit Company did not represent a squeaky wheel in the high-decibel category. Management changes at Nabisco had resulted in their forgetting who had done this or that commercial in the past, so it wasn't difficult for McCann to slide me over to their real problem account, Coca-Cola.

The way they did it represented skilled management at its very best. They used the "anybody can do *that*, but only you can do *this*" form of flattery. I don't mean to be critical. I've used flattery many times to help smooth management changes. But here was this enthusiastic, self-confident guy fresh from a happy stint in the new music world, and young enough and dumb enough to believe he was a giant-killer. "All we have to do is tell him he's right, and show him the giant. But do it quickly, so he doesn't have time to check out the giant with some of those who have returned home bloodied and beaten by him." That's what management must have said to itself.

I fell for it, so I guess I deserved some of the anguish that was to follow.

Anyone working with ideas faces constant internal pressures that come from deciding what's good and what isn't and, further down the road, from deciding how much to compromise when the sit-on-its and filterers get hold of the project. Big money exacerbates those pressures. Because the bigger the money behind an idea at maturity, the higher the profile it will have.

Screenwriters can hide—and they often do—by demanding that their name be taken off the list of credits when they feel the final film has been hopelessly butchered by subsequent rewrites or incompetent direction or production. An inventor or marketer of new products can generally avail himself of the low profile offered by a test market introduction. But people in advertising agencies who head up creative groups on major brands with major budgets are destined to spend many sleepless nights. If they are wrong, their mistakes will be so visible that there will be no place to hide.

But working on Coca-Cola involved far more pressure than what is normally applied by big money alone. There was also the nature of the product itself and its unique place in marketing history worldwide. What tea was to England, and beer to Germany, Coca-Cola was to America.

Added to those pressures was the nature of the Coca-Cola Company's relationship with an organization located 756 air miles to the north entrusted with presenting the product to its public. The Coca-Cola/McCann-Erickson relationship had been a stormy one since the day Marion Harper and Paul Foley had wrestled the account from the D'Arcy agency in St. Louis in 1955. With the help of hindsight it is not difficult to ascertain why. As with most sour agency/client relationships, the fault with this one lay on both sides of the fence, and it was some fence. It even had a name: the Mason-Dixon Line.

Although Atlanta, to my way of thinking, was not, and is not today, a Southern city in the sense that Charleston is, or Savannah, Richmond, or New Orleans, the Coca-Cola Company itself was a Southern company. Its most loyal market was in the South. Its most prosperous bottlers were Southern, and the product's roots were in Doc Pemberton's drugstore less than half a mile from company headquarters.

Robert Winship Woodruff, the controlling stockholder and monarch of all he surveyed within the halls of the Coca-Cola Company, was a native Georgian. But he had been vice president and general manager of the White Motor Company of Cleveland, Ohio, before he became head of the Coca-Cola Company in 1923. In Savannah, his years in a Yankee company might have been viewed as a break with tradition, but in Atlanta when you and your stock controlled the Coca-Cola Company and you were the richest man in town besides (perhaps that's redundant), you could rise above the recent unpleasantness between the North and South that left Atlanta in ashes.

Woodruff wasn't from Atlanta by birth, but he *was* Atlanta during his active days. And as heir to the kingdom of Coca-Cola he was the high priest of what was worshiped by many inside and outside the company almost as if it were the grail of a religion—a brown liquid in a six-and-one-half-ounce pinch waisted bottle that had been born in 1885 when an Atlanta druggist named Doc Pemberton began mixing up some ingredients—which included coca leaves—with his mortar and pestle to produce a brown tonic for Southern gentlefolk who were "feeling poorly."

To the advertising people in New York in the late 1950s, Coke was a nice little bottle of pop with a funny name that existed on a lot of rusting tin signs along back-country roads, mostly in the South. But in limiting their views of Coca-Cola to a northerner's sense of reality, the agency was wrong.

However, the Coca-Cola Company was also wrong in the way it viewed its market. The South was changing just as the North was. The heavy users of Coca-Cola no longer wore their hair in beehives or sported crew cuts. They were Dick Clark's audience with a drawl.

But the structure of the company kept it from seeing the new qualities of its market. It was a company of filterers with Woodruff at the top. As I've noted before, Woodruff summed up his advertising philosophy very clearly and simply: "The purpose of advertising Coca-Cola is to be liked." The only problem was that we could never form an Idea Channel, sit around a table, and ask, "Liked by whom? Our serious drinkers or our serious stockholders?" Woodruff would have answered, "Our serious drinkers, of course." But he didn't get to meet them very often, so the territorial chiefs that filtered the work mostly tried to outguess him. I don't think they were totally influenced by what they thought Woodruff had in mind for his target audience. In their heart of hearts they longed to agree with what they *guessed* was his vision of the world, even though some of them already knew better.

I walked in like a referee between two opposing teams without even knowing what the game was. Like most people in the creative department of an advertising agency, I thought everything could be fixed by "good advertising." And like most people in advertising, I was sure I knew what "good advertising" was. And furthermore, I was the one to do it.

There had been a long line of predecessors who had suffered Career Shock in the spot where I now found myself. What saved me was timing, the Beech-Nut experience, and the fact that my view of the product came from Broad Street in Charleston instead of Broadway in New York. To me, since earliest memory, Coke had been The Pause That Refreshes us all. So what if in its infancy Coke had contained a trace of cocaine? Well, way back then all evil seemed less evil. For instance, there were no "alcoholics" where and when I was growing up—just quite a few relatives who on occasion (like every day) drank too much. And not one of them was crazy, just a bit eccentric. The profile of every problem was lower in those days, for better or worse.

As an example, my pediatrician stepfather saw nothing illogical in recommending Coca-Cola syrup for babies that had colic, and at the same time limiting my intake of Coke—enjoyed at Poulnot's drugstore, corner of King and Broad streets—to two fountain Cokes a week, one on Friday after school, and one on Saturday on the way home from the movies. A Coke was still referred to as "a dope" by the older generation on occasion, but not with a sneer. The South felt it was entitled to prioritize the world's various sins in its own inimitable way, and on the South's list of sins you would find "a dope" in the column headed "good sins" along with the word "damn" when coupled with "Yankee." Even the preacher didn't argue with that column.

The fact that I had elected to go into advertising instead of the law or medicine was a sore subject—but a hidden one—until I became responsible for Coca-Cola advertising. Then suddenly "what Bill was doing in New York" could come out of the closet and be openly discussed on Legare, Church, or Meeting streets. So my view of Coca-Cola was the same as the company's view, and that represented a big advantage.

But the way I saw their main market was diametrically opposed to how they saw it. I was not on "their side." I had spent too much time inside the Little Theater on West Forty-fourth Street listening to what was coming out of Tennessee, Alabama, Louisiana, and Mississippi. And I had come to realize that the music of the New

North was coming from the New South, the South that the company wished to neither see nor hear.

The route that advertising ideas traveled on the way to Robert W. Woodruff ran through two large territories—those of E. Delony Sledge, director of advertising, and Lee Talley, president of Coca-Cola USA. Both were people of considerable talent and experience, but not in the area of advertising on electronic media.

I had been told that Talley had been a preacher—Baptist, as I remember—before he joined the ranks of the Coca-Cola Company. I never had the privilege—and I gather it was a privilege—of hearing him address a large group of Coca-Cola Bottlers. But I understand that no one in the entire company could rally them like Talley when he preached the Gospel According to Coca-Cola.

If you grew up in the South, I can easily describe Sledge to you, otherwise you are on your own. Delony was one of those small, wiry, thoughtful gentlemen of the Old South whose hobby was classical literature, whose values were yesterday's, and whose prognosis for the future of civilization in this country was gloomy at best. He wrapped all this in a warm, dry, self-deprecating wit so it was neither pompous nor boring. But it was his towering disdain of the habits of conspicuous consumption that were just beginning to take hold in America that kept his peers shaking their heads and saying, "When they made Delony they broke the mold."

He drove a nondescript twelve-year-old car that stood out in the executive parking lot of the Coca-Cola Company like a sharecropper would in the Atlanta Driving Club. His suits were so old their wide lapels were coming back into style—only this time accompanied by pegged trousers. His TV set was small-screen. On his infrequent trips to New York—which he hated—Delony stayed in the simplest hotels, and his luggage was often a corrugated box tied with a stout string.

At home, he often lunched at a downscale but convenient eatery called The Yellow Jacket across the street from the Coca-Cola Company. Delony never let me pick up the tab. "I don't want to be beholden to you, William," he would say. "Delony, how beholden can you be for a dollar and quarter?" I countered him one day. I knew he broke up inside, but I never saw him laugh outside, ever. He would just tighten the corners of his mouth so it kept the mirth inside where he could savor it like a cow with her cud.

I think what Delony first saw in me that attracted him—other than our mutual roots—was that I was willing to stand up to both

Margo

A goal to skoal

There's a television commercial in which an international choir of young people is singing on a mountain top:

"I'd like to buy the world a home
And furnish it with love,
Grow apple trees and honey bees
And snow white turtle doves.
I'd like to teach the world to sing
In perfect harmony,
I'd like to buy the world a Coke
And keep it company."

The song is clearly a plea for world understanding. It is also a hint that Coke would like to increase its sales.

There are, after all, more than three billion people in the world, and a Coke for every one of them would cost about a cool $300 million.

The Coca Cola Company appears to be indulging in wishful thinking. How many people, realistically, could afford to pay for such a treat? There's John Paul Getty, Queen Elizabeth, the United States government, and I can't think of too many more. Certainly none of those kids on the mountaintop could foot the bill.

Anyway, Coke's dreams of glory aside, I thought I detected an inference in the commercial that Coke was a brotherhood drink, which could, in fact, help us to solve our problems.

TO FIND OUT WHY such a claim might be made, I called Coke's advertising agency and talked to Bill Backer, the man who wrote the lyrics to the song.

Backer told me that he did, indeed, have brotherhood in mind. "Coke," he said, "is a world-wide product. We would like it if people all over the world could sit down and talk things over over a Coke."

Why shouldn't they like it, I thought, remembering the $300 million. But as Backer talked, I began to see his point. Traditionally, people have exchanged ideas "over a drink." It has seldom, however, been Coke.

Maybe there was something to what he said. People would certainly remain clear-headed if they stuck to Cokes. It might be a sensible drink for talking things over, after all.

WELL, LOOK, SO far nothing else has worked to secure world peace and harmony. Maybe the government SHOULD buy the world a Coke. It couldn't hurt to try. Foreign aid, for example, has cost a lot more than three billion soft drinks, and it hasn't gotten us all that far.

Wouldn't it be fantastic if the solution to international problems had been available to us all along, and we just never noticed? What if the answer IS to buy the world a Coke?

Come to think of it, people have been using it for many more things than just the pause that refreshes.

In the south, particularly, Coke has been a substitute for mother's milk, coffee, and even antiseptic. The formula is also notoriously secret, so how do we know what's in it? Coke might very well have properties which would, in fact, encourage everyone to get along.

THE PRESIDENT, however, is the one who will have to decide whether it's worth a try. The fact that the suggestion would have originated on Madison Avenue need not be a negative point. After all, the Madison Avenue crowd has done all right by Mr. Nixon in the past.

Since world relationships seem to be going nowhere, we hardly have anything to lose. On balance, I'll drink to that.

him and the agency and say what I thought about Coca-Cola advertising or anything else. The campaign Delony had initiated earlier on, "Sign of Good Taste the Whole World Over," was, in my opinion, a view of the world held only by rich bottlers and stockholders. It was a world full of Georgia Peaches making their debuts with Coke in their hands—comforting perhaps, but very limiting for Coca-Cola. And I said so.

The campaign the agency had subsequently foisted on him was perhaps worse. "Zing, What a Refreshing New Feeling."

A bit of puffery is acceptable in advertising, especially in a single commercial. But long-term relationships between products and consumers are similar to relationships between people—if they are going to last, they have to be built on respect and truth. "A long-term campaign can't be based on bullshit," I remember saying to Sledge. I don't know that Delony agreed with all my opinions or the way I stated them. But the first time I brought him something I had done that had bombed, and told him it was terrible and I had blown it, our friendship was sealed. I may have been the first guy who didn't feel he owed a "yes" to anyone on the account, including Sledge. So to him I represented a unique asset and one on whom he would increasingly rely for candid, if not always qualified, opinions.

If the fact that I could be counted on to be candid was what kept me from wearing out my welcome with Delony, what made it worthwhile for me to keep trying was his unique sense of loyalty to the brand. Most people are loyal to themselves or to their jobs first. Delony's loyalties lay to the brand first. He had long ago succumbed to the pull of the worldwide institution—the basic idea—that a bottle of Coca-Cola represented. And I was rapidly yielding to the same pull.

I still remember the day I came to realize exactly how deep was Delony's commitment to Coke.

Like every writer who had ever worked on the Coca-Cola account, I wanted to try my hand at describing the taste of Coke. Delony had not requested a script of that nature. I wrote it on my own—and found occasion to read it to him alone in the vacant boardroom after an official meeting had disbanded. When I had finished, he sat for what seemed like forever and then said, "William Faulkner tried to describe this product. So did James Dickey [the author of *Deliverance*]. So have many of your peers over the years. I don't think it can be done. I don't think the words exist. What suffices for me is for you to understand that the taste of Coca-Cola is the greatest taste ever invented by man"—by now Delony was on his feet standing next to the boardroom doors—"or God, either, for that matter." Exit Sledge. End of scene.

I was to hear him deliver this oration on several other occasions. It was his Saint Crispin's Day speech to any new troops on the account. I never ceased to marvel at the fact that he believed every word. And, there have been times—on a hot day when the road has been long and the syrup comes fresh and plentiful from an old-fashioned dispenser—when I say to myself, "Y'know something, the old man was right."

As impossible a pair as we were, we stayed together for so long because we were both hooked by the bigness of it all. We were refreshing the multitudes. But the truth is that those were some of the worst years of my life. There were a few times—and I am not being melodramatic here—when I sincerely considered suicide. The pressures were no greater than they were in later years on the Coke account. But early on I was too young and naïve to assemble an Idea Family to help me, and Delony was too old and stubborn to get one for himself. So we both went it alone.

Delony, accountable only to Talley and Woodruff for advertising the best-known product in the world, could have driven a Power Car and gone to Power Lunches at Power Clubs wearing Power Clothes, all the while delegating many of the details of his job to assistants whose presence in the company would have made his job appear to be even more of a Power Job then it already was. And he could have had a half dozen yes-men for writers. But he would have none of the above.

And I, who was being courted by most of the major agencies—especially my old friends at Young & Rubicam—and could have had a half-dozen better shots at the freedom I wanted, I hung in there. Because the bigger the idea, the harder the pull.

For three years he and I wrestled for the helm of The Good Ship Coca-Cola, Delony constantly wanting to tack into the wind and me longing to run with it. I have been on similar boat races since then, and they all ended up with a wreck or at least a dismasting. But when Delony and I crossed the finish line at the end of the season, he ended up with the best win/loss record in his division. And I think I was happier for him than he was for himself. And when it was all over—when he retired relatively unheralded (he would have hated a grand send-off), I knew I would miss him—really, really miss him. What I did not know then, but I know now, is that after forty years in this business, I would look back on E. Delony Sledge as the client I liked and admired the most, not because he was right, but because he was wrong in the right way. He did what he thought was right for the brand, not the man.

Early on in our relationship I had brought down a simple statement of what the product meant to people in my opinion. "Let's not go back to defining what it is, 'The greatest taste ever known to man,' et cetera," I said. "Let's talk about what it does for people." Delony's files were full of letters from people—mostly harassed and poor—for whom a Coke provided a wonderful little escape—The

Pause That Refreshes. For them, it was true. But the young were not pausing. They were drinking on the run.

Delony knew that and he easily understood "Things Go Better with Coke" when I presented it. Also he liked the music I had written. It was in the folk-pop idiom of the day—à la the Kingston Trio—and sung by another well-known folk group, the Limelighters (Delony would forever call them the Lamplighters). It wasn't Elvis. It wasn't eight-to-the-bar. But it was straight out of one genre of contemporary music and much younger than Coke had ever gone. "If you can sell it to your gang, I think I can sell it to mine," Delony had said. I thought he would have it tough, and me easy. But it turned out to be the other way around.

The existing campaign, "Zing, What a Refreshing New Feeling," had been checked out at the agency and signed on to by every major figure in the company. It was now "politically correct." So I never got "Things Go Better" officially sold at the agency. But Woodruff liked the message. Its basic honesty appealed to him, I was told. And Talley liked "the beat." So Delony and I sort of sneaked "Things Go Better with Coke" into the stream of American advertising, but not the mainstream—not onto TV or into magazines. It was introduced on radio alone. And it was an instant take.

Some time elapsed before it appeared in print and on TV, but the limited introduction via radio turned out to be more of an advantage then a disadvantage. Because it revealed an area the Coca-Cola Company had not previously explored, if they even knew it existed, the new world of "youth radio," as the Coca-Cola Company called it. They thought of it as a wasteland, degenerate and degrading. But they knew it was inhabited by millions of very thirsty young people with change in their pockets, so Coke had to be there. And the self-appointed Conrad who would take them into the heart of this jungle was me.

It was a job nobody understood or wanted to learn. I was back home, and once again I would be home alone. Delony, from the very beginning of our relationship, had shown little interest in the details of commercial execution for TV or radio. He would pore endlessly over a retouched dye transfer, commenting on every droplet that ran down the Coke bottle, but storyboards and demo tapes were not for him. He would review the finished commercials as if they were a series of still photographs cut together. He would stop the projector and look at each scene the way he would at dye transfers or transparencies. After the torture of dozens of these sessions, I got the idea of putting some of America's premier still photographers into the film business. And doing that represented another first for the campaign.

In this vacuum it was easy to grow a small Idea Tower, let it house all TV executional ideas up to rough cut and all "youth music," period. For youth music I secured an independent budget, like I had had on Dick Clark's show—and I started a system called The Album Concept. It was based on the fact that most singers got one hit from an album of twelve songs. I said I needed to write three Coke songs

for every singer in order to get one hit. And that's how it worked and why it worked. There was no approval of anything until the finished recordings were delivered.

During Delony's time and the years that immediately followed, no youth music was allowed in television advertising for Coca-Cola. The excuse given was that it didn't appeal to adults, but the real reason was, I suspect, that occasionally Woodruff and Talley might watch TV. And God forbid they should hear what was happening to Coke music.

Delony and I were breaking most of the executional barriers necessary to bring the advertising for eighty-year-old Coca-Cola into the second half of the twentieth century without disassociating it from its heritage and the heart and soul of its franchise. We were the first to put a well-known rock group, the Shirelles, on a national advertising campaign (or a local one, as far as I know); we were the first to put black stars behind a major product; and we took the first steps in getting away from the confining form of the jingle, that list of rhymed product attributes put to music that had first put Pepsi in the scene. We also put the first of the famous still photographers into the film business—Bert Stern (he had done one tabletop commercial for a local pancake client) and Mark Shaw, already relatively famous as the photographer of the Kennedy family.

In the years that followed, Sledge and his successor would work with me to develop commercials in the form of songs, and we would unite the two worlds of popular music and of Coca-Cola as no product group had ever done before, or would do in the future. At one time nearly half the singers in the Top 20 were singing for or had sung for Coke. They did not sing jingles or undisciplined songs, but sang about the moments in the life of America's youth that songs love to capture and Coke likes to make go better—the beach parties, the walks in the park, the dances, the first dates, even the smaller and less significant heartaches. And in none of the situations did a Coke seem forced, and all of them quite naturally went a little better when Coca-Cola was present.

But to write for many different singers took a greatly expanded Idea Family, some of whom were the professional songwriters who knew the artists' styles better than anyone else. Luckily, my organization accommodated them all. Otherwise we could never have written separate songs for Paul Anka, Diana Ross and the Supremes, Petula Clark, Roy Orbison, Tom Jones, the Moody Blues, Ray Charles, Aretha Franklin, Ray and Aretha in a duet, the Bee Gees, the Everly Brothers, Dottie West, the Beach Boys (the recording was never released), the Fortunes, Bobby Goldsboro, Neil Diamond, the Seekers, the New Seekers, Marvin Gaye and Tammi Terrell, Freddy Cannon, Lesley Gore, Wayne Fontana and the Mindbenders, Joe Tex, and Billy Jo Royal, to name some of them that still stick in my mind.

Before Brian Epstein, the Beatles' manager, died, he and I had had several conversations regarding his group. I thought the Beatles should own a bottling company, build it up, and take a capital gain some day, meanwhile singing for Coke. Brian did not dismiss the idea. In fact, I think he liked it. But as events later showed, he had other, much sadder, priorities.

As I say, the reason I have gone into such detail about Delony Sledge and "Things Go Better with Coke" is not to blow our long-forgotten trumpets but to try to explain what it was that brought us together and held us together. That neither of us could have done it alone is obvious. As the odd couple of marketing united by the pull of an enormous idea, we produced a unique synergy that helped us overcome our inadequacies as well as the obstacles presented by the Coca-Cola Company. We had no Idea Channel to follow. We were merely outguessing Woodruff. Neither Sledge nor I had an Idea Family; we were from diverse backgrounds and separated by an age gap that was widened by a changing culture.

The idea of combining a little sugar, flavoring, caffeine, and water as a pickup is a basic idea as old and as big as the world itself. Naming and bottling that liquid over one hundred years ago, and doing it consistently ever since—and extra carefully for added confidence—made the basic idea of Coca-Cola not just a big one, but one that was beautifully executed from the start. And many years of communications executed by people who truly believed it was "the greatest taste ever invented by man . . . or God either" and that the taste of the Real Thing would make "things go better for millions of people all over the world" gave it an added value of "mystique" that grew organically from the basic idea.

At worst, what Delony and I did was merely not screw up one of history's best examples of a big basic idea that already had some fine executions. At best, we helped guide it to an identity that fit in a new era. And to do that we successfully pushed back the frontiers of marketing/advertising communications in many areas. But the credit doesn't go to us. It goes to the pull, to the fact that says the bigger the idea, the stronger the pull. Were we naïve? Maybe you have to be to get caught by the pull. For better or worse, we weren't nearly as concerned about our futures as we were with the future of America's entry in the worldwide competition for biggest and best-executed idea in the category of refreshers.

CHAPTER TWENTY-THREE

Beyond the Pull

I **HAVE NEVER** met anyone who could consistently predict whether an idea would be a hit with a large audience above and beyond normal expectations. For instance, you can put millions of dollars behind the execution of a tried-and-true basic idea like enjoying eternal childhood, and if the execution is *Peter Pan,* then normal expectations must be that the resulting film will have wide kid appeal. Beyond that, when it's on to teens and adults, you are into educated guessing, nothing more.

No one at the agency who saw the rough cuts of "Buy the World" with me would predict anything—good or bad. We all liked what we saw. So did K. V. Dey, and later on Ike Herbert. And the signal was given to go ahead, finish up the rough cut and ship a print to Europe, where the commercial was slated to make its debut. The attitude was not "We've got a hit on our hands." It was more "This is definitely something that should be given a fair chance." In other words, the priorities were still in order but now they were being dictated not so much by the pull of the idea as much as by the importance of giving every seemingly sound idea a chance.

We weren't protecting our flanks, and none of us were being influenced by Backer's Laws. Opinions were based on various assessments of the quality of the basic idea and the execution that it spawned, and the prints were shipped as soon as the opticals were in and approved.

Most of the major troubles for "Buy the World" had started the day the basic idea got shipped to England and then Italy for production onto film, and as soon as that finished film landed overseas, it would face the next of its big troubles. At home, it had, and would continue to have, the advantages of a classic Idea Channel, the head of which was a Power Who Could Say Yes with a conviction based on years of experience as a Judge plus a clear set of priorities. It also had its entire Idea Family still intact and still—in spite of all their internecine in squabbles abroad—100 percent devoted to the execution they had developed. So even though the executions were risky, because they were original and untried in the area of soft drink advertising, the environment in Atlanta and New York was still positive, the result of a meritocracy that said, "May the best ideas win," and Backer's Laws had no real effect. But none of that was true in Europe.

I have noted that the priorities in most mature companies are on monitoring the daily flow, not on ideas. At the time "Buy the World" hit Europe, the priorities of many overseas divisions of American companies, including those of the Coca-Cola Company, were not only on monitoring the flow, but on making certain the flow went through customs. By customs I don't mean customs at the country's borders, I mean customs that surround the company's walls, like "It is the custom here to discriminate against foreigners." And the customs that surrounded the divisions and protected them from foreign "interferences" included, of course, foreign ideas. And I don't mean ideas that were necessarily foreign to the local customs and cultures, but all ideas that had been originally captured and executed by foreigners. "Buy the World" certainly fell into that last category.

Technically, Idea Channels did exist and ran into someone with the power to say yes in each division. But every idea had to be stamped "approved" by customs first, so "Buy the World" didn't stand much of a chance. And its chances were made even slimmer by the fact that America's position as undisputed leader of the post-war era was beginning to be questioned in certain spots around the world. "Yankee Go Home" wasn't topping the graffiti charts in England and on the Continent yet, but that sentiment was on the rise. And why not? A new generation was beginning to move into the lower ranks of commerce, and that generation had been kids when America saved their daddies' butts on the beaches of Normandy. So Coca-Cola, that quintessential American product, probably fanned the flames of European nationalism faster and higher than other American products, even though Coke was being bottled locally.

It was perfectly natural, then, for people all over Europe to start trying to be competitive with anything and everything American and to try their hand at "doing it better." And when someone who had a high profile in the world of Coca-Cola advertising, like me, sent a piece of film over that featured a Chorus of the World singing about a wish for the future of the world, everyone in the creative departments of the overseas branches of the agency, with the full encouragement of their clients at the local divisions of the Cola-Cola Company, decided they could be the kid who shot down Jesse James.

In this environment, "Buy the World" had no chance to add to its Idea Family. It was in the hands of people who refused to get close enough to the idea to feel any pull at all.

A few weeks after the films had been shipped abroad and my mind had turned to other problems, the following scene took place in my office. As I remember, I was alone, the door was open, and Gina Gaylord strode in knocking on the open door, as she often did to get my attention. Gina, a large, handsome woman with close-cropped curly hair and a determined step, was the head of the production department reporting to me. In addition to her many duties as head of production, she also represented the agency's clients in negotiations with the New York film unions.

Ordinarily Gina would have said, "May I come in for a minute?" before barging into my office, but not today. Today she cut out the niceties and opened with, "We are in trouble." A day never went by without some sort of trouble, but the manner of her entrance caught my attention.

"What's up?" I asked.

"We can't put the Coke commercial on the air." That really got my attention.

"Why not?"

"Because it has to run overseas first."

"But we've known that all along. We just have to wait for confirmation that they have aired it in some market."

"McAllister just called me and said he had been informed that Coca-Cola Europe has said it is inappropriate for their markets. Too American."

"Those bastards. All they have to do is air it one time in one market. Nothing is so American that it can't be acceptable for one airing. Hasn't Sid pointed that out?"

"You know Sid. You can bet he has."

This was the end. After all the hopes and sweat and tension and dedication, "Buy the World" could never be aired. Not even in the U.S. of A. Let me explain why. There was a ruling in effect by the American film unions that branded all overseas production of commercials "runaway productions" unless you could prove otherwise. Very simply, runaway productions were illegal because they were seen as attempts to skirt union restrictions—which was often the case.

On the other hand, if there were an "artistic reason" for shooting abroad, such as the need to show a specific landmark like the Eiffel Tower, or a specific location like the beaches of Normandy, then overseas production was justifiable. Also, any commercial that a global company such as Coca-Cola had aired abroad was considered a "foreign commercial" and as such it had every right to be shot in a foreign country and aired in the United States. But without the "foreign commercial" label, "Buy the World" was a textbook example of a runaway production. Without proof of overseas exposure, it probably represented sixty seconds of the most expensive commercial footage ever not to run. And the cost would be ours, not theirs.

Priorities, when dictated by the goals of a bureaucracy instead of a company and its culture, keep everyone at a safe distance from the Pull of an Idea, and when there is no Idea Channel to get the idea close to even a few Judges, this is especially true. Only a company culture that represented a Meritocracy of Ideas could have saved "Buy the World." But heavily influenced by nationalism, other priorities had prevailed over the priority of "ideas first, all else second."

"Isn't there a gray area in which we might negotiate this with the unions?" I asked. Gina was beyond the Pull of the Idea itself, but still her priorities were with it. She was necessarily a member of every Idea Family in the agency. But she was also a realist. She shook her head and we just sat there looking at each other. Then a thought struck me. "Gina," I asked, "how come we can air the New York Racing Commercials?"

"Because the story line demands you shoot in England for authenticity. The opening lines are, 'There came to England three Arabian stallions.' "

"Suppose I could justify our location?" I asked.

Gina wasn't biting, but I could tell she was circling the baited hook.

"What more natural location to sing about love and harmony among all peoples than just outside of Rome?"

"How will anyone know where your group was singing? In the racehorse commercials the copy tells the audience where the location is." Gina was still nervous.

"I'll tell them in the Coke commercial, too. With written words instead of spoken ones." On a piece of yellow paper I jotted down the following words: "On a hilltop in Italy we assembled young people from all over the world to bring you a message from Coca-Cola Bottlers all over the world. It's the real thing. Coke." And I handed the paper to Gina. "Suppose we brought these words on as a crawl over the last scene?"

I knew what was going on inside Gina's head. It was the age-old war of priorities. "Who should come first—me and my future, or the idea?" Gina was a distant relative in the Idea Family. She wasn't another me or Delony Sledge ready to risk all for an idea that had us in its grasp. Her job was not to judge the efficacy of ideas, but to see that they were produced efficiently and on time. During her career, however, she had seen thousands of commercials and could easily recognize the risky ones—those that were so unconventional that clients would often doubt them after they were on the air and had received negative comments from the public, and try to get some sort of price adjustment out of Gina's department. Beyond its union problems and its already evident budget problems, Gina was fully aware that "Buy the World" fell into the category of future risks by the very nature of both its basic idea and its executional one. She was also fully aware that the unions would be more suspicious of an execution involving thousands of kids than one that involved a few horses. And she knew that win or lose, going to bat for this one would make her life tougher with the unions for months to come. She wasn't a Parent, Aunt, Godmother, or Judge. But she also knew how important getting ideas on network TV was to the company that employed her. Ideas were its lifeblood. Ideas had to get top priority. She hesitated while the classic battle of priorities, influenced on one side by Backer's Laws and on the other side by a thorough understanding of the care and feeding of ideas and their importance to the company, swirled around her head. Another thought probably crossed her mind as well. Though she reported to me, if she let this one fail she could very well end up with a new boss. Although she liked me, that fact was not a tiebreaker. I think it was the commercial in its entirety and the hopes, energy, and care that had gone into it that moved her the most. Finally she said, "Put the crawl on. We'll try it." I did, and she did, and she won. "Buy The World" broke on all three American networks some six weeks later.

As more and more companies become multinational, the problems of caring for and feeding ideas increase, especially for companies that are not in the idea business on an everyday basis. It is obvious that an idea's magnetism decreases the farther it travels from its core family. Brilliant and, ideally, multilingual Powers Who Can Say Yes at the end of an Idea Channel provide the best answer to the ever-prevalent issues of ego and turf that block the passage of ideas in companies, groups, and political organizations that circle the globe. But in my experience there are not enough of these brilliant, perceptive people trained in the care and feeding of ideas to go around. And Idea Families with the time, energy, and talent to represent their ideas in foreign countries thousands of miles from home are also very scarce. In the absence of these ideal people, it seems to me that your best bet is a company culture that says, "In this company, ideas—from whatever source—have unalienable rights, and these rights override the race, color, sex, status, and physical location of any and all members of an Idea Family."

It is pretty evident that these priorities are not in place in most multinational companies. If they were, we would see Americans rising, on occasion, to the position of a Power Who Can Say Yes in a Japanese company, and

Have a Coke, World

A creative ad director will often steal from a popular hit tune to jazz up a commercial jingle. But now comes one of the fastest-rising hits on the singles charts, "I'd Like to Teach the World to Sing (In Perfect Harmony)," which is nothing more than a spin-off of that catchy soft-drink pitch, "I'd Like to Buy the World a Coke."

"It is a universal idea," says Sid McAllister of McCann-Erickson, the agency that dreamed up the Coke song. "What the hell—that kind of idea has to appeal." That it did—far beyond anyone's expectations. Looking for a way "to get young people involved with our advertising," the admen went to Rome last fall and scoured embassies and schools for hundreds of bright-eyed, fresh-scrubbed youths of every color and nationality who would be willing to assemble on an Italian hillside and mouth the words to the newest Coke commercial as sung by a British group, the New Seekers: "I'd like to teach the world to sing in perfect harmony / I'd like to buy the world a Coke and keep it company . . . It's the real thing . . ."

Revised: The project was expensive (one McCann executive estimates the cost at $225,000), but the payoff was overwhelming. Within a month of the commercial's release on prime-time television, requests for lyrics and music were pouring into Coca-Cola bottling plants all over the country. Coke sent out sheet music and 45-rpm pressings of the jingle and asked disk jockeys to play it as part of their regular programing. When the deejays balked, the next move was obvious: excise the explicit pitch for Coke and get the creative boys at McCann to fill in substitute lines. In short order, the New Seekers were rounded up to rerecord the revised song, and a new, appropriately named group, the Hillside Singers, surfaced to serve up a country-and-Western version. By last week, the two recordings had sold a combined total of a million copies.

Both Coca-Cola and McCann-Erickson are being careful not to exploit their unexpected bonanza. The admen who collaborated on the song—creative director Bill Backer and music director Billy Davis—will turn their share of the royalties over to UNICEF, as, in all probability, will Coca-Cola. "It's nice just to have helped get such a good message out," says Davis, who is black, a former executive at Motown Records and one-time pop singer with the Four Tops. For Coca-Cola, it is even nicer to have come up with a sure-fire form of subliminal advertising—in other words, the Real Thing.

women rising to that same position in General Motors, for instance.

As more companies stretch themselves beyond borders, the top executives are going to find themselves getting there more easily and quickly if they keep looking around and behind them as well as straight ahead. Even the strongest and best ideas will run out of the energy to attract Idea Families by the time they get off the slow boat to China or the bullet train to Kyoto. Only a company culture can save them there, and that is where they will have to prevail in the years ahead.

CHAPTER TWENTY-FOUR

A Barfly Catches a Firefly

IN THE INTRODUCTION to this book I postulated a theory that "most Americans are capable of having good basic ideas." I then went on to say, "You don't have to be 'creative' in the everyday sense of the word to have good basic ideas. . . . The people you think of as 'creative types' . . . may be no better at coming up with basic ideas than engineers, accountants, or lawyers."

I can think of a lot of examples inside and outside of advertising that support this theory, but the one you will probably know the best is "Tastes Great . . . Less Filling," the campaign that ran for Miller Lite Beer for over fifteen years, and for almost all that time led the charts as the American male's all-time favorite. The basic idea for that campaign, plus the insight that gave it its first breath of life, did not come from someone in the creative ranks of the advertising business, or indeed, the creative ranks of any business. The basic "firefly" was spotted and caught in much the same manner as I had caught the idea that Coke was a catalyst for understanding between diverse peoples. Only in the case of Miller Lite, the guy who saw the spark was a research scientist, not an advertising writer.

In 1973 the Miller Brewing Company in Milwaukee had purchased a small Chicago brewery named Meister Brau. Meister Brau brewed several beers in the regular beer category and had entered one in the category of low-calorie beers, a category that would soon be judged a dumb one to enter because its first major entry, Rheingold's Gablinger, failed miserably and expensively after a promising start. Meister Brau's Lite had pretty much been a runaway failure as well. But John Murphy, then head of Miller Brewing, had learned something from Gablinger's failure that piqued his interest. Even though Gablinger's advertising had been cold, clinical, and clearly addressed to dieters, the real, two-fisted beer drinker had been willing to give the new beer a try. In fact, nearly 90 percent of the guys who drank a six-pack or more a week had tried Gablinger's—but just once. What Murphy spotted then was the basis of a big idea—a big need or desire among a large population of American men. He wasn't sure what the best way was to satisfy that need, but he was very sure he would not drop little old Lite from the ranks of brands Miller would promote in the future. The instructions to the agency were to find "the way."

The head of the agency's research department at that time, Francis Van Bortel, began to dig into the Lite numbers. They were dismal at best in almost every market but one. In Anderson, Indiana, a small steel town near the Ohio border, Lite Beer was a hit. In fact it was the number-two-selling beer in town, a town where the bars and supermarkets carried pretty much every national and regional beer, as they do in most manufacturing towns.

Van and several cohorts flew to Anderson, or the closest town that had an airport, and settled in to find out why Lite was a heavy there. Just as I had done in Shannon, they hung around the people whose needs and desires were being taken care of by Lite. Only Van did it voluntarily and in local bars, while I had been forced to do it in Shannon Airport by the bad weather in London.

What Van found out was that the steel workers were drinking Lite because it seemed to leave them less bloated. And the less bloated the belly, the more beer it can hold. The lack of calories didn't seem to attract them so much as the lack of bloat. Lite had become to them a sort of symbol, not of a feminine tendency to watch one's waistline, but rather of a real beer drinker who wanted to consume more beer than the wimps who had to pause, bloated and satiated, when the count reached two.

Any scene that involves a couple of academics from New York trying to act like one of the boys at the Hard Hat Saloon is the stuff of comedy. I wish I had been there to see it. What counts is they got back to New York unbruised and with mission accomplished.

Van and I both knew that even if a real beer drinker were to be concerned about the size of his belly, he would never admit it to his closest friend, much less to a scientific suit from the East. So we buried the calorie story and launched Lite as the symbol of the most masculine of beers—one preferred by those who would ask the beer drinkers of America, "Imagine a great-tasting bear that's less filling. What more could a man want on a long lonely night?" Of course, the alternative way of making a lonely night less lonely was a shapely blonde, and she was very much in evidence to show that even Lite had to be viewed in proportion to a man's other pleasures.

But the first executions of Van's basic idea did not emerge as simply and easily as it might appear. In fact, the basic execution, from which hundreds of others sprang up over the years, actually had no Father, just a group of Uncles who had worked together for many years, trusted one another's abilities, and understood one another's weaknesses. I said earlier that an idea, basic or executional, without a Father usually fails because the core energy and enthusiasm needed to see it to maturity are lacking. Lite Beer's original executions represent an exception to the "Father Theory." And I think the core energy really came from the TV-viewing beer drinker in the first test markets. And up to the end of the Miller Lite campaign, that energy continued to be his. It was never what I call a "boardroom" campaign. It was a populist movement in advertising and it took a long time for the Miller Brewing Company and the Cousins and Judges themselves to become enthusiastic and dub it an unqualified success.

The reason for things working out the way they did was that the original executional brainchild was conceived more out of desperation than inspiration. Everyone agreed that the basic idea was brilliant and some very sophisticated research bore out the premise. But when it came to executions that grew organically from the basic idea, we all seemed to head in different directions at first. That happens, but seldom as drastically as it did this time. The brewery wanted executions that represented traditional beer advertising with gutsy male heroes and a big "beer song." I tried my best to write a gutsy beer song for Miller Lite, but the basic "reason why," the fact that the beer was less filling, was simply too involved for lyrics. I kept telling them "If we try to sing, 'One-third less calories than their regular beer, and no carbohydrates,' we're going to take jingles back twenty years." They nodded, but I know they thought I was merely being stubborn because I had something else in mind. And maybe I was being stubborn, but I sure as heck had nothing else in mind as the months wore on. I was out of executional ideas and so was everyone else in the Idea Family. What the Idea Family finally recommended was an execution that involved a cinema verité look at the bars and people of Anderson, Indiana. But the people in Milwaukee thought that was "too artsy," and looking back I think they were right. But what they wanted was equally wrong, because it just wasn't believable.

We had meeting after meeting and failure after failure. We were working as a team with the client. We had an Idea Channel. We had everything this book says you need. We were given a second, third, fourth, and fifth chance. (Today you get three at most, and with Powers Who Can Only Say No, which is one reason why there are so few advertising campaigns that are sufficiently thought through to have real staying power. Style has triumphed over substance, and style goes out of style each season.)

We were given a *sixth* chance. But the night before I was due to fly to Milwaukee, we still had nothing. I mean zip. I was going to walk away from the game 0 for 6.

Years before, while I was at Young & Rubicam, I had created a daytime TV show called *Mother's Day*, which had a brief run on ABC. One of the junior producers in my short-lived production company (Young & Rubicam encouraged outside creative projects as long as they were not advertising projects per se) was named Gil Cates. Gil's brother, Joe Cates, had produced a legendary movie called *Safe at Home*, which told the story of a kid who ran away from home to be a batboy with the New York Yankees while they were in spring training in Florida. The actors in the film were the Yankees themselves, playing themselves. They had the time to take part in the movie because the formal baseball season had not yet commenced, and they were much cheaper as actors than as players. So the picture, which involved only one professional actor, the kid's mother, came in for peanuts and popcorn. The result was a kind of a cult hit with sports lovers (a pretty big group) and a home run at the bank. I had seen the movie and it made a big impression on me. There was something so believable about real guys playing themselves even though they were rough as actors. The roughness, or lack of slickness, only added to the believability.

At the agency that night, as I sat looking at a pile of storyboards labeled disaster, I remembered another movie I had just seen, *The French Connection*. It too starred a real-life character, but in a minor role, a tough detective named Egan who had actually figured in the real-life drug bust around which the plot of the movie revolved. He too had been entirely believable. I thought to myself, believability is a must; since the audience must really believe that this erstwhile diet beer is really the choice of the two-fisted beer drinker, why couldn't I take a page from Joe Cates's book and present a commercial starring Egan, a tough detective who would certainly drink a man's beer. I grabbed hold of someone to draw a single frame storyboard of a guy with many empty bottles of beer in front of him, swiped a catchy line from the cinema verité campaign, "Everything You Always Wanted in a Beer—and Less," and patched together a jiffy spot. I left six or eight seconds free at the end for a joke or a favorite line of Egan's. I didn't make Egan a spokesman, he merely read the message off of the label. The rest of the spot he was supposed to be talking in his own parlance. Next morning I was on the early bird to Milwaukee.

It was at best a grudging sale, under the heading of "Well, if that's the best the agency can do," but at least it was a sale. However, it turned out to be a short-lived one. The following week when the newspapers broke the story that Egan was suspected of having made off with some of the real cocaine from the real-life drug bust (he was later cleared), the campaign went back to ground zero. I was pretty shook up.

What saved the project was its Idea Family.

They were an ideal group. Like the one that had gathered around "Buy the World" they came from all walks of life, areas of the country, and ethnic backgrounds.

The one area where we lacked diversity was in our mix of sexes. In those days women drank very little beer, and inclusion of them in beer spots was rare and then they were seen only from a traditional male point of view. Otherwise we were a large assembly of diverse talents which would, over the next fifteen years, grow to be (arguably) the largest Idea Family in the history of advertising.

After the Egan fiasco nothing happened for nearly a week. Then one rainy afternoon Bob Lenz, who was soon to take over as head Uncle on the campaign, took a bus up Madison Avenue. Bob's image with the rest of us was of someone who, when criticized by senior financial management for "taking too many limousines" wrote back "there is no such thing as 'too many limousines.' " But according to legend, or at least his legend, Bob saw an ad inside this bus that featured the friendly but very masculine mug of Matt Snell, a famous linebacker recently retired from the Baltimore Colts.

The next day Bob suggested that Matt Snell succeed Egan, and the spot went back out to Milwaukee. This time, it had a gag line at the end—something like "at six foot four, two hundred fifty pounds, there's a lot of me to fill up." It was supplied, I believe, by another member of the Idea Family, either Pacey Markman or Bob Meury, and TV's longest running campaign was born—well, almost.

Our Idea Channel practically disappeared—for a variety of reasons—as we were starting to shoot the first spots. Backer's Laws took over in Milwaukee, and after the first day of shooting I got a call from a distraught account man saying the new client wanted to cancel the rest of the shoot. This time I was the one who had to authorize the agency's money to continue. That level of authority I did not have in my job description, but when Powers Who Can Say Yes are replaced by Powers Who Can Only Say No, people with blood in their veins either become revolutionaries or get out of town. In this case, I decided to stay and fight, but I don't recommend that as a standard course of action. Unless you have a basic idea you are willing to mortgage the home for, plus an Idea Family that almost never misses, it's sometimes wise to live to fight another day. But had I done that in this case, TV viewers from coast to coast would have never had the chance for an extra smile or two each night with Red Auerbach, Yogi Berra, Buck Buchanan, Nick Buoniconti, Dick Butkus, Corky Carroll, Don Carter, Wilt Chamberlain, Bob Cousy, Dave Cowens, Randy Cross, Rodney Dangerfield, Ben Davidson, Dave DeBusschere, Frank Deford, Eddie "Popeye" Egan, Gary Fencik, Whitey Ford, Joe Frazier, Boom Boom Geoffrion, L. C. Greenwood, Grits Gresham, Rosie Grier, Tommy Heinsohn, Whitey Herzog, Jim Honochick, Paul Hornung, the Jamaican Bobsled Team, LeRoy Jolley, Bert Jones, Deacon Jones, K. C. Jones, Sam Jones, Joe Klecko, Sparky Lyle, John Madden, Billy Martin, Lee Meredith, Steve Mizerak, Don Nelson, Ray Nitschke, Numazawa, Carlos Palomino, Joe Piscopo, Boog Powell, Freddie Powell, Jerry and Mike Quarry, Buddy Rich, Brooks Robinson, Frank Robinson, Mendy Rudolph, Jim Shoulders, Bubba Smith, Matt Snell, Mickey Spillane, George Steinbrenner, Marv Throneberry, Bob Uecker, Tom and Dick Van Arsdale, and many, many others. I list them to make a point. Different as they were in their backgrounds and abilities, they were all united by a solid basic idea and executions that were organic both to them as individuals and to the basic idea.

Over the years, the argument that sprang up between "Tastes Great" and "Less Filling" became one of America's favorite chants at sporting events, and the country's favorite advertising became the campaign for Miller Lite. The beer became the number-two-selling beer in America—by a huge margin over number three. Writers lined up to join the Idea Family as Uncles and have a hand at writing a Miller Lite spot. The standard got raised higher and higher, but almost all of the spots stayed true to the original executional idea of guys who were known to be rugged in real life playing themselves and being seen as true to themselves, never as shills for the product. Occasionally we gave them foils like Rodney Dangerfield, but for a good reason, not just for entertainment. The basic idea remained, "Real beer drinkers don't want to get filled up."

When I said in the introduction that "the people you think of as 'creative types' . . . are mostly in the business of executing ideas," I failed to add, "After you grab hold of a good basic idea, go out and co-opt the most talented executors you can find." The guys who wrote the hundreds of scripts for Miller Lite over the years represented the largest and best string of barroom humorists ever assembled to execute one basic advertising idea. What gets the most credit? The basic idea? The early executions that set the tone and pattern? Or the later ones that had the highest profiles? Which represents the horse and which is the carriage? As the song says, "You can't have one without the other."

CHAPTER TWENTY-FIVE

On a hilltop in Italy,
We assembled young people
From all over the world...
To bring you this message
From Coca-Cola Bottlers
All over the world,

Backer's Definition of "Creative"

"**BUY THE WORLD"** made its July air date and the first mail started arriving on the corner-office desks in Atlanta, Georgia, three days after its initial showing. By the time ten days had passed, the daily piles of letters and cards were significant enough to be called stacks. And the letters kept arriving. They were addressed to local bottlers of Coca-Cola; to The Coca-Cola Company, Atlanta (no state listed in some instances); to the President of Coca-Cola (no further address given); to Coca-Cola's Ad Agency, New York, N.Y.; and most of all just to "Coca-Cola, Atlanta."

I don't know how many ended up in the postal service's dead-letter office, but I suspect that most eventually arrived at their intended destination, forwarded by local bottlers, who tend to get anything addressed to generic "Coca-Cola" delivered to them first. The letter writers all seemed to be in a hurry to say what they felt. They seemed to assume they could scrawl any sort of address with the name Coca-Cola on it and expect it to arrive unscathed on the desks of whomsoever was responsible for putting the first United Chorus of the World on a TV screen singing, "I'd like to buy the world a home and furnish it with love." It was as if they saw the commercial and three minutes later were writing their feelings to "Coca-Cola," often with the opening lines, "I feel I have to write and say . . ."

Over 90 percent of the letters requested copies of the lyrics, and what struck me was what many of the letter writers wanted to do with the lyrics when they got them. The younger writers wanted to add—and they did—third, fourth, and fifth verses. I wish I had saved some of them. One teacher wrote a play around the theme for her high school class, and in St. Louis, it was used as part of Up With People's Sing Out program.

How many church choir directors used the music and lyrics in Sunday services at that point we never knew, but when the song broke later on we know its sheet music stimulated choral versions all over the country.

In a press interview shortly after the commercial broke, K. V. Dey said, "It's interesting that over three-fourths of those writing are under thirty, and those over thirty who write in make a special point of telling us their age."

The special point I got from K.V.'s quote was that while a nation's institutions may be in the hands of those over thirty, the stars in its eyes and its dreams for tomorrow will always reside with those who have the most tomorrows coming to them.

Large quantities of mail will often be sent to American companies after some piece of their communications has pleased, or displeased, their audience in a big way. What distinguished the mailings prompted by "Buy the World a Coke" was they kept on coming. The commercial broke all the previous rules of commercial "wear-out" to which I have ever been exposed. Many of the writers wanted to know when and where the "Buy the World" commercial would next be aired so they could be certain of seeing it again soon.

It is important to keep in mind that what stimulated the letters was not an Oscar-winning motion picture or a well-reviewed Broadway musical, but rather a bit of communication that hailed from one of this country's least-liked addresses, Madison Avenue.

How and why it turned out that way is the subject of this chapter. It is the most controversial subject I will deal with in this entire book, even more so than the Idea Channel. I have avoided it up to now because I have a normal—my assistant, Ann Silverman, tells me it is above normal—tendency to postpone really tough decisions in the hope that they will go away. But we are almost at the end of this book, and if I am going to shed any light at all on why some big ideas do better than others when executed, I have to face up to one more definition—a definition of "creative." Because if I don't define that, I can't begin to explain why one execution, such as the one for "Buy the World," is better than another even if both are organic to the same basic idea.

"Creative" is the buzzword today in every corner of the advertising world. In fact it is an operative world in defining opinions in all forms of communications—motion pictures, art, music, and so on. We have thousands of movie critics, drama critics, music critics, advertising critics, book reviewers, and entertainment reviewers using the word in verb, noun, and adjective form. In all of their areas but one I am an amateur. I read their reviews as an outsider, and like many outsiders, I am often left bewildered by the difference between what is said and what, in my own opinion, should have been said. I'd be more willing to accept the experts' opinions on what is "good" or "great" in their area of expertise if they were more willing to define "why"—what are their definitions of "great creativity," or "brilliantly creative," for instance?

In the field of advertising, however, I am an insider. At least that's where over thirty years of making a living in the advertising business should position me.

My area of expertise was labeled early on by the press "the creative side" of the business, because the agencies themselves named my department, and hundreds like it, "the creative department." That meant nothing more than "the department that houses those who create the advertising." And it still means that.

But somewhere along the way the word "creative" got separated from the verb "to create" and became something else. The press, the clients, and the judges of advertising award shows, joined by the film critics, the theater critics, and the Fern Bar Experts developed a set of unwritten, and therefore invisible, standards that they felt allowed them to say, "This particular piece of communication is more creative than that." And, armed with these invisible standards that gave them the power to say what was good, better, and best, they went on to invest the word "creativity" with a new mysterious meaning above and beyond Webster's simple definition: "the power to create." After that, they were in the catbird seat. They could award trophies for "creativity," devote column after column of press coverage to "creativity," influence fortunes of art, theater, movies, and advertising in the name of "creativity," and all in all live the happy life any group lives when it can live by its own set of unwritten laws. Certain voices in the wilderness cried out from time to time against what was happening. Bill Bernbach, one of the founders of the Doyle Dane Bernbach advertising agency, said in 1981, "Today everybody's talking creativity, and frankly, that's got me worried. I fear all the sins we may commit in the name of creativity. I fear that we may be entering an age of phonies."

And David Ogilvy, founder of the Ogilvy and Mather advertising agency, said in a much-publicized speech to the Association of National Advertisers in October 1991, "I'm supposed to be the number one creative genius in the whole wide world, and I don't even know what the hell the word 'creativity' means."

Meanwhile, the rest of the communications world has been either too cagey, too lazy, or too cowardly to step forward and offer a clear, concise definition of what they think is meant by "creativity" and "creative." And up to now I must admit I have been a happy camper in the tents of the cowards. But I can't seem to wrap up this book without pulling the tent flap back and stepping outside to where the hyenas are waiting to laugh, because I am faced with the task of explaining why some big ideas end up bigger than others. If I skip over that, I can't get to why I think "Buy the World" ended up as big as it did.

If I had the power to demand a written copy of these unwritten standards being applied to the worlds of fine arts, commercial arts, popular entertainment, and advertising, I am certain they would put their highest premium on "originality," and hinge their definitions of "creative" on one of Webster's, which is "having the quality of something created rather than imitated." But if you stick with them and this definition of Webster's, you end up, when judging two creative executions that are both organic to the same basic idea, by giving the nod to the one that is the more original. Which, of course, leads to awarding the highest contemporary honors to "art" that consists of used syringes stuck to old license plates with rhino dung, or advertising film that's no more than a succession of sight bites, each involving an image or a bit of technology never seen or used before.

I am not taking sides for or against any of the techniques described above. I am taking a stand against praising them merely because they are "original" and not "imitative." As an amateur theatergoer, I can criticize Frank Rich of *The New York Times* without the fear of reprisal that mutes many of Broadway's most successful producers, directors, and writers. I am disenchanted with reviews that feel it necessary to offer a lesson in the history of the American theater in order to prove that this or that production is or is not 100 percent original, or is imitative of something written ten years ago or staged in 1934. Broadway calls for ideas that fill a need or desire for many people, not just a few. That means big ideas. Off-Broadway is for experimental theater, where the newest of the new is to be given a chance and praised for originality first and content last. By the same token, advertising destined for network TV or national magazines with broad coverage calls for big ideas as well.

Big ideas are all about filling a large number of people's phychological or physiological needs or desires. A big idea can fill the hole in the tummy or the hole in the soul. It can satisfy a desire for something that stimulates the head or the heart. And any form of judgment or criticism that doesn't thoroughly understand this ends

Bill of Particulars.

Bill Backer. Co-founder and president of Backer & Spielvogel. Beneath a soft accent and gentle Southern ways are sharp views about advertising and the agency business. Here, from a recent conversation, are the views of the man whose thoughts and actions have long filled the bill.

On leaving home:
I had an idyllic childhood in Charleston, South Carolina. Charleston specializes in looking backward, in venerating the past. I don't denigrate that, but when you're young and you want to do something creative, you need a different environment. I left to attend Episcopal High in Alexandria, Virginia; then after the Navy, went off to Yale. Finally to New York where I've been ever since. This is the place to be if you're creative; it's where it all happens.

On how it all happened:
My first agency job was at McCann-Erickson. After three years I went to Young & Rubicam. But McCann called back with an attractive offer. So I went back to stay, or so I thought. The last few years, though, I wasn't writing, I was *meeting*. I wanted to get back to what I'm good at doing. That's making advertising, not talking about it. So I left, planning to go into the music business. I bumped into Carl Spielvogel who'd left Interpublic and—as the trade press might say—the rest is advertising history.

On goals and ideals:
At the start, Carl and I had one goal: to return to a "classic agency" where top management works at a client's business, not their own. Our personal goals? To have some fun, and make some money. We don't intend to be the largest agency in the world. We want clients with good products. We want to keep working. We don't want to become "managers." We don't try to be all things to all people. We believe that what we do, we do better than anyone. We want to keep doing it—for clients who need and want it.

On advertising and sales:
Advertising is a substitute for a salesperson, so it should be likable. You wouldn't buy from a salesperson who's rude, arrogant, insulting, would you? Americans *like* to shop and they like to buy from people they *like*. That's why we want our advertising to be the best liked in its category. Over the long term, consumers like to do business with people they like, and they respond to advertising created by people who like people.

On dressing your advertising right:
We try to dress our advertising to fit the occasion. How you dress your sales force is very important. So is how you dress your advertising. We call that *tone* and *mood*. Some clients may think that sounds arty. But it's critically important to your sales message.

On hiring and firing:
Good people are hard to find—and hiring the wrong person is worse than having no person at all. We want decent people with talent who make life exciting when they come in all revved up in the morning; self-starters who don't need prodding. Some people *need* tension and crisis. They won't like it here. When they don't work out, we tell them they don't have as bright a future here as they might somewhere else. After all, it's not a matter of who's right or wrong. The environment has to fit the person—and vice versa.

On invisible advertising:
Much advertising seems based on the theory you can beat the clutter if you only yell loud enough. There's no idea, just more noise. The result is advertising that's invisible. To beat clutter, you need advertising that isn't part of the din, advertising that works harder on the third exposure than the first. You don't get it with the boring formulas on which so much advertising is based.

On thinking and the idea:
To work, advertising needs an idea. That requires sharp thinking, about the product and the problem. Television fools advertising people by substituting glitz for ideas. We won't let a tv commercial go to a client until we've done it as a print ad. Print strips away the show business. You find out if there's an idea. With music, we won't take a jingle to a client until we've played the tune with one finger. People don't hum chords and rhythm. There have to be melodic and lyric ideas. You need ideas, in music and all forms of advertising.

On advertising as an energy business:
Advertising is described as a people business, but I believe it's an energy business. Sure, we depend on people but the differences in talent count only if you can turn on the *energy*. If you can get eighty percent of anyone's red corpuscles working, you're going to have a big edge. I don't believe you can hope to get one hundred percent of anyone's energy—most agencies get ten percent, maybe twenty percent at the most. All of us get up in the morning with just so many *ergs* in us. If eighty percent of those ergs can be applied constructively and not destructively you're going to *feel* the difference.

On The Wall Street Journal:
I've been reading The Journal for years—oh, not every story on every page, but day-in and day-out for what I think is a good reason. The Journal gives me the most unbiased news in print. I'm anti news media for the most part because too many let their biases show—and not on the editorial pages where bias belongs but in the news reporting. The Journal is remarkably free of bias; you get the facts, straight-on, with no slant. I can count on The Journal to give me the important news, the real news that matters. It's the one publication most apt to become the world's number one news source—not simply for business but for everyone who needs the news. There's no glitz to The Journal, so I wouldn't put a glitzy ad into The Journal. But if I have a good product that's made to appeal to thoughtful people, there couldn't be a better place to advertise it than The Journal. As I said, there's more than chords and rhythm to music, and to a medium. You need ideas. And nothing carries an idea like The Journal.

The Wall Street Journal.
It works.

up more influenced by the craft of "creativity" than by what has been "created," at least by Backer's Definition of "Creative":

CREATIVE IS WHATEVER MAKES MORE OUT OF LESS.

Please don't knock it till you try it.

Originality, of course, is an important factor in this equation, because if your combinations of "less" have been used before—in exactly the same way—to make a "more" that's exactly the same as one that somebody else has already made, your result will have little or no impact. After all, the earlier "more"—whether it's a song, a building, a painting, a TV commercial, a speech, a campaign line, or a tube of toothpaste—is already out there satisfying the intended need or desire. The only way to make your particular effort effective is to put money, power, and influence behind it, and muscle into and around what already exists. That is how and why many companies introduce "me-too" products. They see a way to use their superior muscle in the marketplace as a substitute for an original "more."

If you buy the above definition of "creative," then judging between various executions of the same basic idea becomes easier. Very simply,

THE EXECUTION THAT MAKES THE BASIC IDEA THE BIGGEST IS THE BEST.

By "biggest" I don't necessarily mean the one that appeals to the widest audience. In popular arts that can often be the most important criterion. But in advertising it doesn't make sense to worry about having your shaving cream commercials appeal to millions of teenage girls. What I mean by "biggest" is whatever takes the edges of the envelope that holds the basic idea and pushes these edges wider, higher, or deeper into the hearts or minds of its intended audience. That represents the execution that makes the basic idea the "biggest."

Let me say right now that my definition of "creative" is not very creative in the sense of being 100 percent original. It is, frankly, imitative of definitions of "good" that various artists and craftsmen have already used. The one I best remember is attributed to the great architect Mies van der Rohe: "Good architecture is where the whole is greater than the sum of its parts."

Let's go back now and judge two of the examples of basic and executional ideas that I used in Chapter 2, Hopper's paintings of loneliness and a song from what I call Irving Berlin's "loneliness trio," "All by Myself." The basic need or desire to be fulfilled was the same, and the period in which this need or desire was felt is the same. But the audience is different for each, because the medium, and therefore the price and availability of the executions, varies markedly. So I am not going to compare one to another, but rather to the basic idea itself.

In Chapter 2, I pointed out that the 1920s was a time of acute loneliness in America. Hopper and Berlin somehow saw the same perceived desire or need, and that resulted in the same basic idea: "People who are alone and lonely in the world want to feel that someone out there shares their agony and understands it." And Hopper and Berlin both came up with the same abstract answer: "Make loneliness a theme in painting or song."

I discussed the specifics of their various executions in Chapter 2, but I didn't attempt to answer whether or not the executions were "creative" and, if so, "how creative." I know I'm about to step on the toes of every art and music critic from New York to San Francisco, but since I never had to fight their bull, I can play matador in their arena without a real sword or cape. At the end of this chapter, when I try to explain the success of "Buy the World," my peers in the advertising field will have a go at me, I'm sure.

But right now, I am going to start out furthest from my field of expertise, and tackle the creativity of Hopper's paintings using my definition and rules for judging.

Unquestionably Hopper made the basic idea bigger than it was then or is today. I don't think he did this, however, by making it broader or higher. "Broader" would be extending the understanding and shared feelings of loneliness beyond dispossessed white Anglo-Saxons. "Higher," it seems to me, would have been to politicize his paintings as the Depression painters would do fifteen years later, a goal that Hopper insisted he never intended to pursue. I think the way Hopper made the basic idea bigger was to "deepen" it. He pushed the intensity of the feeling of loneliness deeper than any American painter ever did before or since.

My observations on how he did this are not original, merely apt. And certainly oversimplified. What Hopper did was to illustrate how alone his people were by putting them in settings that were ordinarily full of people and then removing all but one—his specific one. Hopper's people are in New York, the largest city in America, but nobody else is there. Nobody. They are more intensely alone than the basic idea of "make loneliness a theme in painting" cries out for. The edges of its envelope have been severed.

Removing all other people wasn't the only element that Hopper used, but it was the most effective. I don't know whether or not it was original. By my definition it doesn't matter. What matters was that the totality of his creative executions—the combination of "lesses," if you will—made the basic idea bigger by making it go deeper. *He made less into more*, and in doing so he created a new—and therefore original—depth of feeling for the loneliness of a specific group of people. That's creative, in my book.

By the same analysis, Irving Berlin made the envelope both wider and deeper. Wider because he painted a picture with words, notes, and a rhythm in which every listener who was lonely and approaching the sunset years could see herself or himself. No one is excluded, except, perhaps, those too young to see that far into the future. The word picture, as I pointed out in Chapter 2, is actually of Berlin's mother, who was then in her fifties, but the scene is broad enough to be anyone, of any sex, color, or creed, who is nearing, or is already in the age of what we now call a senior citizen. Berlin's person, unlike Hopper's, isn't alone because he or she lacks a *world* around them that cares and tries to understand. Berlin's person lacks just *one other person*—someone with whom to share a life.

So his lyrics go:

All by myself in the morning
All by myself in the night
I sit alone with a table and chair
So unhappy there
Playing solitaire
All by myself I get lonely
Watching the clock on the shelf—

At this point the lyrics, the notes, and the rhythm pattern come together to make "All by Myself" the most intense loneliness song ever written for anyone over forty:

I'd love to rest my weary head
On somebody's shoulder
I hate to grow older
All by myself.

'Nuff said.

Now, how come "Buy the World a Coke" ended up a classic in its particular field? We have to go back to the basic idea (as described in Chapter 1): "To see Coke not as it was originally designed to be—a liquid refresher—but as a tiny bit of commonality between all peoples, a universally liked formula that would help them keep each other company for a few minutes."

How can you get any bigger than "all peoples keeping each other company over Coke"? In a literal sense you can't make an idea bigger than "all peoples," but you can give it extra depth and height.

To begin with, it is very difficult to achieve intense depth of feeling when you are asking an individual to identify with "all peoples." That same person has a similar difficulty when he or she goes to vote. He just can't seem to approach the horror of an administration and a group of congressmen whose lax oversight has allowed S&L's to overdraw America's bank account by well over five hundred billion dollars with the same intensity of feeling he or she summons up over the fact that some of that same group of congressmen have overdrawn their individual bank accounts by a few thousand dollars. When the game is one-on-one, Americans can feel for or against each player with a high degree of intensity. But we have shown a marked inability to become emotionally involved with people in the abstract millions or billions.

So when the lyrics of "Buy the World" reduced "all peoples" to a family of people small enough to live in one house, the basic idea gathered intensity of feeling. And when what was wished for the family of man went well beyond a bottle of pop all the way to the basics of life for everyone, such as a house full of love, sufficient food, and above all harmony with one another, a certain height was added to the basic idea, which saw the family of man merely sitting together with a bottle of Coca-Cola.

And later on, what Harvey Gabor did when he translated the "I" of "I'd like to build the world a home" into a chorus of hundreds of "I"s was to increase the intensity by that amount. He and I called it a United Chorus of the World, but actually it wasn't a chorus in the conventional sense of the word. It wasn't the usual group united by a common background, such as a central school or single chorus master, and it wasn't united by dress or sex or religion. It was actually a thousand different voices, each with different background, race, color, creed, and country of origin, united by a common wish—that everyone in this world could have a secure home full of love, good food, worldwide harmony, and, of course, the daily pleasure of keeping each other company over their favorite refreshment, Coca-Cola. In that sense it was a chorus of a hundred "I"s wishing the same wish.

The envelope that contained the basic idea was definitely stretched by the executions in song and pictures. But were any of the individual elements "firsts"? Some were. It was the first United Chorus of the World. But the music it sang and the parlance of the lyrics were both in genres that had been around for years. The camera work broke no new ground, nor did the director, if there was one in the strict sense of the word. But none of that mattered to the people of America, and, later, of the world. They felt both the extra heights and depths that the executions had added to the basic idea. So "Buy the World a Coke" ended up as the most awarded and lauded commercial of the year in America. It was called "great," "brilliant," and "creative" over and over again. But nobody that I can remember ever said what they meant by all those adjectives. And I certainly didn't know. All I can say now is that the executions made a big basic idea bigger than it started out to be—much bigger. They made *less into more*. By definition, my definition at least, they were truly "creative."

CHAPTER TWENTY-SIX

One Last Idea

THE STORY OF "I'd Like to Teach the World to Sing," which was the the song version of "I'd Like to Buy the World a Coke," probably belongs in Chapter 13, where we talk about extending an execution. However, it fits here chronologically, and since the question most people have asked me over the years is, "Which came first, the song or the commercial?" the story of how the song came to be will come here, after the commercial has been aired, because that's where it occurred.

The song represented a further extension of the basic idea. Its success also provided the energy that finally brought the commercial to Europe and the rest of the world. Without the song, the commercial would never have been selected to run globally the way it did, certainly not in the United Kingdom or in most of the countries on the Continent.

Shortly after the commercial broke in America, Billy Davis came to me and said the New Seekers were in New York for a few days and he had a thought that if I could change and extend the basic execution to a song form, he could get them to record it. Where would the money come from? From Billy and me. The New Seekers' recording company did not have sufficient confidence in the idea. Once again, we had to be the Keepers of the Faith.

Time was of the essence. Billy needed to bring the song to the New Seekers in a few days. I had already written the lyrics for a "song version" for a group formed for the purpose of recording the song and called, appropriately, the Hillside Singers. Bill brought those lyrics to the New Seekers. Very simply they replaced Coke with a hug, explained the United Chorus of the World and added a final wish—for peace. The final lyrics for the song were:

I'd like to build the world a home
And furnish it with love
Grow apple trees and honey bees
And snow white turtle doves
I'd like to teach the world to sing

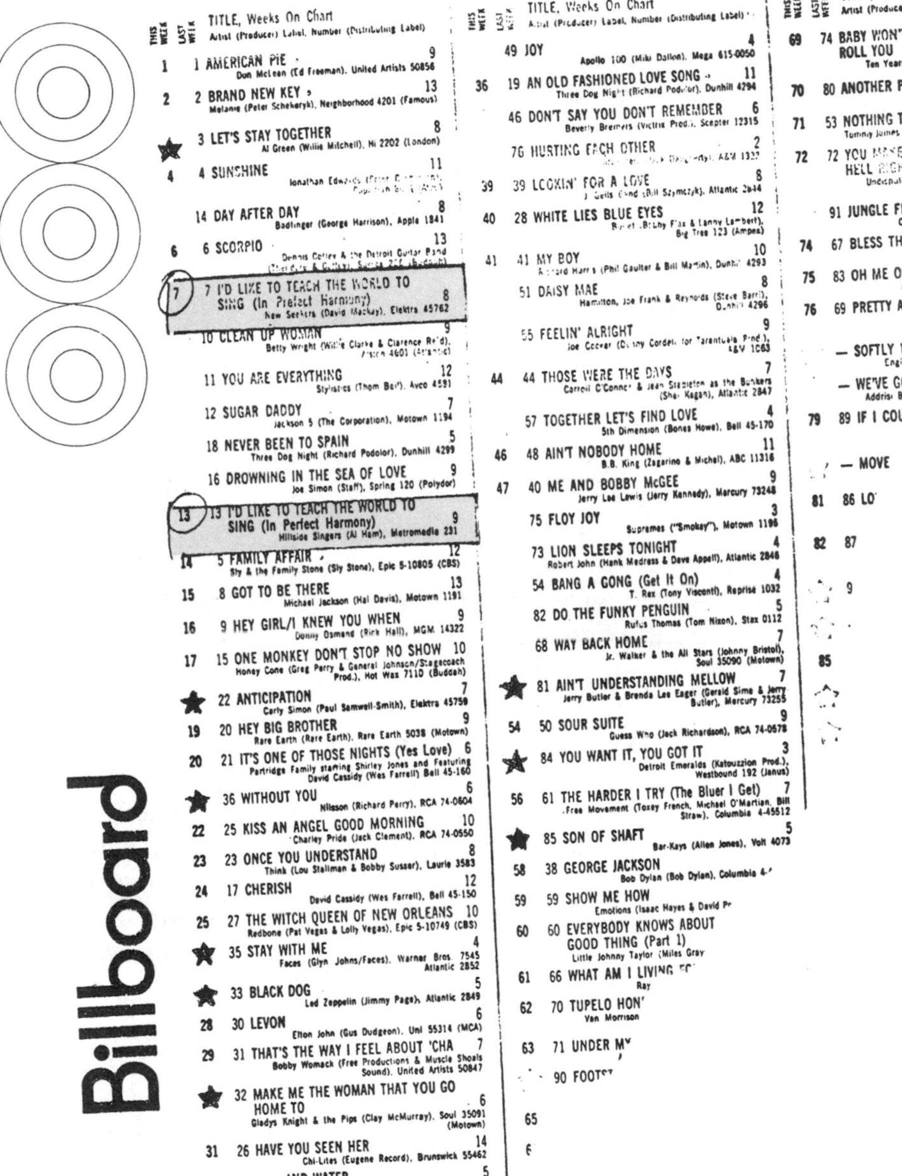

THIS WEEK	LAST WEEK	TITLE, Weeks On Chart / Artist (Producer) Label, Number (Distributing Label)	
1	1	AMERICAN PIE — Don McLean (Ed Freeman), United Artists 50856	9
2	2	BRAND NEW KEY — Melanie (Peter Schekeryk), Neighborhood 4201 (Famous)	13
★	3	LET'S STAY TOGETHER — Al Green (Willie Mitchell), Hi 2202 (London)	8
4	4	SUNSHINE — Jonathan Edwards [illegible]	11
	14	DAY AFTER DAY — Badfinger (George Harrison), Apple 1841	8
6	6	SCORPIO — Dennis Coffey & the Detroit Guitar Band [illegible]	13
7	7	I'D LIKE TO TEACH THE WORLD TO SING (In Prefect Harmony) — New Seekers (David Mackay), Elektra 45762	8
	10	CLEAN UP WOMAN — Betty Wright (Willie Clarke & Clarence Reid), Alston 4601 (Atlantic)	9
	11	YOU ARE EVERYTHING — Stylistics (Thom Bell), Avco 4591	12
	12	SUGAR DADDY — Jackson 5 (The Corporation), Motown 1194	7
	18	NEVER BEEN TO SPAIN — Three Dog Night (Richard Podolor), Dunhill 4299	5
	16	DROWNING IN THE SEA OF LOVE — Joe Simon (Staff), Spring 120 (Polydor)	9
13	13	I'D LIKE TO TEACH THE WORLD TO SING (In Perfect Harmony) — Hillside Singers (Al Ham), Metromedia 231	9
14	5	FAMILY AFFAIR — Sly & the Family Stone (Sly Stone), Epic 5-10805 (CBS)	12
15	8	GOT TO BE THERE — Michael Jackson (Hal Davis), Motown 1191	13
16	9	HEY GIRL/I KNEW YOU WHEN — Donny Osmond (Rick Hall), MGM 14322	9
17	15	ONE MONKEY DON'T STOP NO SHOW — Honey Cone (Greg Perry & General Johnson/Stagecoach Prod.), Hot Wax 7110 (Buddah)	10
★	22	ANTICIPATION — Carly Simon (Paul Samwell-Smith), Elektra 45759	7
19	20	HEY BIG BROTHER — Rare Earth (Rare Earth), Rare Earth 5038 (Motown)	9
20	21	IT'S ONE OF THOSE NIGHTS (Yes Love) — Partridge Family starring Shirley Jones and Featuring David Cassidy (Wes Farrell) Bell 45-160	6
★	36	WITHOUT YOU — Nilsson (Richard Perry), RCA 74-0604	6
22	25	KISS AN ANGEL GOOD MORNING — Charley Pride (Jack Clement), RCA 74-0550	10
23	23	ONCE YOU UNDERSTAND — Think (Lou Stallman & Bobby Susser), Laurie 3583	8
24	17	CHERISH — David Cassidy (Wes Farrell), Bell 45-150	12
25	27	THE WITCH QUEEN OF NEW ORLEANS — Redbone (Pat Vegas & Lolly Vegas), Epic 5-10749 (CBS)	10
★	35	STAY WITH ME — Faces (Glyn Johns/Faces), Warner Bros. 7545 Atlantic 2852	4
★	33	BLACK DOG — Led Zeppelin (Jimmy Page), Atlantic 2849	5
28	30	LEVON — Elton John (Gus Dudgeon), Uni 55314 (MCA)	6
29	31	THAT'S THE WAY I FEEL ABOUT 'CHA — Bobby Womack (Free Productions & Muscle Shoals Sound), United Artists 50847	7
★	32	MAKE ME THE WOMAN THAT YOU GO HOME TO — Gladys Knight & the Pips (Clay McMurray), Soul 35091 (Motown)	6
31	26	HAVE YOU SEEN HER — Chi-Lites (Eugene Record), Brunswick 55462	14
		...ND WATER	5
	49	JOY — Apollo 100 (Miki Dallon), Mega 615-0050	4
36	19	AN OLD FASHIONED LOVE SONG — Three Dog Night (Richard Podolor), Dunhill 4294	11
	46	DON'T SAY YOU DON'T REMEMBER — Beverly Bremers (Victrix Prod.), Scepter 12315	6
	76	HURTING EACH OTHER — [illegible] A&M 1322	2
39	39	LOOKIN' FOR A LOVE — J. Geils Band (Bill Szymczyk), Atlantic 2844	8
40	28	WHITE LIES BLUE EYES — Bullet (Bobby Flax & Lanny Lambert), Big Tree 123 (Ampex)	12
41	41	MY BOY — Richard Harris (Phil Gaulter & Bill Martin), Dunhill 4293	10
	51	DAISY MAE — Hamilton, Joe Frank & Reynolds (Steve Barri), Dunhill 4296	8
	55	FEELIN' ALRIGHT — Joe Cocker (Denny Cordell for Tarantula Prod.), A&M 1063	9
44	44	THOSE WERE THE DAYS — Carroll O'Connor & Jean Stapleton as the Bunkers (Shel Kagan), Atlantic 2847	7
	57	TOGETHER LET'S FIND LOVE — 5th Dimension (Bones Howe), Bell 45-170	4
46	48	AIN'T NOBODY HOME — B.B. King (Zagarino & Michel), ABC 11316	11
47	40	ME AND BOBBY McGEE — Jerry Lee Lewis (Jerry Kennedy), Mercury 73248	9
	75	FLOY JOY — Supremes ("Smokey"), Motown 1195	3
	73	LION SLEEPS TONIGHT — Robert John (Hank Medress & Dave Appell), Atlantic 2846	4
	54	BANG A GONG (Get It On) — T. Rex (Tony Visconti), Reprise 1032	4
	82	DO THE FUNKY PENGUIN — Rufus Thomas (Tom Nixon), Stax 0112	5
	68	WAY BACK HOME — Jr. Walker & the All Stars (Johnny Bristol), Soul 35090 (Motown)	7
★	81	AIN'T UNDERSTANDING MELLOW — Jerry Butler & Brenda Lee Eager (Gerald Sims & Jerry Butler), Mercury 73255	7
54	50	SOUR SUITE — Guess Who (Jack Richardson), RCA 74-0578	9
★	84	YOU WANT IT, YOU GOT IT — Detroit Emeralds (Katouzzion Prod.), Westbound 192 (Janus)	3
56	61	THE HARDER I TRY (The Bluer I Get) — Free Movement (Toxey French, Michael O'Martian, Bill Straw), Columbia 4-45512	7
★	85	SON OF SHAFT — Bar-Kays (Allen Jones), Volt 4073	5
58	38	GEORGE JACKSON — Bob Dylan (Bob Dylan), Columbia 4-	
59	59	SHOW ME HOW — Emotions (Isaac Hayes & David P	
60	60	EVERYBODY KNOWS ABOUT GOOD THING (Part 1) — Little Johnny Taylor (Miles Gray	
61	66	WHAT AM I LIVING F — Ray	
62	70	TUPELO HON — Van Morrison	
63	71	UNDER M	
	90	FOOT	
65			
6			
69	74	BABY WON'T YOU LE ROLL YOU — Ten Years After (Chri	
70	80	ANOTHER PUFF — Jerry Reed	
71	53	NOTHING TO HIDE — Tommy James (Tommy Jame	
72	72	YOU [illegible] HELL [illegible] — Undisputed Truth (No	
	91	JUNGLE FEVER — Chakachas (R	
74	67	BLESS THE BEAST — Carpenters	
75	83	OH ME OH MY — Aretha Frankl	
76	69	PRETTY AS YOU FE — Jefferson A	
	—	SOFTLY WHISPE — English Co	
	—	WE'VE GOT T — Addrisi Broth	
79	89	IF I COUL	
	—	MOVE	
81	86	LO	
82	87		
	9		
85			

bottle of pop as a catalyst for world understanding was, they implied, in questionable taste.

I myself dislike and fear many things in advertising—more so today than in the 1970s. And at the top of the list is misapplied emotions. When I turn on my TV set and see giant public corporations with millions of stockholders claiming to be motivated by

In perfect harmony
I'd like to hold it in my arms
And keep it company
I'd like to see the world for once
All standing hand in hand
And hear them echo through the hills
For peace throughout the land

That's the song I sing
What the world wants today
A song of peace that echoes on
And never goes away

The result was a pop song that went top ten all over the world, earned a platinum record, and was recorded by many other singers of the day.

More important to Billy and me was how and where it finally ended up—being sung by church and school choirs in many parts of the country. In other words, the song originally started by the first United Chorus of the World ended up being sung by choruses in churchs and schools all over America. The execution of the song, then, added a lot of extra height to the basic idea and left a spark of pride in the original Idea Family that remains today.

For the Coca-Cola Company, the song added something else. The sheer energy generated by its worldwide success forced the local Coca-Cola Companies around the world to temporarily reexamine their priorities. If the populace of your country—the folks who will be buying and drinking your product—are paying good money for a recording of a song, it's pretty hard to say they will find it "too American" or "too sentimental" or "in bad taste" when they are hearing it for free through a commercial. The united will of the people will win out over a united bureaucracy every time, but time is what it takes to make the Berlin Walls come tumbling down.

Before the song reached the peak of its popularity, however, the flow monitors on the other side of the Atlantic put up one last-ditch stand. It was started by a negative review of "Buy the World" in *Campaign* magazine, a widely read trade publication in England. The criticism was not about whether "Buy the World" was, or was not, effective advertising. It was about "taste." The British felt we had gone too far. Coca-Cola, they argued, had no right to put itself on such a lofty pedestal, at least not in Europe. Presenting a little public welfare rather than private profit, and further pretending to have a human heart that loves eleemosynary causes instead of the cause of self-interest, I writhe. America expects businesses to base their decisions on logic, not emotion. Corporations exist to provide products and services that fill basic needs or desires—in other words, that have a worthy basic idea. And executions that make something more out of that basic idea instead of diminishing it will be in good taste.

On the other hand, any execution from any group that degrades the spirit of the people whose needs or desires it is trying to serve is to my way of thinking in bad taste.

Movies, plays, books, and songs that attempt to shed new light on liars, cheaters, philanderers, and families who hate one another have a basic idea that they try to illuminate with an execution. But if the public doesn't buy it, they can avoid it. Advertising that uses paid-for media to force its messages on people, however, makes less out of less when it deploys stereotypes that are mean-spirited and diminish respect for the human race.

More and more American companies seem willing to degrade the American spirit in order to sell their products. If a spaghetti sauce—in blind taste tests—really tastes as good as homemade, I am happy to buy the proposition and promote it with executions that have a high degree of involvement. But when I see commercials that show the daughter-in-law deceiving the mother-in-law by claiming that she made the sauce with her own little hands, I get depressed. Because in my book that is bad taste. The same goes for devices European advertisers keep finding so convenient—extramarital affairs, unhappy families, nagging wives, and evil little children. When the basic idea is about the needs or desires that a bowl of porridge will take care of, those devices make less out of less, not more.

I have always been suspicious of people who are so sure they know what good taste is that they try to impose theirs on everyone else. But I also lose respect for people who are so insecure about their sense of taste that they will snuggle up to someone else's.

I won't try and impose my taste on you. I will only point out that while the basic idea was rooted in a desire to sell more Coca-Cola by adding extra value to the product beyond sensory satisfaction, it was nonetheless TRUE. The world can keep company with almost everyone over a bottle of Coke.

And if, while wishing for that, the Coca-Cola Company expands the basic idea with compassionate wishes for world peace and prosperity, doesn't that compassion also represent an honest wish for any worldwide company to make if it sells a worldwide product to the people? Peace and prosperity are as good for the Coca-Cola Company as they are for the individual.

As it turned out, the Idea Family in America didn't have to argue any of the above. The song made the opening argument in Europe and after that the commercial spoke for itself. Whether or not it had the same impact around the rest of the world that it had in the United States we would never be allowed to know. Back home you could see on a sales curve the effect that the combination of the commercial and the song had on sales. Overseas, at least at that time, it was more difficult for Coca-Cola USA to get unbiased sales reports than at home. All I know is that the orders for prints kept pouring in for more and more countries. There were also a few requests for us to tinker with the footage. The office in South Africa, for instance, asked me if I could cut a version with no blacks in it. I said I could but I wouldn't. I knew from where I sat that if I took sides politically I would lose, so I simply stood behind the idea itself and explained it was not about building the white world a home, but building a home for the whole world.

Four Versions of Hit In Cola Push

By RITCHIE YORKE

TORONTO—A unique promotion launched here by Coca-Cola, Ltd., is bringing new attention to the current hit, "I'd Like to Teach the World to Sing (In Perfect Harmony)."

Coke, through its advertising agency, McCann-Erikson, has recorded four separate versions of the song on two disks, which are being distributed as a premium offer.

A reported 110,000 copies of a soul version by Doctor Music and a version by the Laurie Bower Singers have been pressed. A similar number of copies of two different versions in French by Donald Loutrec, the leading Canadian pop star, have been prepared. The French renditions are titled "Terre d'Amour."

Peter Clayton, Coca-Cola account executive at McCann-Erickson produced the English disk. It also contains the original Coke commercial whence the song came. Copies of the disks are offered for cap liners or ring-pulls from cans of Coca-Cola.

The promotion is being backed with media campaigns, which incorporates leading AM stations in each market.

Seven years ago, Coca-Cola initiated a premium rock album, "A Wild Pear" which was responsible for bringing together the talents of producer Jack Richardson and members of the Guess Who for the first time.

The other day a friend of mine told me he had heard his six-year-old daughter singing "I'd Like to Teach the World to Sing," and he asked her where she had heard it. She replied, "We sing it at school. It's one of our happy songs." I find that depressing.

"I'd Like to Teach the World to Sing" is a song about wishes for a happy tomorrow. I think six-year-olds should have happy songs that sing about a happy today—songs about having a mother and father who love them, enjoying a happy home, being surrounded by gentle people they can lean on, getting rid of gloom, and feeling the skies are shining bluer just for them. I realize they have a few such songs courtesy of Sesame Street, Raffi, and Sharon, and others. But the songs from the adult world that they might share with their parents are not about a happy today, as they often were when the country was younger and hopes were higher (and when times were actually tougher). Songs like "Home Sweet Home," "Dear Hearts and Gentle People," "If I Knew You Were Comin'," "The Pessimistic Character (With the Crab Apple Face)," "High Hopes," and "Blue Skies" tend to sound pretty dumb today. And I am afraid that even if the best contemporary songwriters rewrote them, the ideas they are based on would not be given a chance. The real needs and desires they address have been buried beneath so many layers of cynicism that you can't awaken them, even with the best executions. After all, people today are likely to ask: "What's so sweet about home?" "Aren't gentle people a myth or, worse yet, stupid?" "Aren't pessimists more often right than wrong?" The problem, then, is probably more content than style. And, as I say, I find that depressing. Because, whether it's content or style, the cynic files away most adult happy songs, probably under "sloppy sentimentality." And I wonder how long my friend's daughter will sing "I'd Like to Teach the World to Sing" before she too becomes cynical and thinks its wishes are too good to ring true and are therefore sentimental or, maybe worse, dumb. Will that come when she's eight? Or nine?

If any of the wishes in "I'd Like to Teach The World to Sing" are going to become reality before the song is relegated to "sloppy sentimentality" (I'm surprised it's lasted this long) by some future class of six-year-olds, I would suggest we're going to need a lot of good basic ideas about how to make the world a happier place and those basic ideas will need to get cared for and nourished to successful maturities by some pretty creative executions.

The fireflies are out there, but they need to be seen and handled with care. They're going to need Idea Families who can not only keep the faith, but who, right at the beginning, understand the difference between a basic and an executional idea. They're going to need Idea Channels headed by Powers Who Can Say Yes who surround themselves with people chosen on their merit, plus a corporate culture outlined by people at the top who understand the dangers of bureaucracy and the negative pull of Backer's Laws of Corporate Gravity.

Although you now know how to identify most of the standard

obstacles ideas will face along the way, I have made no attempt to identify which of the many fireflies you might try capturing. The ones that light up the needs or desires of the people you serve in order to earn your daily bread are easy for you to identify. But only you can prioritize them. They are too specialized to use as subjects for the mythical idea loop I wish to set up for this book's final exercise. So we'll look to tackle a problem in some more generalized area.

When we go beyond commerce to the needs or desires of America or the world as a whole, the subject of determining which firefly is the most important to try to capture first becomes one for another book. And that book should be written by someone who has honed his or her vision, philosophy, and conscience by spending most of his time thinking about, and trying to solve, the problems and ills of society itself. I am not eligible to be included in that list. So as we near the end of this book, and I suggest a huge need or desire to practice your newfound skills on, you should remember the limitations of my background.

The professionals who write daily about America's most urgent needs or desires seem to identify the following as those that need our attention first: education, jobs, the family, the deficit, competitiveness. I have not attempted to list the above in any order of priority, but those six seem to me to be the top six, and I am going to choose from that list.

I feel like a quiz show contestant. I'll choose the category of "Education and Jobs."

The reason I chose that category is I already have a basic idea that falls in it. The firefly lit up some years ago in a location similar to the one where the basic ideas of "Buy the World" occurred—in an airport, but not Shannon. I can't remember which airport, but it was probably La Guardia. I do remember I was reading one of the news magazines and suddenly an article hit me—hard. It was about some companies in the Midwest who couldn't fill their job requirements because the applicants, though high school graduates, couldn't read well enough. So the companies were running courses in remedial reading. I felt the hair on the back of my neck rising. Here we are, a country desperate to have our companies become competitive with those of Japan and Germany, and yet we ask them to allocate and channel their stretched resources into remedial reading courses. We can't even deliver to them high school graduates who can read.

"I'D LIKE TO TEACH the world to sing," a record based on Coca-Cola's "I'd like to buy the world a Coke" jingle, has made No. 26 on Billboard's Top 50 hit tune chart, and sold 500,000 copies. The artists are the Hillside Singers, and the song has been produced on Metromedia Records by Al Ham, also a broadcast commercial music producer. Also rising: The New Seekers' version on Elektra Records (they also sing the original jingle), now No. 28 . . .

Coke Record

If you've been enjoying the new Coke commercial that has those young people from many lands on an Italian hillside singing "I Want to Buy the World a Coke," you haven't been alone.

Coca-Cola reports that its company headquarters has received 3,000 letters about it, which it says is the most mail it has ever received on one subject. So Coke has had a London group record the number and records will soon be shipped to bottlers for local distribution. If you can't wait, Coca-Cola will send you sheet music.

BILLY DAVIS MCCANN ERIKSON
485 LEXINGTO NAVENUE
NEW YORK

NEW SEEKERS NUMBER ONE BBC CHART STOP SOLD 95000 COPIES
UK YESTERDAY TOTAL SALES UK APPROACHING HALF A MILLION ALREADY
STOP THANK YOU KINDEST REGARDS
KEITH AND DAVID

Somebody had better have some ideas in this area that are drastically different from those that have failed so miserably.

BASIC IDEA: Reconceptualize "reading" not as one of the list of subjects taught as part of an EDUCATION—not even as one of the three R's of readin', 'riting, and 'rithmatic—but as a subject apart from all the rest. See "reading" as the most important element in PREPARATION, as opposed to EDUCATION.

EXECUTIONS: (a) Rename what we now call "education" as far as the first through the fifth grades. Instead identify it as what it should be called, "preparation."

(b) Press certain schools to specialize in preparation, that is, preparation for the pursuit of happiness and respect through having a job, and view education as an attainable goal for anyone who can read. (c) Encourage these schools to introduce the written word as the key to everything that is fun and exciting to kids. For instance, make words and sentences a part of a host of new interactive video games created by the world's great game experts, like Nintendo, in concert with experts in the art or science of teaching the young to read. The following words might flash on the screen: "Avoid the Red Planes," "Follow the Blue Pac Man," "The Cat Is Your Friend," and they would not take the fun out of the hand-to-eye-contact that kids find so tantalizing. But you'd get zapped if you couldn't read. (d) Encourage the "preparation schools" to treat the written word the way Berlitz treats a foreign language, i.e., you must speak it to get along in your class. Only in preparation schools almost nothing would be spoken but pleasantries. Instead, everything would be written, so you'd

better learn to read. What is read can run the gamut from simple stories to history to lyrics to instruction manuals on how to assemble toys for the class. (e) Encourage local businesses to promote reading contests instead of spelling bees. Local restaurants should have "reading days" on which any child who can read every word on a specially prepared menu gets a free meal. (f) Because most educators agree that children whose parents read to them have a permanent advantage over other children, local TV stations would be encouraged to substitute "It's nine o'clock, have you read your child a story yet?" for "It's nine o'clock, do you know where your child is?"

Obviously, what I am doing is taking reading out of the politics of education and putting it first among equals. There are so many fingers being pointed today at our system of education, which manages to turn out high school graduates who can't read a basic sentence, that I am not about to single out just one reason why the system has broken down. But anyone who has ever put together anything, from an advertisement to an organizational structure, knows that by emphasizing every thought equally you ensure failure. One has to have the insight and the guts to set priorities. Maybe we should have the insight, or basic idea, to say that "preparation" comes before "education" and jobs come before the history of art.

Even at the college level there is no agreement on what constitutes an education. Professors at my well-regarded Ivy League college told me, "What we are trying to do is give students the basics of an education so they can educate themselves over the years." In other words, after we had spent four years and a great many dollars, they were not willing to stamp us "educated," merely "literate" and "grounded in the basics."

Obviously, the executions I have suggested for the basic idea concerning jobs and education are in areas where I have no practical expertise. But since I wrote this, I note that certain software companies have begun to develop software along the lines I have suggested. The executional idea has friends already.

I told you at the start that "this book does not guarantee to make you head of sales or ultimately CEO of your company." But I did promise the following:

> On the way to becoming head of your engineering group or even CEO of your company, or on the way to creating advertising for new products, you are going to need ideas, either yours or somebody else's, and you are going to have to be part of either the team that executes them or the team that judges them, or you are going to have to help pull the process together so that the ideas get marketed. And then you are going to have to exploit the power of those ideas once they begin to be successful.
>
> This book will help you do all of the above.
>
> After reading it, your opinions of your own ideas or someone else's will not only be more soundly based than before, but you will also be better able to articulate them in a manner that others can understand and respect. And your insights on basic ideas and what to do with them will be equally sensitive and thoughtful whether you are looking at five lines of poetry, hearing some lyrics sung to a folk melody, or deciphering the design for a revolution-

ary new valve. You will understand that behind them all must be an idea that fills somebody's need for something. If that need is shared by a whole lot of people, so much the better.

So whether you are the Father or Mother of a basic idea, an Uncle or Aunt who helps it grow with executions, a Godfather who moves it along, a Judge who says, "That's good or that's bad," or a Power Who Can Say Yes, (or No, if necessary)—whoever you are in your next idea loop—you should find that you represent a stronger, more secure link. Because you have been exposed to a number of theories—most of them proven in practice—about how to feed and care for ideas so that they can reach a useful maturity. You now know something about looking for the spark of a firefly and what to do when you catch it. If you are an Uncle or Aunt, you know enough to look at your executional ideas and ask yourself, "Is my execution organic to the basic idea, or is it an ego trip to the land of new techniques?" Or if you find yourself as a Godfather, you now know the risks, the tricks, the pitfalls, and the ethics of that game. If you are in an organization that needs a supply of ideas to keep it competitive—and what organization doesn't?—you now know the value of Idea Channels in keeping ideas alive and well and in avoiding bureaucracy and Backer's Law of Corporate Gravity. You know what it takes to be a successful Power Who Can Say Yes, and you know the necessity of maintaining 360-degree vision if you ever get to the very top.

While all that was not backed specifically by a money-back guarantee, I want you to know it is backed by a pretty impressive cast of Uncles, Aunts, and Judges. I would like to thank them all, and say to you on behalf of each of us, that if just one idea can come out of this book, get cared for and nourished to maturity with the help of what has been said here, and finally be big enough to make a difference, then the hours spent devoted to writing, judging, reviewing, and rewriting will have been well spent.

THE CAST

(in order of appearance)

Mike Cohn (agent)	Godfather
Bill Backer (author)	Father
Ann Nita Silverman (scribe)	Aunt
Paul Golob (editor)	Uncle and Judge
Ann Backer (consulting editor)	Judge
Al Scully (authenticator)	Idea Family Member and Judge
Sid McAllister (authenticator)	Idea Family Member and Judge
Billy Davis (authenticator)	Idea Family Member
Phil Messina (authenticator)	Idea Family Member
Robbin Schiff (jacket design)	Aunt

Additional material authenticated by Joe Brooks and Bob Cox, special acknowledgment to Mark Morris for initial encouragement, and special thanks to Carl Spielvogel for continued understanding and patience.

PERMISSIONS ACKNOWLEDGMENTS

Grateful acknowledgment is made to the following for permission to reprint previously published material:

BPI Communications: Excerpt from the Top Single Chart that appeared in the January 22, 1972, issue of *Billboard*. Copyright © 1972 by BPI Communications. Reprinted by permission of *Billboard*.

Coca-Cola USA, a division of The Coca-Cola Company: Excerpts from Coca-Cola advertising campaigns, "Coke," "Coca-Cola" and the Dynamic Ribbon device are trademarks of The Coca-Cola Company. Permission for use granted by The Coca-Cola Company.

Irving Berlin Music Company: Excerpt from "All by Myself," words and music by Irving Berlin. Copyright 1921 by Irving Berlin. Copyright renewed. International copyright secured. All rights reserved. Reprinted by permission of Irving Berlin Music Company.

Miller Brewing Company: Two lines of lyric and two pages of sheet music from "If You've Got the Time" by Bill Backer. Copyright © 1971 by Miller Brewing Company. Reprinted by permission.

MPL Communications, Inc.: Excerpt from "Palisades Park" by Chuck Barris. Copyright © 1962 (renewed) by Claridge Music Company, a division of MPL Communications, Inc. All rights reserved. Reprinted by permission.

The New York Times: "Advertising/Campbell Switching to B&S" by Philip N. Dougherty, May 26, 1981, and "A Small Agency That's No Small Beer" by Lydia Cravez, June 21, 1981. Copyright © 1981 by The New York Times Company. Reprinted by permission.

Pepsi-Cola Company: Three lines from a Pepsi jingle. Reprinted by permission of Pepsi-Cola Company.

Shada Music Co., Inc.: Excerpts from the lyrics to and three pages of sheet music from "I'd Like to Teach the World to Sing" by Bill Backer, Billy Davis, Roger Greenaway, and Roger Cook. Copyright © 1971 by Shada Music Co., Inc. One page of sheet music from "Look Up America" by Bill Backer, Billy Davis and Rod McBrien. Copyright © 1974 by Shada Music Co., Inc. International copyrights secured. All rights reserved. Reprinted by permission of Shada Music Co., Inc., 1650 Broadway, Suite 1405, New York, NY 10019.